Family,
Community,
&Disability

Series editors:
George H.S. Singer
Ann P. Turnbull
H. Rutherford Turnbull, III
Larry K. Irvin
Laurie E. Powers

Children with
Acquired Brain Injury

Also available in the Family,
Community, & Disability series:

Redefining Family Support:
Innovations in Public–Private Partnerships
edited by George H.S. Singer, Ph.D.,
Laurie E. Powers, Ph.D., and Ardis L. Olson, M.D.

Family,
Community,
&Disability

Children with
Acquired Brain Injury

Educating and Supporting Families

Edited by

George H.S. Singer, Ph.D.
University of California
Santa Barbara

Ann Glang, Ph.D.
Teaching Research–Eugene
Eugene, Oregon

and

Janet M. Williams, M.S.W.
University of Kansas
Lawrence

·P A U L·H·
BROOKES
PUBLISHING CO

Baltimore • London • Toronto • Sydney

Paul H. Brookes Publishing Co.
Post Office Box 10624
Baltimore, Maryland 21285-0624

Typeset by PRO-Image Corporation, Techna-Type Division, York, Pennsylvania.
Manufactured in the United States of America by
Thomson-Shore, Dexter, Michigan.

Gender specifications for both students and support services providers alternate throughout the text at random.

All examples in this book are completely fictional. Any similarity to actual individuals or circumstances is coincidental and no implications should be inferred.

Library of Congress Cataloging-in-Publication Data
Children with acquired brain injury: educating and supporting families /
  edited by George H.S. Singer, Ann Glang, and Janet Williams.
    p.   cm.—(Family, community, and disability; v. 2)
  Includes bibliographical references and index.
  ISBN 1-55766-233-9
  1. Brain-damaged children—Family relationships. 2. Parents of
handicapped children. 3. Brain-damaged children—Rehabilitation.
4. Family social work. 5. Social work with mentally handicapped
children. 6. Caregivers—Services for. I. Singer, George H.S.
II. Glang, Ann.   III. Williams, Janet M., 1960–   .   IV. Series.
RJ496.B7F35   1996
617.4'81044'083—dc20   95-24213
                                                                      CIP

British Library Cataloguing-in-Publication data are available from the British
Library.

Contents

Series Preface

The purpose of the *Family, Community, & Disability* series is to provide a forum for contemporary work on the challenges and issues that families face, as well as effective ways of supporting families as they fulfill their roles in the lives of people with disabilities. The authors for each volume strive to create a vehicle for making state-of-the-art theory, research, and practice readily accessible to a diverse audience.

In the United States, the institution of the family has undergone revolutionary changes during the last half of the 20th century. Fundamental changes have taken place, increasing the rates of women's employment outside of the home, the prevalence of divorce and remarriage, and the numbers of single and never-married mothers, as well as in the traditional roles of men and women in homes and geographic mobility. Demographic changes, including the rapid growth of non-European ethnic populations and the burgeoning numbers of older adults, also contribute to the transformation of U.S. families. At the same time as these trends are evident, the percentage of people with long-term disabilities has grown dramatically—a trend that will continue during the first quarter of the 21st century. Families are the primary source of day-to-day assistance for people with disabilities. They are crucial to the quality of life for people with developmental disabilities, chronic illnesses, mental illnesses, and disabilities associated with aging.

Much progress has been made in recognizing the key roles of families in early intervention, education, transitions to adulthood, and supported living for people with disabilities. However, the knowledge base about practical ways to strengthen and support families in their multiple roles is still in a nascent stage. Theories of family change, adaptation, and life-span development need to be tested against the phenomena of modern family life. Ethical and social policy issues need to be articulated and analyzed. And, perhaps most important, effective ways of supporting families need to be tested and disseminated. We will endeavor to address these topics in this series.

No single discipline has a primary claim to the field of family and disability studies and much is to be gained by the cross-fertilization of ideas from many traditions, including psychology, history, anthropology, education, sociology, economics, medicine, law, and philosophy. It is also essential that the voices of family members and people with disabilities be heard in this forum.

We hope to address a number of essential topics in this series, including social support, the changing roles of fathers and mothers, the training of family support workers, the demonstration and evaluation of family support models, the roles of various community institutions in assisting families, the implications of ethnic diversity for family policy and practices, the role of self-help and advocacy, and the prevention and treatment of family dysfunction, to name but a few.

An inherent goal of this series is to enhance the long-term development of the field of family and disability studies in such a way that families will benefit from new programs and practices that are informed by an emerging body of knowledge.

Editorial Advisory Board

Foreword

I have been avoiding writing this piece because I did not want to have to relive old memories and reopen old wounds. In the 8 years since our daughter Kara's brain injury, my husband and I have written, as well as spoken to community, educational, and conference meetings, about the impact of ABI on our family. We have shared the steps, stages, and passages that our family has undergone. I have found that it does not get any easier to "go down that road" again—even when sharing what we have learned with others. In fact, most of the time, it triggers a wide array of emotions in me—fortunately, the rage, anger, sadness, and sorrow are all very short term.

Talking and writing about Kara's acquired brain injury make me think about our previous hopes and dreams for her, our perfect child, our only child. Then the reality and impact of her injury strike me anew, and I focus on the impairments in her and the ongoing challenges facing our family. We usually look at the strengths, gifts, and talents she now possesses as well as the strengths we have had to develop to endure this most shattering of life experiences. But the uncertainty of long-term recovery from severe ABI and the degree of unpredictability for the future will continue to sadden me.

Kara sustained severe ABI on December 21, 1986, at age 5. She was in kindergarten and full of life, love, and laughter. Our family was skiing 10 miles from our Colorado home—one of our favorite activities. Kara took a spill and, before she could get up, was hit by an out-of-control skier whose ski tip shattered her skull. She was transported by helicopter to the closest hospital equipped to deal with such trauma, 90 miles from our home.

In the ensuing 8 long weeks of coma, multiple surgeries, near-death experiences, and complications, we certainly felt as if we were on a roller coaster ride. Our life was a constant series of dramatic ups and downs. Once the long-term rehabilitation began, our family began to face many more challenges related to the future: What will come next? Where do we go from here? Where can we obtain the supports and services we need? (We lived in a small community of 7,000 people, with the nearest hospital-rehabilitation center 90 miles away.)

We opted to remain in our home of Glenwood Springs for the community support we felt we needed. We had a gut feeling that Kara would progress if we surrounded her with familiar friends, places, and activities. We were able to find the private therapists (physical, occupational, speech-language, etc.) to work with her, and we adjusted to the 90- or 150-mile drive for the more specialized evaluations and treatments she needed. Yet, we were completely caught up in the medical model, focusing on Kara's deficits instead of her strengths. We continually looked at what was wrong with Kara and how to fix it—this is what we were comfortable with and could understand, as both my husband and I are registered nurses. Still, we constantly questioned ourselves, wondering if we were doing everything we could to help her regain her old self.

When Kara returned to school, the emphasis was placed on specialized services and supports and labels (i.e., special education), which was good for a while but became too specialized and too restrictive. We just wanted her to go to school and be like other kids again.

Through those gut-wrenching, topsy-turvy, emotional times, it became increasingly difficult to try to live with the many professional recommendations we were receiving as they tried to reshape our lives. We were trying frantically to reintegrate the new Kara into a world we did not want to be in ourselves. We wanted to move beyond what was wrong and learn how to be a family again. Somehow, we had lost the ability to have fun.

Even the most caring, considerate, compassionate, and educated service providers could not truly understand the depth of our loss and grief as we dealt with the day-to-day, long-term impact of ABI. They did, however, have the tools to teach us how to begin to cope. Every service provider must remember that putting families back together again is a delicate process—there is a time to provide maximum support and services and there is a time to foster the independence that families require to be sustainable. Families need to be acknowledged for their expertise.

Still, it is those families who have "been there," parents of children with disabilities, including ABI, who have led the way for us by sharing their feelings, successes, hopes, and dreams. This system of families supporting families in informal networks of support has brought much into our lives as we continue to face the never-ending challenges of life with Kara. Family after family has shown us how to be an equal member of Kara's support team, whether it is educational or medical, and stressed the importance of teams. We are all in this together.

Today, we find we still have the same hopes and dreams for Kara. We want her to be happy, to have friends, to have meaningful work when she is an adult, and someday to be able to live away from home—dreams not so very different from other parents. As with most parents, the question is how to create the supports within the community to allow that to happen. We have established a special group of friends, families of children with all kinds of disabilities, that meets as often as possible; we all live many miles apart. This group gives Kara a chance to be "just a kid" with others who face similar challenges and it gives us an opportunity to discuss, often in heartfelt conversation, the meaning of life. We also share our coping strategies as well as celebrate the accomplishments in our lives.

We consider school as Kara's primary community and realize that she needs to be viewed as both a member of and contributor to that community. The inclusion that comes from being a part of the school carried over into making connections with kids at the mall, movies, McDonald's, or church. She is now considered just another kid, more alike than different. We believe that this inclusion and community acceptance at school is vital to the long-term well-being of any child with a disability. And once children grow up with and become accustomed to diversity among their classmates, there will be much more acceptance and support. As it is, I look to Kara's classmates to help support her as she moves into young adulthood—another informal system of support being built for her.

Although I have great respect for the teachers and therapists who continue to work with her, there is nothing quite like "kid power." These kids challenge all of us to let Kara be who she is and support her in these endeavors. Yet, there are still times when we rely quite heavily on the support of the experts. In moments of pain and sorrow even 8 years later, I need someone else to explain Kara's learning styles to a new teacher; I need someone to work with the town recreational department to modify the activities to allow Kara and other children with disabilities to participate fully; I need help in advocating for her rights. Certainly, the Americans with Disabilities Act (ADA) of 1990 has helped, but there is much work still to be done.

I've shared Kara with you to a degree—her strengths, gifts, and talents—but in order for you to understand what she has faced, I need to share some of her impairments too. She is 14 years old now; she has a seizure disorder; she has a severe visual field loss; she has hemiparesis and no use of her left arm; she walks with an ankle-foot orthosis on her left leg; she is essentially a nonreader; and she has great difficulties with math, writing, and many other academic skills. She also has behavior problems—some are the usual teenage tantrums and others are related to her injury. She has a part-time teaching assistant who helps her in the general education classroom to participate in the same curriculum as her peers. The teaching assistant—working in collaboration with the general classroom teachers, the special education teacher, and us—helps to modify Kara's curriculum to meet her needs and ensure that it is meaningful. For instance, Kara learns best auditorally, so much of her curriculum is presented orally.

She also has a crooked grin, a wonderful loud laugh, and a group of friends who enjoy her and accept her for who she is. With support, she managed the seventh–eighth grade girls' basketball team last year, she swims, she has been a Girl Scout and has gone away to camp with her troop, she has played softball on a recreation league in town, and this past winter she relearned how to ski. She also loves rock and roll, to dance, and to talk on the telephone, and is very interested in boys. Like other kids, she has household chores, pets, a 3-wheel bicycle that has allowed increased independence and the capability to do what the other kids are doing. The bottom line is that we are a family and we do family things. The cost of Kara's injury is unknown, but the value of helping her to be a useful, productive, life-filled, love-filled member of our community and world is priceless.

One of the most frequent comments my husband and I hear is, "It must be so hard to have had a normal child and now to have one with disabilities. How do you do it?" To this question, I try to reply, "Kara *is* normal; she just faces some different challenges in her life." Also, we are so grateful to still have her with us, we never stop being thankful for the fighting spirit within her that allowed her to survive and sustains her throughout all of her difficulties.

Kara brings us a simpler, less complex view of the world. She has made us focus on what is of value and importance in our lives. She has a sweetness and gentleness and an incredible sensitivity toward others that naturally draws people to her. She is honest and without pretense, not afraid to express any feeling she might have—a trait that has carried over into many aspects of our lives. We now know how quickly life can change; if there are things we want to share, we are not afraid to share. There may be no tomorrow. I will always remember the little girl she used to be. I celebrate and rejoice in the confident, self-assured, happy young lady she is now. Her sense of humor, her ability to find good in almost everything around her, and her motto of "never say never" have taught me life's lessons in ways I would not have had a chance to experience otherwise. Kara's injury has changed our lives, but it has not ruined them.

We have had many people tell us of the contributions Kara has brought to them as well. Not just adults, but kids, too, have said what an inspiration Kara is. This has helped us to see the positive side of ABI and make meaning of its occurrence in our lives.

Our family has come an incredible distance since we first encountered ABI, but our journey is far from over. I feel encouraged that there are books such as *Children with Acquired Brain Injury: Educating and Supporting Families* to enlighten many more professionals and families. The ranks of those who have sustained and survived ABI will only continue to grow and will increasingly require the knowledge and expertise professionals are gaining from taking the time to learn about them.

Alice Brouhard

Contributors

Elizabeth Cooley, Ph.D.
Senior Research Associate
Far West Laboratory for
  Educational Research and
  Development
730 Harrison Street
San Francisco, California 94107

Roberta DePompei, Ph.D.
School of Communicative
  Disorders
Polsky Building, Room 188 H
University of Akron
225 South Main
Akron, Ohio 44325-3001

Karen Gibson, B.S.
Rehabilitation Research and
  Training Center on Supported
  Employment
Virginia Commonwealth
  University
Post Office Box 842011
1314 West Main Street
Richmond, Virginia 23284-2011

Ann Glang, Ph.D.
Associate Research Professor
Teaching Research–Eugene
99 West 10th Avenue, Suite 337C
Eugene, Oregon 97401

Karen L. Kepler, Ph.D.
Senior Neuropsychologist
Department of Rehabilitation
  Medicine
Mt. Sinai Medical Center
Box 1240, East 98th Street
New York, New York 10029

Sally Kneipp, Ph.D.
Community Skills Program
Counseling and Rehabilitation, Inc.
1500 Locust Street, Suite 1505
Philadelphia, Pennsylvania 19102

Marilyn Lash, M.S.W.
Director of Training and Principal
  Investigator
Research and Training Center on
  Rehabilitation and Childhood
  Trauma
New England Medical Center
and
Assistant Clinical Professor
Department of Physical Medicine
  and Rehabilitation
Tufts University School of
  Medicine
750 Washington Street, #75K-R
Boston, Massachusetts 02111

Ellen Lehr, Ph.D.
Pediatric Psychologist
Private Practice
19105 36th Avenue, West, Suite 206
Lynnwood, Washington 98036

Joseph M. Lucyshyn, Ph.D.
Specialized Training Program
College of Education
1761 Alder Street
University of Oregon
Eugene, Oregon 97403

Karen J. Morales, C.S.W.
Senior Case Manager
Hilltop Manor of Niskayuna
1805 Providence Avenue
Niskayuna, New York 12309

Charles Nixon, Ph.D.
Co-Director
Direction Service Counseling
  Center
1240 Charnelton Street
Eugene, Oregon 97401

Laurie E. Powers, Ph.D.
Assistant Director
Hood Center for Family Support
Dartmouth-Hitchcock Medical
    Center
Assistant Professor of Pediatrics
    and Adolescent Medicine
Dartmouth Medical School
One Medical Center Drive
Lebanon, New Hampshire
    03756-0001

Penny R. Reed, Ph.D.
Wisconsin Assistive Technology
    Institute
Post Office Box 268
Amherst, Wisconsin 54406-0268

Ronald C. Savage, Ed.D.
Director of Behavioral Health
    Systems
The May Institute
35 Pacella Park Drive
Randolph, Massachusetts 02368

George H.S. Singer, Ph.D.
Professor of Education
Graduate School of Education
2321 Phelps Hall
University of California
Santa Barbara, California
    93106-9490

McKay Moore Sohlberg, Ph.D.
Assistant Professor
Department of Communication
    Disorders and Sciences
College of Education
University of Oregon
Eugene, Oregon 97403-5252

Bonnie Todis, Ph.D.
Associate Research Professor
Teaching Research–Eugene
99 West 10th Avenue, Suite 337C
Eugene, Oregon 97401

Darlene Unger, M.Ed.
Rehabilitation Research and
    Training Center on Supported
    Employment
Virginia Commonwealth
    University
Post Office Box 842011
1314 West Main Street
Richmond, Virginia 23284-2011

Julie Weis, M.Ed.
Franklin County Alcohol, Drug
    Addiction, and Mental Health
    Services Board
447 East Broad Street
Columbus, Ohio 43215

Michael D. West, Ph.D.
Rehabilitation Research and
    Training Center on Supported
    Employment
Virginia Commonwealth
    University
Post Office Box 842011
1314 West Main Street
Richmond, Virginia 23284-2011

Janet M. Williams, M.S.W.
Research Associate
Research and Training Center on
    Independent Living
Life Span Institute
Dole Building
University of Kansas
Lawrence, Kansas 66045

Volume Preface

Modern medicine has propelled many families into becoming lifelong sources of care and concern for children who experience acquired brain injury (ABI) resulting in severe disabilities—an unprecedented circumstance in American family life. Prior to the 1960s, most children whose brains were seriously hurt died soon after the trauma. Changes in emergency treatment, imaging technology, and surgical and pharmaceutical treatments have begun to routinely save the lives of approximately 30,000 of these children each year.

The response to this growing population has been primarily medical. A majority of the resources, both financial and personal, that have been allocated to the care of children with brain injuries have been concentrated in acute care hospitals and rehabilitation programs instead of with families—a necessarily grave mistake. Families are, in most cases, the only continuing source of support to people with ABI. For children, they are indispensable and irreplaceable. The nature of the family's support to a child with acquired brain injury is, over the long term, one of the primary determinants of that child's quality of life.

The purpose of *Children with Acquired Brain Injury: Educating and Supporting Families* is to provide a resource for parents and service providers, detailing the kinds of supports needed and describing the practices of some programs that promise to be exemplary.

The first four chapters of this book, as well as the Foreword by Alice Brouhard, aim to reveal the experience of acquired brain injury from a family perspective. These chapters are designed to help parents connect with and relate to the experiences of other families and to help students and professionals begin to develop an understanding of the complex effects of ABI on the family. Although these accounts discuss painful and often tragic experiences, they are written with the confidence that many families adapt to a child's injury with the help of numerous forms of evolving community support.

The remainder of the book provides examples of the key kinds of support that hold promise for assisting families. These chapters, though, by no means cover all of the different supports that families may require. Contemporary thinking about family support emphasizes the importance of flexibility and individualization in tailoring assistance to match the needs and preferences of family members. Such individualization collides with inevitable pressures to establish programs and standardized approaches to helping. One way to reduce the conflict is to design programs that allow for optimal variation. Another way is to maximize informal sources of support—support from friends, extended family, co-workers, fellow churchgoers, and other voluntary associations. Self-help groups, including parent-to-parent programs, should also play a vital role. It will, however, still be necessary for professionals, especially those trained in counseling and behavior therapy, to be involved and wrap their services around families. They must first learn the specific nuances of ABI and its effects on the family, though, to be completely effective.

We hope that, in these pages, family members will find the encouragement and motivation for uncovering the kinds of supports they require, as well as useful ideas about assistance and the goals of advocacy efforts. We hope, too, that this volume will contribute to the growth and development of family support efforts on behalf of families of children with acquired brain injury.

To the families of
children with acquired brain injury
who have taught us about their challenges and needs
and shown us their courage and persistence,
often against great odds.

They have shared their humor and love
as well as their suffering, and
have made us think and think again about what it
means to be a parent, grandparent, brother, or sister.

Children with
Acquired Brain Injury

1

Constructing Supports

Helping Families of Children with Acquired Brain Injury

George H.S. Singer

Annually, more than 100,000 children and youth (ages birth to 21 years) are hospitalized with acquired brain injury (ABI); roughly one third of these injuries are so severe that the children experience long-term disabilities (May Institute, 1993; Rivara & Mueller, 1986). As this population is cumulative, over a decade, at least 300,000 families will have to adjust to having a loved one with long-term disabilities and more than 1 million will have to cope with the severe stress of acutely caring for a member with a mild or moderate acquired brain injury and, then, its aftereffects. This volume focuses specifically on the families of children with severe ABI, meaning that the child was comatose following the injury, lost some functional skills, and is expected to require special lifelong accommodations to participate in typical community living. The needs of children with ABI and their families have emerged as an important social issue since the 1980s. Because families serve as most children's primary social support networks and socialization agents, any efforts to assist children with brain injury must make the family a central focus.

The centrality of the family in education and rehabilitation for children and youth with disabilities has been widely accepted in regard to other disabilities, including children with developmental disabilities (Singer & Irvin, 1989; Singer & Powers, 1993; Turnbull &

1

Turnbull, 1986), infants and toddlers with disabilities (Mallory, 1995), children with emotional and behavior problems (Friesen, 1996), and children with chronic illnesses (Patterson, 1988). However, the development of family support services for children and youth with ABI has lagged behind that of other disability fields. Pediatric and adolescent rehabilitation services have been driven largely by a biomedical model that emphasizes damage and recovery within the biological systems contained in a child's body. Interventions usually take place in hospitals, clinics, and rehabilitation centers where medical methods of intervention prevail. Although a few exceptional programs have begun to emphasize the role of the family beginning with the initial trauma, most do not. Treatment centers are often located long distances from family homes and are usually funded for limited time periods by private insurance. Often, funding does not cover the kinds of family supports that are required to maximize the child's recovery and long-term adaptation to the family and community.

This chapter briefly reviews an alternative to the biomedical model of care for children with ABI—a biopsychosocial model that views the child's physical systems as parts of a whole person and, in turn, sees this person as nested in a social ecology. It also describes recent thinking in the design of family supports that enhance the family's ecological niche.

THE CASE FOR THE CENTRALITY
OF THE FAMILY IN REHABILITATION

Why should an emergency technician, transporting a young girl from the scene of an injury, care about her family when his first and foremost concern is keeping the child alive and getting her to an emergency room as quickly as possible? Why should the emergency physician, who must assess and treat urgently, care about the child's relatives in the waiting room? Similarly, why should the neurosurgeon, who must remove bone chips and reduce brain swelling, care about the distraught parent down the hall? These questions can be extended to all professionals who will treat the child's injuries—the neurologist, the neuropsychologist, the physical therapist, the special education teacher, and the adaptive recreation specialist, among others. There are two answers: One is humanitarian and the other is functional.

First, from a humanitarian perspective, anyone who has ever had a child or sibling who experienced a severe injury knows that it is an enormous, usually catastrophic, event for all members of the family. Because a large proportion of brain injuries occur in automobile accidents, very often other family members also undergo injury or emotional trauma. Severe brain injuries almost always entail a possible loss of life and injured children often hover on the brink of death, while their family members desperately hope and pray for their survival. Often the child is comatose for periods of time that range from hours to months. Thus, the experience of an acquired brain injury is a multiple series of the most stressful kinds of events for parents and siblings: experiences that involve near death, pain, physical disfigurement (either temporary or long-term), physical separation, and protracted uncertainty. Interviews with parents, even years after the accident or injury, often reveal memories that are extraordinarily vivid and painful (see Chapter 2).

Interview and survey studies consistently indicate that parents want more information and involvement at every stage of the treatment and rehabilitation of their children with ABI (see Chapters 2 and 10). Thus, people who work with children and youth with brain injuries should care about families because members are directly affected by the injury and require information, care, and assistance; also, parents' experiential trauma is as real and challenging as their children's biological trauma.

The second reason is more functional: Children and youth are unlikely to recover as fully as possible without the support of their families. Families serve as the intermediary between the child and the outside world, including such rehabilitation institutions as hospitals, clinics, residential rehabilitation facilities, and specially designed education programs. Families bring children into contact with rehabilitation workers by arranging appointments, providing transportation, filling prescriptions, carrying out assignments, and keeping track of the many, interrelated needs of their child. Families provide continuity, emotional support, and connections to adults in the community. Parents and siblings know the injured child in the context of a typical, 24-hour-a-day life and, thus, are able to observe the child's recovery and the residual effects of an injury more fully than a professional who sees the child only in a therapeutic setting. Furthermore, families, as guardians of a child, have the legal authority sometimes needed to obtain services from reluctant schools and other community systems. Families also provide continuity for the injured child well into adulthood; many young adults with ABI continue to live at home well into their 30s. By contrast, professionals' involvement is much more transitory. These and other family functions have a direct impact on the way a child recovers and adapts to the long-term effects of brain injury.

In their study of children with ABI 1 year after injury, Rivara and Mueller (1986) found that a significant portion of the variance in the children's academic performance and behavior problems could be attributed to family functioning. In fact, family functioning was almost as potent a predictor of the children's functioning as the severity of the injury 1 year postinjury. Although these findings must be viewed as preliminary given the small sample number and short time interval of the study—especially in comparison to the long-term course of ABI recovery, they are consistent with research on children with other kinds of disabilities, which also strongly suggests that family functioning is an important predictor of child outcomes, including physical health (Patterson, McCubbin, & Warwick, 1990) and school adaptation (Nihira, Meyers, & Mink, 1980). The data suggest that one of the most effective interventions for children with ABI is to ensure that they have a parent who is an effective, committed advocate and source of long-term support (see Chapter 5). Efforts to encourage and sustain family resources are likely to be as important in the long term as most medical and therapeutic treatments.

Models for Building a Cognitive Framework of Family

In order to understand how to support families, it is important to have a consistent cognitive framework for organizing the enormous number of variables that occur in families of children with ABI. Table 1 presents several of the key variables that constitute the contemporary view of families in relation to childhood disability. These variables are interactive factors that help determine the listed outcomes for children and families affected by pediatric ABI.

Various models have been proposed to describe family adaptation to disability and/or ABI. These models differ in what they choose to emphasize: Some describe the processes that families undergo in response to acute crises while others focus on the longer-term adaptation to a child's disability (Billings & Moos, 1985; Patterson, 1988; Singer & Irvin, 1989). The model presented in Figure 1 is based upon current models of adaptation to stress in individuals and families; it serves as a way to organize the variables presented in Table 1. Without this structure, the number of variables and possible combinations for interaction would be overwhelming and, thus, not useful.

It is important to examine each of the components in Figure 1 both before and after the brain injury, as a child's brain trauma always takes place in family contexts that vary in their levels of day-to-day stress and effectiveness of coping skills. For example, families that are undergoing severe hardship and having difficulty coping with their environment are likely to be at risk for negative adaptation to their child's ABI. By contrast, families with more preinjury coping skills are likely to adapt more effectively.

Table 1. Key components of a family social-ecological model for children with ABI

Child-centered variables
Child's age and development at
time of injury
Health status
Severity of injury
Preinjury social and behavioral
adjustment
Child's current age and cognitive
development
Length of time since the injury
Speed and extent of recovery
Presence of behavior problems
Child's peer social network prior to
injury
Child's peer network postinjury

Family background resources
Culture
Family structure
Socioeconomic status
Family size and membership
Education
Stage of family life cycle
Family strengths in carrying out
family functions

Family resources
Preinjury family cohesion
Preinjury family adaptability
Informal social support network
Availability of rehabilitation services
Availability and quality of school
services
Insurance or availability of public
funds
Family members' skills as advocates
and intermediaries
Family commitment to rehabilitation
goals

Family coping processes
Communication skills within the
family
Communication skills with the
outside community
Group problem-solving skills
Family's cognitive adaptation
Family's cohesion
Family's adaptability
Family's ability to activate and utilize
supports
Family's ability to maintain a balance

Community resources
Informal helping networks
Relatives

Community resources—continued
Friends
Co-workers
Church members
Service organization members
Formal helping institutions
Rehabilitation programs
Local primary care medical
providers
Special education services
Family support services
Case management
Information and referral
Advocacy
Mediation
Fiscal assistance
Linkage to other families
Support groups
In-home behavioral assistance
Counseling and mental health
services
Housing, food, and fiscal
assistance
Adaptive technology
Vocational rehabilitation programs
Transportation
Alternative living arrangements for
adults with ABI
Housing, food, and income support
Support groups

Outcomes
Positive adaptation
Long-term family cohesion
Balanced meeting of all family
members' needs
Acceptance of the child's
postinjury condition
Family integration into community
Maximized recovery by child
Typical morale in family members
Family's continued ability to
perform culturally expected
functions
Negative adaptation
Family dissolution or long-term
discord
Neglect of some family members
Rejection of the injured child
Social isolation of family
Potential for child's recovery
unrealized
Demoralization in family members
Family's failure to perform
culturally expected functions

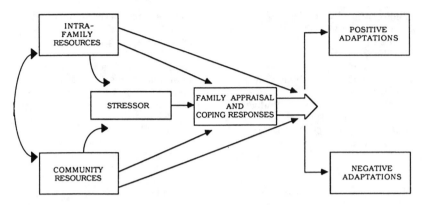

Figure 1. Model of family stress. (From Singer, G.H.S., & Irvin, L.K. [Eds.]. [1989]. *Support for caregiving families: Enabling positive adaptation to disability* [p. 6]. Baltimore: Paul H. Brookes Publishing Co.; reprinted by permission.)

THE NATURAL COURSE OF AN ACQUIRED BRAIN INJURY

The onset of ABI triggers a series of events that involves families with multiple institutions that have their own rules, norms, and goals. These institutions and systems include ambulances, emergency rooms, intensive care wards, hospital wards, rehabilitation centers, clinics, special education programs, vocational rehabilitation programs, and specialized residential centers. Families must adapt to these settings, while their children chart the natural course of brain injury—ABI and its aftereffects unfold within generally predictable phases.

Phase One

ABIs usually begin with a sudden, unwanted event—often, a vehicular accident. Although any child is vulnerable to ABI through an accident, some groups of youth are more at risk than others. The highest rates of ABI occur among teenage males who engage in high-risk behavior—driving fast, using alcohol or other drugs and driving, skateboarding without protective equipment, and so on. Consequently, a child's or youth's ABI often begins for family members with the notification that their child has been in a serious accident.

Usually an ambulance carries the injured person to an emergency room. During the ambulance ride and subsequent hours in the emergency room, the family is typically kept away from the injured child or youth. The possibility of death is everpresent, yet families are given very little information about their child's condition. In part, this informational vacuum results from the urgency of the situation and the lack of medical clarity about the nature of the injury. Medical personnel are guarded in their statements as they have very little solid information to rely upon during the period immediately following the injury. All of these variables constitute stresses: the violence of the accident, the separation from the child via ambulance and emergency room, the hours of waiting with little information, and the great uncertainty concerning life and death matters.

Phase One for Severe Brain Injuries Children with severe brain injuries are comatose during this initial stage of trauma. Often they are kept alive with respirators, intravenous feeders, and a variety of electronic monitoring devices. During deep coma the child is noncommunicative and in a state resembling deep sleep—no two-way interaction is possible. The duration of the coma is unpredictable and can range from hours to months. Often, families maintain an around-the-clock vigil over their child, wanting to do anything they can to promote survival and recovery. This period of hospitalization disrupts typical work schedules and household routines: Meals, laundry, transportation to school, and supervision for siblings must be altered. Parents must attend to these details while living out of the injured child's hospital room. The crisis that engulfs the family during the injury and coma is a crisis of belief and emotion, as well as a practical crisis involving the disruption of typical and essential daily living patterns.

Phase Two

Recovering from coma is a gradual process that varies with the severity and location of the brain injury. Emerging from coma can be confusing for family members whose only knowledge may be from the mass media that depicts emergence from coma as akin to waking up from a deep sleep. Instead, it is a gradual and variable process that occurs in stages. Levels of awareness often fluctuate and family members' hopes can soar and then be dashed, often several times within the same day. Interviews with parents reveal the intensity and hopefulness of this phase. Parents described how they became hypervigilant for any sign of change in their child. They told how they believed they must ward off any pessimistic statements from the staff and hold on to hope at all costs.

Phase Three

After emergence from coma, the full extent of the child's injuries starts to become apparent. Cognitive and motor difficulties appear as the child returns to typical levels of awareness. However, the impact of brain injury is not stable nor is it easy to grasp at any one moment in time. Some consequences of the injury do not become apparent until the child returns to his original school or community setting. Also, the process of regaining skills and functions that begins when one emerges from coma can continue for several years. Thus, the family is faced with the challenge of understanding the fluid, indeterminate effects of ABI. This changeability and lack of clarity can be a source of stress, particularly if family members have different interpretations of the severity of the injury and its consequence.

If the child has the appropriate insurance coverage or public funding and if a program is available, he may live in a residential rehabilitation facility for several days to several months. Such centers provide intensive therapies from a number of different professional specialists, including speech-language therapists, physical therapists, neuropsychologists, behavioral psychologists, occupational therapists, recreation specialists, and special educators. In most cases, these professions with their unique foci are unfamiliar to family members who must learn quickly about the enormous range of specialized knowledge that is necessary to rehabilitate an injured child. Increasingly, family members are being invited to become members of the rehabilitation team—a role that offers more of the collaboration and access to information that many family members desire, but one that also brings additional stress including an intensified sense of responsibility for the child's recovery. Again, during the inpatient rehabilitation phase, families must carry on their typical functions at home, which may be a great distance away from the rehabilitation center.

Phase Four

Returning the child to her home ushers in a new phase of recovery with its own set of benefits and stresses. The decision to terminate inpatient rehabilitation is often driven by funding limitations rather than by the child's reacquisition of skills. Also, it is important to note that a large percentage of children are never served in residential rehabilitation settings; in these cases, children receive services directly in their family homes from the acute care hospital. During the child's absence, the family system has had to change in order to accommodate the crisis precipitated by the injury: A grandparent may have moved in to care for young children; an older sibling may have taken on new responsibilities; a parent may have reduced work hours. Upon the child's return home, the family must strike a new balance. If the child requires additional caregiving, as is usually the case with severe ABI, new roles must be assigned and routines modified. For example, a 45-minute period for getting the children on the school bus in the morning may need to be extended to an hour to accommodate the child's needs for dressing and feeding; or, brothers and sisters must respond to questions from classmates and comments from other children on the bus. At the same time, family members must make sense of the child's injury, as well as changes in personality and behavior.

Changes in Personality and Behavior For many families, changes in personality and the emergence of behavior problems pose the greatest challenges. Although the effects of ABI vary tremendously and require any generalization to be qualified, they typically involve some social, behavior, and emotional problems in the injured young person. In research on children with developmental disabilities, behavior problems are some of the most severe stressors for parents and are often associated with parental demoralization (Pahl & Quine, 1987). Studies from the United States and Western Europe consistently show that changes in the personalities and social behaviors of people with ABI are the most difficult aftereffects for families to deal with (Florian & Katz, 1991).

ABI can lead to changes in both internalizing and externalizing behavior problems. Children who experience an increase in internalizing problems show more passivity, lack of spontaneity, decreased initiative and interest, slowness, and fatigue. Young people whose externalizing behavior changes exhibit one or more of the following challenges: reduced ability to inhibit impulses, increased acting out, irritability, outbursts of anger, less patience, emotional lability, and increased aggressiveness. Behavior problems usually involve other people in an aversive event and can contribute to secondary problems for the family, such as social withdrawal (Singer, 1993). It is difficult for families to obtain child care for a child with behavior problems, and social events can be embarrassing or shameful for parents if their child misbehaves in public.

The Transition to Special Services The transition into the world of special services for people with disabilities is often very stressful for family members. A child who was previously not given a label is likely to be coded to become eligible for special education or vocational rehabilitation services, tested, and assigned an administrative label. The services themselves also involve new kinds of interactions between professionals and parents. Parents are likely to experience their first individualized education program (IEP) meeting soon after the child's return home (see Chapter 8).

Many families have to fight for appropriate services for their children with ABI because these children do not readily fit into any existing program. Navigating through the complex world of human services in schools and communities often requires parents to assume new roles and learn new skills—a process that can be extremely taxing. In some states, school systems and vocational rehabilitation programs have developed policies and practices to meet the concerns of people with ABI. However, in the majority of communities, the condition is too new and of such a relatively low incidence that rehabilitation organizations (including public schools) have not yet adapted.

The children may move from a general education classroom to a special education program or may begin to receive the kinds of supports that are typically provided to children with other kinds of cognitive disabilities, such as mental retardation or autism. The stigma associated with such a placement can be painful for the parents and the children if they retain awareness of their prior social identities.

These children's changed identities often result in the loss of previous friends. The cutting of former social ties may be attributed to the change in the child's social skills and personality as well as the stigma that still surrounds children with special educational needs. The children also may not be able to participate in activities that previously provided social contacts. For instance, soccer games and church youth group meetings may no longer be open to them. These changes in social identities and social relationships can have a secondary effect on parents and siblings and add another source of stress.

The Effects on Siblings   All of these stresses also affect siblings (see Chapter 7). The initial phases—injury onset and hospitalization—can disrupt the typical routines that comprise the siblings' days. Brothers and sisters may have to move in with relatives or be cared for by child care workers for unusually long periods of time. The siblings may resent their loss of attention or feel guilty about the injury. When their injured brother or sister returns home they can find his changed personality and caregiving needs difficult to understand, requiring new ways of acting that can be taxing (e.g., helping with wheelchair transfers or special feeding). Changes in the injured sibling's behavior and social status can cause distress at school because of teasing by other children or the avoidance of *courtesy stigma*—the negative social evaluations that can adhere to those who are closely associated with a devalued person.

The Future of Children with ABI   Finally, a child with severe ABI acquires lifelong disabilities, changing the child's future plans and those of the rest of the family forever. In families that expect young adults to become independent, ABI disrupts the move toward separation and independence; the typical transition to a different life stage can be very different from what parents might have once expected. As with the other ABI stressors, the resolution of the child's role in the adult world is largely dependent on the availability and quality of support services, such as supported employment and supported residential living programs. When these programs are not available, parents and siblings have to either become advocates for these services or plan an alternative way for the family to care for their member with ABI. In either case, ongoing involvement with and assistance for the family member with ABI are often required for the remainder of that person's life.

Costs Associated with ABI ABI usually involves enormous hospital and rehabilitation costs. Often, insurance coverage is inadequate or nonexistent, leaving families with huge debts. Employed parents often have to forego work or reduce work hours in order to care for a child with ABI. Consequently, financial stress is often a part of the challenge that families must face. It is not uncommon to encounter parents who have taken on second jobs in order to pay off medical bills or others whose standard of living has changed greatly as a consequence of a child's ABI.

VARIABLES AFFECTING FAMILIES' ADAPTABILITY TO ABI

It is important to reiterate the individuality of people with ABI and the great variability in the effects of brain injury. The child's temperament, level of cognitive development, and skill repertoire prior to the injury all interact with the unique pattern of brain injury. For example, young children injured prior to the development of abstract thinking will react to injury differently from older children. Similarly, there is evidence to suggest that behavior problems prior to ABI are a strong predictor of the severity of behavior problems after the injury (Brown, Chadwick, Shaffer, Rutter, & Traub, 1981). Therefore, the uniqueness of each child and each injury should not be foregone in the effort to construct a usable model of family adaptation to ABI.

Intrafamily Resources

There is not a direct relationship between the severity of a child's brain injury and the family's adaptation. Otherwise, brain scans and X rays could predict how a family will fare. Instead, the outcomes for families are determined by the interaction of a number of factors, with medical and biological factors being only a small part of the overall picture. Among the sets of variables that determine how families cope with ABI are factors that collectively make up the internal resources that the family can use in adapting to the challenges posed by a youth's ABI. Some of these factors are readily apparent and need little explanation: The family's social and economic status, the availability and helpfulness of extended family members, and the family's preinjury resources in meeting the many functions that families perform are some of the more evident resources.

Culture of Origin The family's culture of origin will provide both resources and challenges that should be understood by the rehabilitation team. Concepts of injury, healing, medicine, and the origins of behavior vary with culture. A culture that traditionally values patience and care toward the injured may provide a family with a different set of behavioral and attitudinal resources from a family whose culture or subculture views misfortune as a sign of divine displeasure or punishment. Cultural attitudes toward authority will influence the family's interaction with the rehabilitation team. People from cultures that never question authority figures will have a very different reaction to being included on a rehabilitation team from those of family members from a culture with a less reverent attitude toward professionals. Another major attitudinal variable that is affected by culture is beliefs about independence and separation from the family of origin. In many cultures, the value placed upon self-reliance and independence is much different from the United States, where a majority of the culture expects young adults to leave home and start their own households. Families that expect a family member with a disability to always remain at home will have different priorities for rehabilitation than a family that expects their injured family member to one day leave home and work. Another culturally determined set of attitudes concerns problem behavior. If problematic behavior is viewed as shameful, regardless of its cause, a family may have greater difficulty accepting their injured member than if there is a tradition of acceptance based upon a more tolerant view of behavior.

According to their cultural attitudes, families will bring different resources and vulnerabilities to the experience of coping with a child's brain injury. The traditional medical model has been relatively culture free. However, as a more comprehensive view of rehabilitation is adopted, it is important to understand that cultural factors pervade every aspect of the family adaptation model. Consequently, those who work with the families of children with ABI should become familiar with the cultures of the families they serve. Also, subcultural differences such as social class differences will affect the family–professional relationship. Parents who are middle-class professionals may be more skillful at communicating with the rehabilitation professionals than working-class parents.

Family functioning prior to the injury is also a predictor of post-injury coping. As might be expected, families that have successfully adapted to other crises, have well-developed communication and problem-solving skills, and are able to flexibly assign roles are more likely to adapt positively than families who have experienced great distress and disruption in the face of other challenges (Patterson, 1988). Two dimensions of family interaction are frequently cited in the literature on family adaptation to ongoing health conditions, disabilities, or ABI (Olson et al., 1983; Patterson, 1988; Rivara & Mueller, 1986): family cohesion and family adaptation.

Family Cohesion *Family cohesion* refers to the emotional bonding among family members. It includes the extent to which family members view themselves as part of a family unit, work together to achieve mutual goals, and involve themselves in each other's daily lives. As conceptualized by Olson and colleagues (1983), cohesion exists on a continuum that ranges from disengagement, to separation, to connectedness, to enmeshment. They also theorize that at its extremes (e.g., disengagement, enmeshment), family cohesion interferes with adaptation to stress. Families in the mid-range (e.g., separation, connectedness) are more likely to function well over time. Empirical support for this view of cohesion comes from a large-scale study of 1,124 families. Olson et al. found that families demonstrating mid-range cohesiveness were more likely to have higher levels of marital and family satisfaction and lower levels of stress and use more coping skills.

However, the normative level of family cohesion is, again, largely a matter of culture, which makes it important for rehabilitation personnel to understand the levels of mutual involvement usually expected in families from an array of cultural backgrounds. When families are so disengaged that there is little support for the injured member or when they are so closely engaged that other family members give up their typical lives, there is cause for concern.

Family Adaptability Family adaptability refers to the family system's ability to change its power structure, role relationships, and relationship rules in response to stress (Olson et al., 1983). Family adaptability is thought to be an important contributor to rehabilitation and health outcomes for children with disabilities (Turnbull & Turnbull, 1986). As conceptualized by Olson et al. (1983), family adaptation exists on a continuum that ranges between extremes: from extreme rigidity to extreme chaos. Families who operate in between these extremes are labeled flexible or *structured*, having achieved a workable balance between stability and predictability, on the one hand, and responsive change, on the other. Again, this normative range will be determined by cultural standards, making it important for those involved with the family to understand how different cultures react to change.

An example of the way in which a child's ABI can affect family adaptation involves the family and traditional gender roles. The child's injury often poses a severe financial challenge to the family; at the same time, there is an increased need for home caregiving. In some families, the family may adapt to these contradictory demands by assuming traditional gender roles. For example, in one family, the father took on extra employment, often requiring him to be away from home more than usual, while the mother cut back on her work hours to be able to provide more home care to her son with ABI. In this way, traditional gender roles were reinforced and made more rigid. In this particular family, the assignment was almost automatic; they relied upon an unspoken acceptance of a cultural norm. However, in another family, both parents agreed to adjust their work hours and both took on more home care duties—a change that caused friction and led the family to request help in discussing the assignment of jobs at home and agreements about rest and time off from extra care.

In fact, the families that pose the greatest challenge to professionals are those who fit the general description of a chaotic family. In these families there are few predictable behavior patterns: Meals are not regular, nor are meeting times or leisure activities. There is little that is predictable except a high level of flux. Because most interventions assume some basic level of order and predictability, chaotic families often frustrate interventionists. Family treatment programs often coach families to establish routines before attempting to solve other problems (Fleischman, Horne, & Arthur, 1983). Furthermore, routines are often the easiest and most concrete way for family members to organize their time and assign tasks. Consequently, family treatment specialists, such as Lucyshyn, Nixon, Glang, and Cooley (see Chapter 6), focus on family routines as the basic unit for analyzing the family's behavior.

Family Communication and Problem Solving A child's brain injury poses many problems that the family system must solve. Interfamily communication skills and interfamily problem-solving skills are key in adapting to these challenges, and most of the professionally developed methods for helping families adapt to crises use these two aspects of family interaction. For example, Hawkins, Singer, and Nixon (1993) have successfully used short-term behavior therapy to assist families of children with severe disabilities. At an early stage in their problem-oriented treatment, they help each member identify his or her problems within the family and develop goals that represent a desired solution to these problems.

A key part of this process involves assisting family members to listen carefully to one another and show that they have heard the other family members through the use of such communication skills as paraphrasing and reflecting feelings. Once the family members are able to establish mutual goals, they are shown how to generate ideas about reaching those goals. The therapists are able to suggest solutions that include help from the larger community. The members then agree on who will take steps to reach the goals before the next family meeting. These homework assignments provide them with a chance to work on goal attainment independently of the therapist. As the family gains experience with careful communication and joint problem solving, they acquire skills that permit them to adapt with less internal conflict.

Although this kind of structured family communication and problem-solving approach has been developed under the umbrella of professional therapy, it can also be delivered as a family enrichment program by church groups and trained support staff, or as part of a self-help program.

Cognitive Adaptation within the Family A number of social scientists have studied groups of people who have survived and adapted in the face of extraordinary life challenges, specifically survivors of genocide, rape and incest victims, people with life-threatening diseases, and survivors of combat (Antanovsky, 1987; Herman, 1992; Janoff-Bulman, 1992). Recently, researchers have extended their work to include parents of children with disabilities (Turnbull et al., 1990), including parents of children with acquired brain injury (Singer et al., 1994).

Although each of these theorists and researchers has emphasized somewhat different specific content in his or her theories, they all agree on some basic assumptions about coping with extreme stress. First, these cognitive theorists believe that people actively construct their world through ongoing cognitive processes that shape perception, influence behavior, and strongly influence emotion. They all believe that there are underlying beliefs that serve as a framework for organizing and interpreting many complex stimuli; these beliefs concern such basic assumptions as whether the world is predictable, whether there is a meaning to life, whether the person can be effective in dealing with the world, whether the self is valuable, and whether there is reason to hope for the future. Usually, these basic beliefs operate in the background and are rarely the focus of conscious thought. However, when traumatic events occur, these assumptions are challenged and disrupted. This disruption can shatter a person's world when much of what was previously taken for granted is suddenly called into question.

The process of disruption often involves overwhelming emotions that are experienced as uncontrolled and highly disruptive—feelings of meaninglessness, worthlessness, fear, hopelessness, panic, rage, sorrow, and despair are felt with great intensity. The process of building a new metacognitive structure that allows a person to continue living without a sense of defeat or hopelessness has been labeled *cognitive adaptation*, although all would agree that it involves much more than ordinary conscious thought. The adaptive process appears to involve some key elements including desensitizing the person to the memories of the traumatic event, exposing her to people who can help restore a sense of trust and hope in her community, and modeling ways of thinking about the experience that allow the person to incorporate it into a viable belief system. In other words, this process develops new ways of thinking and new emotional responses in the face of a tremendous challenge. Cognitive adaptation is one of the main ways in which humans come to terms with trauma, whether it be a physical illness, loss, or traumatic event (Janoff-Bulman, 1992).

Cognitive adaptation is made more difficult when the facts about the impact of a trauma are not clear. Ambiguity appears to impede the process of coming to terms with a very difficult circumstance. Boss (1988) has identified two kinds of ambiguity among family members: *physical absence with psychological presence* and *physical presence with psychological absence*. An example of physical absence with psychological presence has been noted in families of prisoners of war or men missing in combat. Often families have unusual difficulty in coming to terms with the loss until verification of survival or death is obtained. As an example of physical presence with psychological absence, Boss (1988) has found that family members of people with Alzheimer's disease can have extreme difficulty in accepting the loss of a family member who is physically present but whose personality and mentality have been altered or lost.

Interviews with parents of children and youth with ABI suggest that some families experience difficulty in cognitively adapting to a child's brain injury because the child is physically present and unchanged, but psychologically altered. The nature of the psychological change often does not make itself clear for a long period of time and can evolve as the child develops. Lehr (see Chapter 3) argues that family members must mourn the loss of the child who existed prior to the injury, while they adjust to and accept the child as changed by her injury. Many families do manage this difficult task and many are able to cognitively adapt. Clinical work with parents of children with ABI repeatedly shows that it is possible to achieve a sense of purpose and acceptance in the face of a tragedy. Singer and Powers (see Chapter 13) describe how parents in support groups have helped each other by sharing their sense of acceptance and the positive attributions of their children. In fact, this volume argues that community resources, such as support groups and family-centered rehabilitation programs, can make an essential contribution to family adaptation to ABI.

Community Resources

Families exist in a social context of neighborhoods, communities, cities, and states with numerous social institutions that provide many different resources including education, jobs, medical care, recreation, housing, worship, public safety, and the goods and services that make up their surrounding economy. However, communities vary greatly in the degree to which they provide family-centered resources. Recent studies have demonstrated that children who grow up in poor neighborhoods with few such resources are less likely to fare well in school, graduate from high school or college, or have gainful employment as young adults than children from communities with richer resources (McLanahan & Sandefur, 1994). Although this issue has not been adequately addressed in the research literature, it is extremely likely that the relative poverty or wealth of family support systems has a major impact on families of children with ABI.

Community resources can be broadly classified into two different categories: *informal* and *formal* support systems. *Informal supports* consist of the social networks that are not mediated by a deliberately structured, paid service system. They include extended family members, friends, neighbors, co-workers, and fellow members of voluntary organizations including churches, school organizations, clubs, and teams. The extent of the network and its strength in the face of a long-term challenge are believed to greatly affect family adaptation to extreme stress. Innovative family support programs should build upon and enhance informal supports rather than supplant them.

Several working groups around the United States have developed methods for convening groups of informal supporters to assist families. These approaches have been given different names, including personal futures planning, circles of support, and support teams (Mount, 1994). All involve gathering and activating groups of people who are concerned about a family or person with a disability. They are gathered informally and use the typical discourse of friends and neighbors as opposed to the more structured and stylized communication forms used by professionals. One of their primary goals is to establish and strengthen relationships. In writing about people with disabilities in the community, Bradley (1994) observes the following:

> Being part of a community means that individuals have enduring relationships with people other than those paid to be with them. With real friendship comes natural systems of support that are often able to forestall relatively minor problems or prevent them from becoming insurmountable difficulties. Most people have these natural supports, but people who have been in the service system for years frequently have lost them to professional intervention. (p. 12)

Although much can be accomplished by tapping informal networks, there is also a need for a set of formal services that are designed to meet the concerns of families of people with ABI. Formal services consist of deliberately structured organizations that provide assistance via paid staff members. Often, formal services are staffed by people who have had advanced training, achieved some form of licensure or artification, and are presumed to have special knowledge and skills. People in formal services are usually governed by written rules and regulations. Their modes of discourse and communication are often specialized and not generally accessible by untrained laypersons. The way that these services are designed and the values implicit in them matter greatly.

Because survival from severe ABI is relatively new, most states and localities have not yet developed adequate systems for meeting the needs of children with ABI and their families. In 1996, many of the new services are driven by for-profit companies that are funded with private insurance dollars. The services are often of limited duration, removed from the family's home community, have a strong therapeutic emphasis, and involve congregating people with brain injuries into specialized living units. Similarly, some school systems have begun to establish special classrooms and segregated programs for students with ABI. Cooley and Singer (1996) have argued that these service models are likely to have severe, unexpected negative consequences; they believe alternative design principles should be adopted.

Since the 1980s, new support services have been created for both people and families of children with other disabilities that focus on constructing *supports* in natural communities rather than creating programs and services. The values that underlie these new service models should be followed in establishing new supports for people with acquired brain injury. The principles behind the new family support disability programs are, briefly, as follows[1]:

1. *Support services must view the family as the primary unit of concern and primary recipient of care. Emphasis is placed on the family's resources and potential to serve as a partner in rehabilitation.* By moving the child's family to the forefront for therapeutic intervention, every step of the treatment and rehabilitation process takes on a different tone and emphasis. For example, when a child is comatose, the nurses and physicians should pay as much attention to the family members as to the child's physiological condition. When planning physical or occupational therapy, the therapists should take into account the typical routines, settings, and objects

---

[1]For an in-depth explanation of the principles behind family support disability programs, see Bergman and Singer (1996); Dunst, Trivette, Gordon, and Starnes (1993); Singer and Powers (1993); and Singer, Powers, and Olson (1996).

in the child's home. In helping the injured child make the transition back into school, the school personnel should incorporate the parents into the planning process, attend to the concerns of siblings, and maintain ongoing cooperation between home and school.

2. *Supports should aim to increase the family's membership in the community by resisting the forces that cause social isolation and building upon informal social networks rather than supplanting them.* This principle acknowledges that most people's primary emotional and practical supports come from friends, family members, neighbors, co-workers, and members of shared organizations, not paid service workers (Singer & Powers, 1993). Family assistance must be designed in ways that do not undermine these informal supports and should help to establish and maintain them when they are not present. Similarly, interventions for children should be designed to help the child preserve and build upon social networks, which often erode as a result of brain injury.

3. *Families should identify their own needs and supports should be designed flexibly to respond to these family perceptions.* By contrast, a more traditional approach to services consists of signing a family up for a specific, established program, such as respite care or transportation; the menu of choices is determined by the availability of programs rather than by the family's concerns. Flexible supports should be tailored to the unique concerns of each family, and these supports should change over time as the family changes.

4. *One consistent person should be the primary coordinator for the family and should be able to act as an advocate, coach, and source of information and emotional support.* The family support coordinator must be extremely knowledgeable about the informal and formal resources available in the community or region. This person should be easy to contact and able to respond quickly. Support coordinators should be very skilled at giving clear information about the many complex issues that arise in ABI treatment and rehabilitation. In the rehabilitation field, these coordinators are typically referred to as case managers.

5. *Family support must address the life-span needs of the child and family.* People with severe brain injury will require some form of assistance throughout their lives in order to participate in typical community living. Thus, services should not be time limited and must change flexibly as the person with ABI ages.

6. *Family support should enable and empower family members to develop a sense of mastery in coping with the challenges posed by ABI.* Family support should be designed and delivered in a way that will trans-

mit the skills, information, and resources necessary to enable family members to become more effective in coping with challenges. By contrast, they should not build dependency or encourage a sense of helplessness. As a corollary to this principle, family members should have a decisive role in the governance of services through boards, policy-making bodies, and staffing.

7. *Family support should be based upon generic community institutions and services whenever possible.* Rather than creating separate programs, such as special schools, sheltered work settings, and separate living centers, services for people with ABI should be located in and made an integral part of the settings where the rest of the community lives, works, and plays. Inclusion, rather than segregation, should be a primary goal of family support.

8. *Family support services should adapt to cultural diversity and variant family forms.* Cross-cultural competence and acceptance of the family's own definition of its membership are essential to providing family-based services. In a multicultural society with rapidly changing family structures, it is essential that family support not inadvertently become an agent for the social control of families outside the majority culture.

9. *Federal and state policy should be designed in order to enhance the capacity of local communities to support families of people with ABI.* This principle points to several important practices. For example, if a state makes a decision to contract with a teritiary care center for people with ABI, it should require the center to offer comprehensive outreach services to the local communities where the injured people will return. If family support coordinators are hired by public agencies, they should be based in a community or regional system rather than a centralized system.

Family support services require a wide array of different kinds of discrete services including financial assistance, housing assistance, employment counseling, marriage and individual counseling, support groups, allied health professions, homemaker services, in-home behavior management assistance, special school supports, supported employment programs, and supported living programs. This array does not exist in many resource-poor areas. Public policy should aim to build these capacities on a local or regional basis over time, rather than centralize these services in ways that will retard or divert local capacity building.

CONCLUSION

This volume aims to make readers aware of the needs of families of children with severe brain injury. This large and growing population will continue to challenge the capacities of a humane society for the foreseeable future. It is hoped that this volume will contribute to an understanding of what families require in terms of supporting their lifelong efforts to care for and relate to loved ones with ABI. The contributors to this volume present a variety of professional viewpoints about essential components of a comprehensive family support system.

REFERENCES

Antanovsky, A. (1987). *A sense of coherence: Unraveling the mystery of health.* San Francisco: Jossey-Bass.

Bergman, A.I., & Singer, G.H.S. (1996). The thinking behind new public policy. In G.H.S. Singer, L.E. Powers, & A.L. Olson (Eds.). *Redefining family support: Innovations in public–private partnerships.* (pp. 435–464). Baltimore: Paul H. Brookes Publishing Co.

Billings, A.G., & Moos, R.H. (1985). Psychosocial stressors, coping, and depression. In E.W. Beckman & W.R. Leber (Eds.), *Handbook of depression: Treatment, assessment, and research* (pp. 940–976). Homewood, IL: Dorsey Press.

Boss, P. (1988). *Family stress management.* Beverly Hills: Sage Publications.

Bradley, V.J. (1994). Evolution of a new service paradigm. In V.J. Bradley, J.W. Ashbaugh, & B.C. Blaney (Eds.), *Creating individual supports for people with developmental disabilities: A mandate for change at many levels* (pp. 11–32). Baltimore: Paul H. Brookes Publishing Co.

Brown, G., Chadwick, O., Shaffer, D., Rutter, M., & Traub, M. (1981). A prospective study of children with head injuries (III): Psychiatric sequelae. *Psychological Medicine, 2,* 63–78.

Dunst, C.J., Trivette, C.M., Gordon, N.J., & Starnes, A.L. (1993). Family-centered case management practices: Characteristics and consequences. In G.H.S. Singer & L.E. Powers (Eds.), *Families, disability, and empowerment: Active coping skills and strategies for family interventions* (pp. 89–118). Baltimore: Paul H. Brookes Publishing Co.

Florian, V., & Katz, S. (1991). The other victims of traumatic brain injury: Consequences for family members. *Neuropsychology, 5*(4), 267–279.

Friesen, B.J., & Poerther, J. (Eds.). (1995). *From case management to service coordination for children with emotional, behavioral, or mental disorders: Building on family strengths.* Baltimore: Paul H. Brookes Publishing Co.

Herman, J.L. (1992). *Trauma and recovery.* New York: Basic Books.

Janoff-Bulman, R. (1992). *Shattered assumptions.* New York: Free Press.

Mallory, B. (1995). Early intervention and family policy. In G.H.S. Singer, L.E. Powers, & A.L. Olson (Eds.), *Redefining family support: Innovations in public–private partnerships* (pp. 151–170). Baltimore: Paul H. Brookes Publishing Co.

May Institute. (1993). *Information on brain injury in children,* brochure. Boston: Tufts New England Medical Center.

McLanahan, S., & Sandefur, G. (1994). *Growing up with a single parent.* Cambridge, MA: Harvard University Press.

Mount, B. (1994). The benefits and limitations of personal futures planning. In V.J. Bradley, J.W. Ashbaugh, & B.C. Blaney (Eds.), *Creating individual sup-*

ports for people with developmental disabilities: A mandate for change at many levels (pp. 97–108). Baltimore: Paul H. Brookes Publishing Co.

Nihira, K., Meyers, C.E., & Mink, I.T. (1980). Home environment, family adjustment, and the development of mentally retarded children. *Applied Research in Mental Retardation, 1,* 5–24.

Olson, D., McCubbin, H.I., Barnes, H.L., Larsen, A.S., Muxen, M.J., & Wilson, M.A. (1983). *Families: What makes them work?* Beverly Hills: Sage Publications.

Pahl, J., & Quine, L. (1987). Families with mentally handicapped children. In J. Orford (Ed.), *Treating the disorder, treating the family.* Baltimore: Johns Hopkins University Press.

Patterson, J.M. (1988). Chronic illness in children and the impact on families. In C.S. Chilman, E.W. Nunnally, & F.M. Cox (Eds.), *Chronic illness and disability* (pp. 69–107). Beverly Hills: Sage Publications.

Patterson, J.M. (1991). Family resilience to the challenge of a child's disability. *Pediatric Annals, 20*(9), 491–500.

Patterson, J.M., McCubbin, H.I., & Warwick, W.J. (1990). The impact of family functioning on health changes in children with cystic fibrosis. *Social Science and Medicine, 31*(2), 159–164.

Rivara, F.P., & Mueller, B.A. (1986). The epidemiology and prevention of pediatric head injury. *Journal of Head Trauma Rehabilitation, 1*(4), 7–15.

Singer, G.H.S., & Irvin, L.K. (Eds.). (1989). *Support for caregiving families: Enabling positive adaptation to disability.* Baltimore: Paul H. Brookes Publishing Co.

Singer, G.H.S., & Powers, L. (Eds.). (1993). *Families, disability, and empowerment: Active coping skills and strategies for family interventions.* Baltimore: Paul H. Brookes Publishing Co.

Singer, G.H.S., Powers, L.E., & Olson, A.L. (Eds.). (1996). *Redefining family support: Innovations in public–private partnerships.* Baltimore: Paul H. Brookes Publishing Co.

Singer, J. (1993). *Social support and coping in families of children with disabilities: The role of parental friendships.* Unpublished doctoral dissertation, University of Oregon, Eugene.

Turnbull, A.P., & Turnbull, H.R., III. (1986). *Families, professionals, and exceptionality: A special partnership.* Columbus, OH: Charles E. Merrill.

2

A Report on the Concerns of Parents of Children with ABI

George H.S. Singer
and Charles Nixon

A relatively new and growing population of children and youth has entered the public school and community service systems for people with severe disabilities: children and youth with acquired brain injury (ABI). The discovery and dissemination of new medical practices has reduced mortality rates for people who experience severe brain trauma (Sachs, 1991), while the use of improved emergency procedures and the increased availability of pediatric intensive care facilities have contributed to improved outcomes. Children and youth with severe brain injuries frequently experience cognitive challenges and often face other sensory and neuromotor challenges. Because of the plasticity of the brain and the typical malleability of children's development, long-term outcomes are not easy to predict.

When a child or adolescent experiences severe ABI, the family also experiences trauma and may need—at least intermittently—special supports to promote typical family life. However, the needs of these families are somewhat different from those of families with children who are identified at birth, or shortly thereafter, as having a congenital disability. Children with ABI experience a sudden trauma

This report was funded in part by Grant #H086P90083 from the U.S. Department of Education. The views expressed herein do not necessarily reflect the views of the funder.

23

that changes them from typical children to ones with severe disabilities.

This chapter describes what parents experience when their children undergo ABI by summarizing the stories of several parents during their first year postinjury. This chapter is based on a study conducted to provide professionals who work with families of children with ABI with a better understanding of the difficulties parents face. Qualitative research methods were used in order to 1) develop an insider's view of the experience (Bogdan & Biklen, 1982); and 2) make the lived experiences of these parents more real to the reader (Guba & Lincoln, 1989).

RESEARCH METHODOLOGY

Study Participants

Twenty-six parents of individuals with severe ABI participated in the study. They were recruited by local chapters of the Brain Injury Association and by the staff of a rehabilitation hospital. Ten of the parents participated in a day-long focus group in which they were asked to recount their experiences surrounding their children's accidents or injuries. Ten of the parents participated in lengthy structured interviews in which they were asked to recall their children's injuries and their means of coping with resultant difficulties. Questions emphasized stress, coping, and social support. The focus group proceedings and the interviews were transcribed for analysis. An additional group of six parents participated in a 2-hour stress management class in which parents were encouraged to recall their experiences surrounding their children's injuries. The authors collected field notes during this 8-week group.

Ten of the subjects came from urban areas in the northeastern United States and 16 from the Pacific Northwest. Subjects included mothers and fathers, married and divorced parents. All of the parents were English speaking and Caucasian. The majority of parents were middle class. Of the exceptions, two were upper–middle-class professionals and two had lower incomes and relied on public assistance. The time since their child's injury ranged from 1 year to 10 years. All of the children and youth with ABI required intensive educational support services. All had severe cognitive sequelae from their accidents. Children ranged in age from 3 years old to 40 years old at the time of data collection.

Data Collection and Coding

Data were collected in group and individual settings. The authors asked a few general open-ended questions (e.g., "Please tell us the story of what happened to your child and how it affected you"), followed by more specific probes (e.g., "Who took care of your other children while you were in the hospital?"). Parents were asked to describe what happened to their child and how they responded. In order to encourage parents to provide as much detail as possible in their answers, close-ended questions were asked to elicit specifics about their thoughts and feelings in response to the situations that they described and the ways in which they coped with extremely stressful circumstances. Parents were asked to tell about other people who helped them in coping with their child's ABI.

Transcriptions and field notes were coded for themes that emerged from a careful reading of the material, as recommended by Glaser and Strauss (1967). Initially, a large number of distinct code categories were developed; these were subsequently reduced by incorporating the smaller categories into broader themes. Critical incidents and key excerpts were then identified to exemplify the major themes.

RESULTS FROM THE PARENT STUDY

When parents of children with ABI talk about their experiences, they organize them into four life phases.

The time of the accident, the occurrence, and what we had to face dealing with the immediacy of it; then the stresses that we faced returning home, in the community, and currently.

The ordering that follows is derived from the major events and stages that unfold in the natural course of a severe brain injury:

1. The accident
2. The period of coma
3. The period of intensive rehabilitation
4. The period of reintegration into the home and school

The Accident

The time of the accident...what we had to face with the immediacy of it.

Parents remember the events surrounding their child's trauma in the vivid detail that characterizes the most powerful life experiences. They are able to recall exactly when and where they learned of the accident and typically communicate a sense of having been instantly plunged into a new and dire dimension of life.

My son, Patrick, called and just from the tone of his voice I knew something dreadful had happened. I knew the minute I heard his voice—it was just like a zombie talking, no change of inflection: "Mother, there's been an accident. Peter's been hurt."

I came on to the accident scene and immediately recognized my boy's bike in a crumpled state. Everything went on automatic at that point.

Involvement with the emergency medical system began very soon after the accident for parents, as most had to deal with emergency transportation. Parents report these encounters as distressing, saying they felt shunted aside.

A lot of damage is done to parents before their children are in the hospital. These EMTs, ambulance crews, and fire rescue people need to understand that not only is the person lying on the ground or in the water injured, but so are the parents and they need to be taken into consideration immediately.

Several themes emerged from the accounts of these confrontations: separation and isolation from the injured child, a lack of recognition of the parent's need for comfort and information, the need to make vital decisions under great pressure, a need for extraordinary efforts and endurance, and a fight against hopelessness. Frequently, parents were told nothing or given negative prognoses.

We had been told nothing. All I knew was that my son was bleeding from his head or skull. Scalp injuries bleed tremendously anyway. I had no concept of what we were looking at, but I stayed with him. I spent 57 hours caring for this kid. He was released to me 24 hours postop and I was supposed to handle this? I was scared to death.

That first night it happened, that really was stressful. They called me up here at 1 o'clock in the morning and asked me if I was his dad and I said, "Yeah." And they said, "There was an accident"; and I said, "Well, how bad was it?" They said, "He's not dead yet."

Another mother was told of the severity of her son's accident at work, when hospital staff called to say that he was not a candidate for survival. There was a strong sense of events being out of control.

You start to learn about the fact that you can't control a lot of things. Like, when you've had a good life, and you've had a good marriage, and you've lived in this garden and watched life grow beautifully—why, you tend to forget these tidal waves that can overwhelm human beings.

Under this extraordinary stress, parents often were required to make major decisions quickly and with little information or assistance. In retrospect, they wished that they would have had some help with these decisions.

I wish I could have had, from the very beginning, someone who was very knowledgeable about brain injury to help me because there are a lot of decisions that have to be made right from day one.

Children who were initially received by small hospitals needed to be transferred to larger care centers. Parents were sometimes asked to choose the hospital but were given little or no information about the alternatives. One parent reported being asked to select a neurologist without any prior knowledge or information about the choices.

The time surrounding the initial accident also had a strong impact on the rest of the family. Several parents reported that extended family members helped out during the first days after the accident. Family members provided such practical help as watching siblings who were left at home and taking care of the house; others stayed in the hospital to keep the parent company. During the emergency room and intensive care unit period, some parents noted that friends provided relief.

The crises also affected the siblings of the injured children. Often, brothers and sisters were cared for by relatives and had little idea of what was happening. In looking back, some parents were concerned that the accident and subsequent separation from parents was also a traumatic time for siblings. One parent said the following:

His [the sibling] emotions have been on a roller coaster near all the time now; I don't know if that's related to the accident or not. I think it had to have been traumatic for him because at the scene of the accident, he was literally handed to a friend and didn't see either my wife or I for over a week—you know, not knowing where his mom and dad were at when he was 4 years old.

The disruptions in family life were often extensive. Typical schedules and routines were cast aside, sleeping and eating patterns altered, and usual patterns of communication distorted by the enormity of parents' emotional reactions.

Parents had very mixed reports about the quality of the emergency medical care that their children received. Reports ranged from one parent who had high praise for the staff of a small rural hospital to reports of alleged negligence and malpractice. Some parents had shocking stories to tell: a child left unchanged and uncleaned in a full body cast for 4 days, another whose wound was stitched in the emergency room without being cleaned, and one parent who believed an ambulance crew was responsible for his child's heart failure and subsequent brain damage on the way to the hospital. For many parents, the encounter with trauma care initiated a very mixed, and often conflicting, relationship with the medical and related health professions that treat people with ABI.

The Period of Coma

All of the injured children and youth described in this study were comatose following their injuries. The comas lasted anywhere from a few days to several months. Several themes regarding this period emerged from the interviews: great uncertainty and lack of information, a struggle to maintain the personhood of the child, a struggle to maintain hope, the value of personal caregiving, and the emotional drama of the recovery of consciousness.

During the time that the children were in deep coma, parents struggled with preserving the personhood of their loved one as well as hoping for survival and recovery. When their children did not respond in any way to the environment, parents had little to go on other than hope. Physicians either communicated negative prognoses or admitted that outcomes were completely unpredictable.

Peter had three major systems breakdowns and had to be fed through tubes. I mean, when you're in a coma a month, your body is really thrown into low. Eight days after the accident, why, they wanted me to take him off of life support...

They just didn't know—he was in coma for, like, 6 weeks and in intensive care for 6 weeks. And, we never knew and the doctors couldn't give us any hope. They just didn't know. They'd keep telling us, "Well, we've got to wait until the swelling goes out of his brain before we know what to expect."

For some parents, negative prognoses at this phase resulted in anger, pride, and determination later on: anger directed at the doctors for not having hope, pride for their children's unexpected recovery, and determination to continue trying to obtain improvements. Still, parents wish that doctors would have been more direct in communicating some hope.

I have survived, and I'm pushing for more because every doctor I have spoken with told me, "Your son will never come out of a coma, and if he does he will be a vegetable." Vegetable now is growing flowers and doing well.

We knew it was serious. We didn't need a doctor to say that. What we needed to hear is there's always hope but it's very serious. I mean, what is it? Six or seven words. And I don't think they have to be able to do any more than that. Perhaps shake your hand or hold it, look you straight in the eye, and say "This is very serious. But there's always hope." But you see, that wasn't given to us at all.

I just had to have someone seeing my son as a real special human being.

In coma, children lay in hospital beds, hooked up to tubes and equipment. They are changed, sponged off, and tested by nurses and physicians, but do not interact or respond to any caregiving efforts. In these circumstances, it is important to parents to maintain relationships with their children as people—people with thoughts and feelings, a personal history, preferences, and wishes; although there is no visible evidence that these personal conditions still exist. At the same time, parents still feel shocked and frightened.

He was really out of it, you know, tubes at his head and a sack gathering up brain fluid, and he looked so bad; he just looked so bad. That was really frightening—scared me.

Parents tried hard to maintain a relationship with their comatose children by talking to them and touching them as if they were responsive. Efforts to communicate were aimed at trying to elicit recovery as well as maintaining person-to-person, close, emotional contact.

We would go in and work with him. We'd take a key and rub on the bottom of his foot when he was in intensive care to see if there was any reaction whatsoever. And it was quite a thrill the day that we saw him move his toes.

I couldn't bear the thought of my son lying in intensive care with people who didn't know him, didn't care about him except as a body that they were responsible for. They didn't notice this gift. And so I collected photographs from different places from the time he was in preschool, well, from the time he was a baby. And I put them in his room in the intensive care unit. I wanted so for him to become a person to somebody. I knew that it wouldn't affect certain people, but then for others that key is a visual image. It was because I just had to have someone seeing my son as a real special human being.

Some parents felt that, in the effort to save their child's life, the medical staff lost sight of the child's individuality and their emotional pain. With some exceptions in which parents believed they received substandard medical care, they felt that the hospital did a better job of taking care of the child's physical needs than of the child's and parents' psychological needs.

Well, of course, I want them to fight for his life. You know, I don't want 1 centimeter of effort lost on his behalf. But I think that, professionally, they certainly did their job. Psychologically, no. I mean it was incredible.

Many parents were critical of the lack of concern they encountered from some professionals. Complaints about professional communications centered on two areas: lack of knowledge about brain injury and lack of concern about what parents and family members were experiencing.

Do you know that, in the early stages when it was getting toward the point where our daughter was returning home, the insurance company had us visit a psychiatrist. It was a total waste. I could have told that girl things; she didn't know beans.

I saw the neurosurgeon for the first time the week following my daughter's surgery and he said, "I suppose you would like to talk to me." Prior to that he said, "If I have anything else to tell you, I will tell you."

Several parents mentioned that nurses were helpful during this period. Some parents mentioned having favorite nurses; others said that the nurses gave them much more information than the doctors. One parent described how a nurse taught him to wash his son—a personal care skill that was very important to the parent. One parent complained that the hospital circulated her favorite nurse and, thus, terminated an important relationship.

The coma and intensive care period often lasted for weeks. Parents had to set aside many of life's typical demands in order to deal with this crisis. Parents whose children were moved to centers far from home had to find places to stay near the hospital or commute long distances. During this period of protracted intensive care, some parents began to first experience social isolation, which later became a major concern.

It's like you're an island. You're isolated. People don't want to step into these situations. I mean, I think that the level of pain is so great and everybody has so much pain already, so many troubles of their own to deal with, that you tend to be shunned from the very beginning.

Other parents continued to have the help of friends or relatives during this time and remembered it with appreciation.

The emergence from deep coma and gradual return of skills marked a new period for parents—most did not know what to expect. One parent said that all he knew about comas came from watching television; he thought that when people emerged from unconsciousness, they wake up and have their full faculties. He also assumed that progress would be steady and without setbacks. When the actual course of recovery was very gradual with many ups and downs, this parent was bewildered. Each step forward represented hope for the child; each step backward raised fear that the child would regress into coma or fail to recover. Once again, parents were not given information about stages of recovery from coma.

Every parent had a vivid memory of the moment he or she first reestablished communication with the comatose child. They recalled these moments with feelings of joy and gratitude and, in retrospect, these occasions were very important to them.

[What] a thrill when we'd say, "Darell, this is Dad. Do you hear me? If you do, squeeze my hand." And he'd squeeze, you'd feel his little squeeze in the hand.

Initially, it was really tough because he was unresponsive. And then when he responded—it was the fourth or fifth day—it really lifted our hearts. And then to be with him and watch him progress from originally not being able to communicate at all to at least being able to say something at the end of the 4 weeks, really did us some good.

By the time he was able to talk to me, there was—I don't think—any shadow of death left. But this would have been sometime during the fourth or fifth week. That was a joyous, joyous, joyous time. And you know, Lord, the smile. Oh, my. He was so glad to see me and I was so glad to see him. We just sat there and smiled like fools.

After hovering near death in a comatose state, this experience of reemergence was a very powerful one. Parents thought it often appeared to defy the negative predictions of the doctors and, similarly, challenged the seemingly impersonal nature of hospital care. In light of this medical defiance, parents felt they had very strong emotional evidence to prove the worthiness of their undying hope. This notion was reinforced by the gradual reacquisition of skills during the first year following the accident. Some parents did not understand that their child was forever changed until long after the accident; they still felt they had strong experiential evidence to encourage them to believe that, eventually, any sequelae would lessen or disappear altogether. Again, in retrospect, parents wished that they would have been given much more information about the long-term effects of severe brain injury. In particular, they wished that they had been informed about the changes in social behavior and personality that are usually associated with severe ABI.

The Period of Intensive Rehabilitation

Most of the children studied required several months of intensive rehabilitation before they were able to reenter their homes and school systems and return to a semblance of their typical daily schedules.

After recovery from coma, children were either transferred to rehabilitation hospitals or, in areas with no services, sent home. In the rehabilitation units, parents learned that the work of these professionals had a different focus for their children. The emphasis shifted from biological survival to the recovery of previous mental and physical abilities. In this phase, the child had to be much more of an active participant and ally. Also in this phase, parents first encountered the scarcity of pediatric rehabilitation services. Some parents had to bring their children home and manage the rehabilitation themselves, as best they could. Others believed that the rehabilitation program their child received was not really designed for children, as staff had worked primarily with adults with ABI whose needs are different. Other parents had to send their children far away from their home community for rehabilitation.

Parents recall the rehabilitation phase as all-absorbing. Typical family routines and schedules, as well as social interactions, were disrupted as parents either spent a lot of time in the hospital or devoted a great deal of time to the child's rehabilitation at home. Several parents described the need to commit large amounts of time and energy to helping their child recover. For many, these efforts were exhausting and isolating. For the most seriously injured children, the demands of caregiving have continued indefinitely; exhaustion began to take a toll the year following the injury.

My wife gets up at 5 A.M. She has a difficult time a lot of days finding the time to go to the bathroom or eat. Many nights my wife doesn't eat because she is doing the laundry and she sleeps in the same room with my [brain-injured] daughter. There is no going to any social meetings. We don't have time for that kind of stuff. Geez, I don't know where anybody finds time to do that.

Parents wanted to believe that absolutely everything possible that could be done for their child's recovery was done; they found any effort less than 100% unacceptable. Given the limitations and tremendous cost of rehabilitation services, this meant that a major amount of rehabilitation and caregiving fell to the parents, who held themselves to very high standards. Still, even the most intense rehabilitation efforts did not ensure success. One boy cooperated with his rehabilitation—anything he was given to do, he worked hard to accomplish, but he refused to go outside of the house. He was still unable to communicate fully and his mother could not understand his resistance.

I finally reached that point where he could give me enough of an answer—he didn't want to go outdoors until he was all well. And I realized that there had to be a great push made to break [his decision] that if he was going to be outdoors, he had to be 100% well. So I got him a puppy for Christmas and he had to walk his dog. That was the only negative I saw in Peter; he didn't want to go outside until he was all well.

Often these efforts entailed a high personal cost, affecting relationships within the family, social ties outside of the family, and the fiscal status of the family. Some parents reported that, eventually, they did begin to learn to balance their own needs with those of their child.

I think some of us learned that from the hospital or from some support person who got to us and said, "You've got to take care of yourself"; or my husband and I would have never realized that we needed sleep or we had to eat, you know.

Others found their child's needs so compelling that, in retrospect, they felt that relationships with spouses and other children suffered. In some couples, the accident and subsequent caregiving strained the marriage to the breaking point.

I think the first thing that came to mind on my list [when asked about stressors] was the family relationships and how Brendon [my husband] and I cope with the stress that occurs between us because of the injury.

It's just that we are always so busy. There is no time for a relationship between us and we are the foundation for our family.

My husband insisted that she [our daughter with brain injury] come home because there was nowhere else, except for a place in Jersey where they wanted to just put her away and forget about her. My husband insisted on her coming back; after about 3 months, my husband left. He couldn't cope with it anymore.

My son was hit by a car 8 years ago. He spent about 4 months in ICU [intensive care unit] for coma and then he went to Sunnyview [rehabilitation hospital] for another 4 months. I just think that this accident ruined our lives completely because my husband couldn't cope with it. I didn't have any help; we went to all the counseling and it still didn't save the family.

We are here [at the focus group] because we survived. I know a person in our situation who cannot cope at all, who can't do it. How many husbands or wives have walked out and washed their hands?

Coping with the accident and its aftermath did not break up every marriage. On the contrary, some parents reported that it brought them closer together. One couple said the accident both brought them together and caused more occasions for arguments.

I think that initially it brought my wife and me closer together, but then it probably pulled us apart. It gives us more instances to disagree—how we should proceed with Fred and do things over dealing with our other children. I think that had we not been where we were, it might have torn us apart. We knew we had to hold together to survive as a family.

Coping with Personality Changes and Behavior Problems

One of the most divisive issues for some families centered around the injured child's behavior problems after the accident. Closed-head injury often traumatizes parts of the brain that are critical to generating the behavior that makes up personality. Children with ABI commonly experience difficulties with social judgment, typical affective behavior, and impulse control. After the child has returned home and begun rehabilitation, these social and behavioral challenges often emerge as one of the most difficult legacies of the trauma for parents. Some of the personality changes in the study group were relatively benign.

Fred was somewhat quiet and introverted before the accident, but he's very outgoing and extroverted now. He's not afraid to go walk up and give someone a big hug. You know, for an 11-year-old boy to do that now, you know, that's not cool. Fred doesn't even think about it. He goes, if he wants to give somebody a hug, he does it.

It isn't that the symptoms are different. It's that the controls aren't there. For instance, I can remember with Bradley, he always had a hot temper but before the accident he was cool. After the accident, it hit the fan. All those controls were gone. His main problem was he was still 17 years old and he thought he was very popular with the girls. He'd try to make out with every girl he saw.

[Before the accident] he just didn't talk much. He was always very close to his mother when he was growing up. Then, after he came out of the coma and started to talk, he never shut up. He'd just talk, talk, talk. And a stranger, he didn't know what a stranger was. And he just about talked us to death [laughter].

The problem of disinhibition—a child's loss of normal constraints on emotional reactions—was much more serious for some parents. It was particularly difficult when the impulsive behavior involved anger and aggression. Parents reported that the onset of behavior problems took them by surprise. Again, they wished that they had been given more information about the behavior problems and personality changes associated with ABI. When these problems first emerged, parents and professionals did not attribute them to brain injury and, in some cases, the children were given inappropriate kinds of treatment.

Like I said, we anticipated physiological problems. We did not anticipate what appeared to be psychiatric problems. My husband and I went through a crisis of our own, questioning [his] alcohol and drug [use]. We ended up forcing him to voluntarily commit himself. Had we realized, had we known, we could have taken the appropriate measures then, taken him to who he needed to see instead of putting him through 60 days in a private psychiatric hospital where he was subjected to [people who experienced] alcohol abuse, drug abuse, suicides, homicides, personal mutilation, all of the things that—when my kids were born—I never wanted them to see.

It is important to note that not every child experienced serious behavior problems and that, in some cases, the kinds of personality changes that occurred were viewed as positive. For example, one parent talked with admiration about the way his child continued to work to recover from the injury and face challenges posed by her altered abilities.

I live on a day-to-day basis. I feel she is doing super. She is a very positive, patient kid. No fear. We can't compare what Kelly is like today to her first 14 years, except she has not lost her determination. We go day by day and each day we learn to accept what we have to accept, but I'm not done and she is not either.

In the interviews with parents of young adults with ABI, some parents were still very concerned about social and behavior problems several years after the injury. One father described his irritation at his son's temper and argumentativeness. Another described continuing embarrassment at the way his son, now an adult, would approach strangers and strike up conversations that were inappropriate.

Behavior problems were cause for dissension within some families. In cases of anger and aggression, the children's problem behaviors raised interpersonal tension among other family members.

It almost got to the point of domestic violence. We were so frustrated, and he was violent, and we had no support.

In other instances, family members became divided over their view of the problem behaviors. In one such family, the mother attributed her son's difficult behavior to his injured brain and assumed that it was out of his control. As a result, she viewed him as essentially blameless. Yet, her husband believed that moral behavior was always under a person's control, regardless of brain injury. Siblings in this family were also divided in their opinions: one sympathizing with the brother with ABI, the other blaming him for acting in problematic ways.

And I told him, I said, "Sean, you know in your mind what's right and what's wrong. And some of the stuff you pull is wrong. And you know it's wrong. Don't do it." But he just won't listen.

His brother Bill, he's the oldest, gets along real good, because Bill was always the bad boy in the family. Now my second boy, he won't have anything to do with Sean. Sean bugs the hell out of him and he won't have anything to do [with him].

Changes in the child's personality pose one of the larger, long-term challenges for parents as they adapt to the effects of acquired brain injury on their child, themselves, and their family. Parents described how this process involved both coping with the loss of the child as he was before the accident and accepting a new, changed person.

Parental experience in coping with a child with ABI involves a simultaneous process of grief and adjustment. For many parents, even years after the accident, there were feelings of deep sorrow as if a child had died. This mixture of emotions was somewhat confusing and parents felt that other people did not easily understand this mixture of thoughts and feelings.

I mean it was like [having] schizophrenia. I'm looking at this kid who looks the same—a little bit of a balance problem, a little deficiencies. But, this is not the same kid. I'm going crazy. My husband is going "You're fine." My mother-in-law is going "You're psychotic." I needed to have someone who I felt was solid, someone trusting, a professional, someone who has the education to tell me, "Yes, Ruth, it is fine. Tear your house apart. Scream and yell and mourn this child."

Many of the children also underwent this process of mourning; that is, they remembered themselves prior to the injury and had to come to terms with their own loss. Some parents expressed bewilderment about what to say to their child about the loss of abilities.

The crucial thing is that the child himself knows he is different. If you can't accept the new kid, the new kid can't accept himself. He is fighting you every day.

For some parents, the accident and loss of their child, as known before, triggered a loss of meaning. One father spoke bitterly about his loss of faith in God. Another mother described the way in which the accident not only caused grief but also brought to the forefront feelings of being cast out by the benevolent side of life.

Do you believe in God, all of you? Did you ask and you receive? Did you ask to receive a brain-injured child?

I no longer believe that if you work at life it lets you walk off into a beautiful sunset. So where does that leave me? Still trying but not really believing? Off the track permanently? Yes, there is a God with His Purpose, but my faith is an imperfect vehicle. My former identities as a wife and mother, I'm sorry, have eroded and disappeared in a cloud of dust leaving nothing in me that is coherent.

Some of the parents also described a period in which they experienced guilt and anger. One parent mentioned the fact that she had bought the bicycle that her son was riding when he had his accident—as if she might have prevented it if she had not purchased the bicycle. Others expressed worries that they were not doing enough for their child's rehabilitation. Parents wished that the professionals who worked with them would know how to counsel them about guilt and grief—or, at least, be aware of these feelings. They felt that social workers, therapists, and counselors needed to be educated about the effects of brain injury on parents.

_____

The guilt encompasses many, many things such as, "Am I doing enough? Could I have prevented this ABI?"

We need to get to our mental health people. [They] need to know that the minute [parents] find out there is a brain injury involved, they are undoubtedly going to feel guilty. They are going to feel the definite mourning process because the moment that accident happens, that child and their lives are changed permanently, forever, completely.

_____

Dealing with such strong emotions and pervasive feelings of doubt was a solitary struggle for most parents. Again and again, they mentioned their difficulties in making themselves understood by others.

The Period of Reintegration into the Home and School

Social Isolation, the Communication of Stigma, and the Creation of a Handicapped Identity An injured child's status is often unclear for a considerable length of time. Realization that the child is permanently changed and will now have a different identity is communicated by key events after the child's return to home and school. During this period, parents began receiving powerful messages from their social community.

_____

The biggest disappointment was later on when his friends just kind of faded away from us.

_____

Several parents thought that the accident and subsequent changes in the family's lifestyle resulted in social isolation for both the parents and child. Most parents indicated that family and friends were available during the immediate crisis following the accident and that their practical support was of critical importance.

_____

My husband's brother's wife had enough objectivity to deal with this. She was instrumental in getting someone to clean my house, mow the lawn, and take care of our other kids.

_____

Others described relatives or friends who visited the hospital while the child was in the intensive care unit: One mother told of a good friend who would sit by the child's bedside at night so that she could get some sleep. The child's school friends were also active during this crisis time. However, after this initial period, supportive people began to withdraw from the family and child; this withdrawal communicated to parents that their child had a new identity—one that was devalued by the larger community.

At the time he was in the hospital, we had several friends who came up to see us and Darell. I guess the biggest disappointment was later on when our friends and his friends found out that it was more of a permanent situation; then, they just kind of faded away from us, especially his friends. They just stopped coming around, didn't see him any more and that was kind of heart-breaking.

The loss of school friends can be partly attributed to the amount of school time that the children miss. They often miss a full year of schooling, which leaves them behind their age and grade mates when they do return. Also, physical and psychological changes intrude on friendships. For example, the father of an 11-year-old boy who had become uninhibited about showing affection to peers since his brain injury described the effect these behaviors had on peer relations. Other children were subjected to teasing because of their altered abilities.

You know, it isn't cool now for him to be doing that [showing uninhibited affection]. He gets peer pressure for that.

It's so awful to have people look at your child like he's stoned or drunk because he doesn't have good balance. I wouldn't care if he didn't have both of his legs. He's still the same person, but it's awful the judgments that we lay on other people. You know, they have these crushing expectations.

People make these assumptions. If you don't talk absolutely clearly, why, you're mentally retarded or else there's something wrong with you. These quick assumptions we use to judge people by are continually working against anybody who is severely disabled with brain injury. And just because you may be slow in the way you speak or because you can't respond to questions quickly, people write you off.

Many of the children were aware of these reactions. One parent described how she learned that her son was sensitive about other children's reactions to him upon returning to school from the hospital:

I asked him once when he came home why he watched the ground so much and he said, "Well, I don't have to see the expressions on other people's faces when they look at me." That was the only inkling that I ever got of how he suffered from awareness.

Thus, the loss of the child's friends and subsequent teasing and rejection communicated this sense of social stigma for those with visible differences in abilities.

The process of isolation appeared to be more complicated for the parents. For some parents, the isolation initially began as a result of their total absorption in their child's care and recovery. This absorption left them with little to talk to other people about beyond their very strong feelings concerning the hospital, their child's health, and related concerns.

I couldn't [wasn't able to] socialize after that accident. It was like I could live intensely in this loving world with my son, but if somebody came to visit and asked how are things going, I could hardly cope with it. It was like I was somebody who was wound up like a toy and once I got started all this, this anger started coming out—and how I was raised, you know, that's inappropriate behavior. You're not supposed to express your feelings like that. And I was appalled with the amount of emotion I was containing.

Caught up in these overwhelming emotions, it was hard for parents even to respond to other family members who were also grieving.

You have your extended family who is there grieving also, but sometimes I think you want to say, "What are you feeling sorry for yourself about? I'm the one in this situation." You have to deal with their grief when you aren't even through dealing with your own grief, so sometimes it's even harder to have them around, depending on the relationship.

Problems with maintaining friendships were also related to the practical demands of caregiving. It was often difficult for parents to get away in order to spend time with family or friends. One couple described the way that their many friends eventually stopped calling to invite them out because they were always too busy with caregiving after the accident. Finally, most parents felt that other people simply did not understand them. This sense of distance partially resulted from the well-meaning, but nonetheless fatuous, comments that people would make. Parents seemed to long for more understanding from the people around them.

You get sick and tired of hearing "I don't know how you people do it. How do you do it?" What [else] are you going to do?

If people were more aware of what you have to go through every day of your life they might be a little bit more understanding. I don't think you would be as isolated if the awareness were a little bit more than what it is, if there was more awareness in everyone around you of exactly what you were going through—the isolation, the social relationships, the burnout, the fight.

Parents also wished for this kind of understanding from professionals, especially in those cases where the child's return to school was isolating. The children in this study were developing typically, both intellectually and physically, prior to their injury. However, when they returned to the public schools after long periods of time in hospitals and rehabilitation programs, most of them no longer were able to be served in their previous, general education classrooms. In fact, all of the children in the study were identified as requiring special education and placed in programs for children with mental retardation. The process of special education labeling and placement gave many parents the first concrete realization that the broader community had given their child a new social status.

Some parents believed that children with ABI did not belong in the same program as children with mental retardation; others believed that the school staff were unprepared to serve children with acquired brain injury. The complex needs of these children often surpassed staff skills. For example, one parent reported that staff incorrectly kept putting on an arm and hand splint that her son needed to wear for an hour a day at school. Another parent reported that it was necessary for her to train the school staff to work with her daughter; she complained that the school's policy of rotating personnel from year to year meant that retraining new staff would always be necessary.

The tremendous variability in school services across regions and communities was evident in parental reports about their children's return to school. Although some parents were distressed at the quality of school programming for their children, others were impressed with the range of services that was available:

[School] has done as much for my daughter as any rehabilitation hospital or anything else. They have licensed therapists, occupational and physical therapists, and the bus comes every morning.

Return to school not only marks a critical milestone in the community's redefinition of an injured child, it also represents a substantial disjunction between two service systems—the medical/rehabilitation system and the public school system. The medical/rehabilitation system usually has much higher levels of funding from private insurance. Therapies and treatments are delivered in one-to-one sessions. Health personnel and services are viewed as part of medical treatment. Thus, reintegration into public school usually follows a period of intensive rehabilitation, either at a hospital or at home. Upon reentering public schools, the children had to share staff time and resources with several others. In some cases, parents were disappointed with the ways in which their children's physical and educational needs were not given as much care as previously.

It turned out that we had to be constantly vigilant to make sure that his individualized education program (IEP) was being followed.

Some parents were also disappointed in the way schools were very slow to implement their children's instructional programs. They expected the IEP to be implemented early in the school year, whereas many services were delayed. Again, it seems likely that expectations established during rehabilitation when children are given one-to-one assistance and programming are not applicable to a school setting where there are many more children and fewer resources.

Parents were also concerned with the way teachers dealt with their children. One parent complained that the school staff was overprotective of his son, allowing the boy to nap regularly instead of requiring him to engage in classroom work. Similarly, parents had concerns about how other children treated their child and about behavior problems. When children return to school, parents still must actively monitor and advocate for services as a child's adaptation to school will not necessarily settle into a predictable pattern.

Concerns About Siblings Parents also described focusing on the brothers and sisters of the injured child, which presents another set of social and emotional issues.

My older boy had a lot of problems dealing with his brother, the illness, and the trauma that he saw.

Some brothers and sisters developed behavior problems; others had difficulty sleeping or trouble at school. Parents attributed these problems to the trauma involved for brothers and sisters seeing the accident, being separated from parents during the hospitalization, and losing parental attention. Once again, parents desired information about the impact of brain injury on other family members and on ways to cope with these effects.

My older boy, he was intact, in other words, alive. So I thought, "Well, I will have to deal with him later." Months and months later, I dealt with the problem.

[I wish I'd had] a checklist to say, "Is this child in trouble? Do you see this, this, and this happening?" Not to the injured child, but to the surviving sibling. My daughter couldn't sleep. She had incredible sleeping problems, all kinds of things; we knew that she needed help.

Like their parents, brothers and sisters also struggled with feelings of guilt, loss, and grief. One particularly poignant story illustrates the cognitive and emotional reactions that siblings can have and their need for someone to attend to them. One mother was away at the hospital for $3\frac{1}{2}$ months while her daughter was in a coma. She tried to explain *coma* to the 4-year-old and 12-year-old brothers.

We had to explain to both kids that Sarah was sleeping and she was hurt. She had hit her head and she was hurt. When I first had gone home after $3\frac{1}{2}$ months, they had in school what they called a journal where the kids would keep a diary that nobody would ever read. And Harry had all the pages stapled closed. I opened it because I wanted to—he couldn't talk to anybody, and I wanted to know what he was feeling. All he kept writing was, "I wish it was me. It should have been me. It shouldn't have been my sister."

Parents were also concerned about the role that siblings should play in caregiving. On the one hand, they wanted the brothers and sisters to be helpful. On the other hand, they did not want to unduly burden them with responsibilities. They also struggled to give enough time and attention to the siblings while assisting their child with ABI.

It's a big one [problem]—making sure everybody gets their time and not putting too much responsibility on the older kids, the more capable kids, in taking care of him [the injured child]; although, I trust my kids with him more than I trust any other stranger in the world.

Financial Worries   In addition to the social and emotional impacts of caregiving on parents and siblings, the people we interviewed also had many practical concerns about finding and paying for appropriate services for their children with ABI. The costs of long-term care were a great concern, as were the many inequities in the medical payment system. Medical treatment at each stage of recovery—from the emergency room, to intensive care during the coma, to rehabilitation and follow-up—is very expensive. Several parents were faced with enormous debts.

With his medical bills alone, I am in debt upwards of $15,000.

I have a lien on me. I have a loan of $450,000 from the New York State Department of Social Services for this kid. Where do you get this money?

Parents discover quickly that money is the key to obtaining services for their children. From the beginning, doors began to open or close, depending upon parental resources.

The first thing the rehabilitators play is they take you in the board of directors' room and sit you down at the table. They want to know if you have got insurance before they even take you. That's the first thing they want to know, and if you don't have insurance, they don't want you.

Those parents who were privately insured had complaints about the difficulties that surround getting payments for items such as special equipment. Also, most insurance policies have time-limited rehabilitation payments; termination of rehabilitation services was often determined by the end of insurance payments rather than by the needs of the child. Other parents were faced with prohibitive increases in the costs of their health insurance once their child became a long-term patient.

Parents receiving public assistance had many difficulties with Medicaid. Many doctors would not serve them because the Medicaid payments were too low or too difficult to obtain. For those children who did not recover from coma and required long-term care, parents said it was difficult or impossible to find services and pay for them. These parents suffered from both a lack of catastrophic health care insurance and the restrictions in public assistance that characterize contemporary health care funding.

Helpful Supports to Parents of Children with ABI

Although this study has emphasized the suffering and frustrations that parents and other family members experienced in coping with the acquired brain injury of a child, there were—of course—positive experiences. Parents described a number of formal and informal supports that were of genuine help. They also described a variety of coping strategies that have been adaptive for them.

From the outset, parents had to rely on the competence and efficiency of medical personnel and systems for their child's survival. Several parents expressed appreciation for the way that local hospitals served their children. In almost every case, children were close to death after their injury and their lives depended upon the availability of emergency treatment and the skills of doctors, nurses, and technicians. These urgent services often were rendered under intense time pressures and in difficult circumstances.

They [hospital staff] have done a fantastic job under the circumstances. I don't want to see my daughter hurt in the brain, but they have done a great job in my hospital.

In retrospect, some parents were able to forgive the poor communication skills and lack of interpersonal concern that so often seemed to characterize the people and the procedures in medical settings.

I guess what I am saying is that they have been schooled many times. They have to protect themselves with this shell, and that shell can hurt you. You can still be coming off of anger for months and years later from it even though you are saying, "Hey, it was good because they saved my son."

When professionals were able to communicate clear information with empathy, parents were very appreciative. Parents desired both professional competence and human warmth—neither by itself would have been sufficient.

The nursing staff was great. They had a set-up in the pediatric emergency room or intensive care room and told all the shifts so we had the same nurse every day for Don. Actually, the same two nurses so we got to know them real well. They were very supportive. Ellen [spouse] and they would talk about Don's condition and we actually got more information from the nurses than we did from the doctors.

Similarly, when parents had adequate insurance coverage and cooperation from the insurance company, they reported being able to obtain services that made an important difference to their child and family. One of the parents who had the most fiscal resources available through full insurance coverage was able to hire a personal case manager to take care of the large volume of paperwork generated by the many agencies and services that his child required. Another family was able to hire private-duty nurses to help with rehabilitation at home. However, the personnel did not always exhibit competence, which made the resource insufficient. The combination of adequate resources, professionally competent personnel, and good communication occurred rarely.

Several parents noted that professionals generally were not well informed about acquired brain injury and its long-term effects. Many parents found it necessary to read and learn as much as possible about their child's condition, which sometimes made them more knowledgeable than the experts. When professional staff were willing to learn from well-informed parents, both sides appeared to benefit. In addition, continuity was particularly important, in both services and personnel, given the need for specialized knowledge. Parents repeatedly expressed frustration with the frequent turnover of personnel, ranging from ICU nurses to special education teachers. When hospitals and schools established procedures that led to continuity of staff, parents were grateful.

In addition, informal sources of care and companionship were at least as important as formal services and financial support. Often, immediate and extended family were invaluable. One mother even asked, "What is greater than a family?" Parents reported that family members helped with practical concerns, such as house care and child care for siblings, and gave invaluable emotional support. Similarly, friends and work associates were important to some parents. One parent described a friend who stayed with her son at night. Another talked about a church group that offered practical assistance, as well as emotional solace. Some of the most helpful contact came from other parents of children with ABI, as it was essential to parents to make contact with other people who could truly understand their suffering.

My son swims for a swimming team for the physically limited and one of the boys that is on the team is brain injured. We just met his mother Saturday and my wife talked to her about the common problems we have and seemed to hit it off.

I need somebody who has been through it or who has been through it with other people; someone who knows what to look for, what problems to look for.

Parents also wanted contact with someone who was knowledgeable about acquired brain injury and its treatment from the time of the accident. They felt that they were left in the dark for long periods of time and had to make many important decisions in the absence of clear information. One parent was able to obtain both information and emotional support from a staff member of the local Brain Injury Association and reported satisfaction with this help.

I think you definitely need somebody right there as soon as it happens who is knowledgeable and knows the ropes.

Respite care was also greatly valued, as the long-term demands of home caregiving can be exhausting and can greatly limit a family's opportunities for typical activities. When parents and siblings were able to have a break from caregiving duties, they usually enjoyed it. However, it was necessary to find someone who was trustworthy and competent to take care of the child with ABI—not always an easy task.

We were in a position to hire someone to come in and stay at home so that our older boy would have care when we were away. This was invaluable to us.

Another kind of personal assistance that was of great value to some parents was case management. This usually involved help with obtaining services, negotiating with agencies and systems, and assisting with the necessary paperwork. Parents often had to fight to obtain services for their children; when they had an ally who could serve as a mediator and advocate, they felt supported.

Parents also reported that community institutions, including schools, youth groups, and churches, could be helpful. For example, one parent described the way the public school gave emotional aid to her son at school while she was away caring for her other child who was in coma. But, once again this program could have benefited from more information.

Our junior high school had a crisis intervention class. They made a point of taking my older son out of the class every day at study hall and allowing him to call the emergency room so that he could find out what was happening at the hospital. They dealt with him on a daily basis.

He really did need the crisis intervention counseling, but the point was, the counselor really didn't have the information, and neither did I, to explain to the 12-year-old what he could expect when his brother came home.

Parental Commitment and Coping Parents also drew upon personal resources and coping skills in the face of their harrowing experiences. Many were required to call upon the full extent of their will and faith. Different parents seemed to emphasize different ways of coping with the many challenges brought on by the injury, including intensive commitment, persistence, aggressive determination, religious faith, appreciating the progress their children made, and taking a view that some good can come from suffering. An example of the kind of commitment these parents have given to their children with ABI is one mother's statement, "I have given 5 years of my life for my son." Another father described his efforts to help his son rejoin the community:

[I] try to make his life as typical as it can be. I saw him as being a very active, outdoors-type boy, so now I find myself helping, like in Boy Scouts. I've been a den leader in Cub Scouts for 3 years. Baseball, I've gotten him into baseball, basketball. I've been there to help with the coaches and have given him some help [to see that] he has individualized help all along.

In those families whose children with ABI had grown up and entered adult life, the interviewers found that some of these parents were still embroiled in ongoing stresses. However, it is important to note that at least six parents expressed a sense of having resolved their anguish. In either case, they were reasonably satisfied with the kinds of lifestyles and options available to their children. In one case, the adult son was living in a group home sponsored by an organization that his father had helped to start. The father's satisfaction with his son's living arrangement and other services played an important part in his acceptance of the situation. Another mother who was interviewed 3 years after her child's injury talked at length about how the experience had given her a new set of values. She viewed her child, primarily, as a major contributor to her quality of life and said she had learned important lessons from the experience.

SURVEY RESULTS AND IMPLICATIONS

A qualitative methodology was used in order to let parents tell their own story and express their own concerns. This methodology attempts to maintain some of the integrity of a parent's experience, while unifying themes from several different people. Here, there is one metatheme that emerges from listening to these voices of people in extremis: The human tragedy surrounding the permanent damage of a child now takes place in the context of a set of social institutions that are only minimally cognizant of the social and emotional effects of the trauma on the family. In this nonsystem, actually made up of several disparate and noncommunicating parts, the child is viewed as a decontextualized entity—a body to keep alive, an arm or leg to restore, or a learning repertoire to enlarge. Rarely is the child viewed as a part of an elaborate social system—a family. Rarely is the family considered to be equally affected by the accident that leaves these children and their relatives forever changed.

From the interviews, it is evident that parents and siblings are vital lifelong resources for support for people with ABI. Yet, from ambulance attendants to insurance agents, the many people who are involved in the treatment, rehabilitation, and long-term support of people with ABI rarely recognize the needs of family members for information, emotional concern and empathy, empowerment to make choices and be partners in treatment decisions, and concern for the social fabric that surrounds the child and family with ABI.

The process of humanizing this treatment and caregiving system will require numerous reforms from many angles. On one level, new services and resources must be created and the medical and educational services that do exist must change their focus. Every stage of the treatment process and long-term care for people with acquired brain injury needs to treat the individual as part of a complex social network and consider parents and family members with equal importance as foci of concern.

Some important limitations of this research must be acknowledged. First, the sample size was relatively small and the generalizability of these findings may be limited. Because there are few formal safeguards against observer bias in qualitative research, it is possible that these findings reflect, to some extent, the authors' opinions. The findings of this study should be compared to data gathered from other methodologies in order to examine their validity.

A recent needs assessment of 119 family members of people with ABI appears to support several of this chapter's themes (Devaney, Kreutzer, & Marwitz, 1992). For example, 98% of the respondents said they needed clear information and emotional support—"to have my questions answered honestly" and "to have a professional to turn to for advice or services when help is needed." A quantitative survey with items derived from these themes could further test the validity and generalizability of the findings. Furthermore, it is important to acknowledge that responses were greatly variable; characterizing parental experience in a general fashion may have glossed over many individual differences.

As briefly noted, about one quarter of the parents in this study appeared to have made considerable progress in adapting to their child's condition. These parents expressed very little distress and seemed remarkably positive in the face of a difficult set of challenges. Future research should examine effective coping responses and positive family outcomes in greater detail. Despite these limitations, these parental accounts are still valid and potentially useful for training professionals who work with families of children with ABI, as well as generating the understanding and support that parents desire.

REFERENCES

Bogdan, R.C., & Biklen, S.K. (1982). *Qualitative research for education: An introduction to theory and methods.* Newton, MA: Allyn & Bacon.

Devaney, C.W., Kreutzer, J.S., & Marwitz, J.H. (1992). Assessment of family needs following traumatic brain injury. *Transmit TBI, 3*(2). Richmond: Rehabilitation and Research Center on Severe Traumatic Brain Injury, Virginia Commonwealth University.

Florian, V., Katz, S., & Lahav, V. (1989). Impact of brain damage on family dynamics and functioning: A review. *Brain Injury, 3*(3), 219–233.

Glaser, B.G., & Strauss, A.L. (1967). *The discovery of grounded theory: Strategies for qualitative research.* New York: Aldine De Gruyter.

Guba, E.G., & Lincoln, Y.S. (1989). *Fourth generation evaluation.* Beverly Hills: Sage Publications.

Sachs, P.R. (1991). *Treating the families of brain-injury survivors.* New York: Springer Publishing.

3

Parallel Processes

Stages of Recovery and Stages of Family Accommodation to ABI

Ellen Lehr

Acquired brain injury (ABI) sustained by children and adolescents is very much a family affair. Not only do family members often feel responsible for the injuries of their children, they are also intimately involved in the care and well-being of their children after the injury. In fact, family members of children with ABI are likely to have been closely involved in the injury itself. For example, children may be injured while riding in the family car or while crossing the street with parents or an older sibling. Statistics show that injuries to children are most likely to happen in their homes, in their neighborhoods, or while they are with family members and friends. The recovery of children and adolescents after an acquired brain injury, then, involves a physiological recovery or improvement as well as an adaptation on behalf of both the children and their families. These are, in fact, parallel processes; however, these processes are not always in synchrony throughout the recovery period.[1]

RECOVERY FROM ABI AS A PROCESS

The combination of physiological and psychological recovery from an acquired brain injury usually progresses along a relatively predictable course. Description of this recovery course did not come from labo-

---

[1]Throughout the chapter, the term *recovery period* refers to the recovery or improvement period.

53

ratory research, but from multiple clinical observations of treating professionals working with a large number of individuals who were hospitalized after brain injuries. The observations began to form a pattern, quite consistent across people, and were eventually compiled into a series of stages termed the Rancho Scale for the Rancho Los Amigos Hospital in California where they were developed (Hagan, Malkmus, & Durham, 1979). Table 1 lists the eight levels of cognitive functioning in the Rancho Scale.

Although the Rancho levels have been helpful, especially for acute care and rehabilitation hospital settings, they do not necessarily reflect the realities of an acquired brain injury, which can have lifelong repercussions, on both individuals and their families. The conceptual model used in this chapter was devised (Lehr, 1990) from clinical practice with many children who have sustained ABI and their families; it extends over many years and throughout childhood developmental stages.

Although the pattern of recovery is generally consistent across patients, the length of time involved can vary considerably and is probably related to the severity of the brain injury. For example, in mild injuries, the child may experience only very brief loss or alteration of consciousness and rapidly progress through the stages over a period of days, weeks, or months. In very severe injuries, a child might be in coma for months and continue to demonstrate recovery over several years. In some extremely severe cases, the individual may persist at a very low level of consciousness for years with little to no improvement. Also, there is no guarantee that a child with ABI will go through all of the stages. The severity of injury can limit the degree of progress and a child can plateau at any of the stages. Then, there will be little further improvement in levels of consciousness or functioning.

The following sections illustrate the stages of recovery from both the perspective of the child who has been injured and the perspective of his family members while reacting to the child's accident and at-

Table 1.　Rancho Scale: Levels of cognitive functioning

1. No response to stimulation
2. Generalized response to stimulation
3. Localized response to stimulation
4. Confused, agitated behavior
5. Confused, inappropriate, nonagitated behavior
6. Confused, appropriate behavior
7. Automatic, appropriate behavior
8. Purposeful, appropriate behavior

From Rancho Los Amigos Medical Center, Downey, California, Adult Brain Injury Service; reprinted by permission.

tempting to cope with and adjust to the injury and its effects. Table 2 shows a schematic presentation of the stages.

Initial Injury Impact and Coma

If children are severely injured, they will experience a period of coma or unresponsiveness to their environment. It is difficult to express the impact of seeing one's child—who is usually walking, talking, playing, and even getting into trouble—incapable of any of her typical activities, even those she could do as a baby. Children in coma are usually not aware of themselves or what is going on around them, but they may have very brief experiences that they can recall after emerging from coma. For example, they might remember the ambulance doors closing but nothing else from the accident or early hospitalization, or they might remember a family member sitting by their bed but have

Table 2. Stages of child recovery and family issues in ABI

Child	Family members
Initial injury impact and coma	Shock, grief, crisis, disruption of family routines and sense of loss of control over their lives
Beginning response to commands	Resurgence of hope, continued disruption of family life, fatigue
Agitation	Fears of regression and painful experiences, continued disruption of family life
Early cognitive recovery	Initial fears of confusion resolving to recognition that their child, siblings, and family members are expected to go through the motions of typical activities
Continued cognitive recovery	Reestablishment of family routines with adjustment for recovering child, sibling reactions, need for assistance with planning and management
Social-emotional recovery	Emotional and behavioral concerns, social rejection and isolation, coping with child's reaction to injury, emerging awareness of the extent and impact of child's limitations and changes on the child and family functioning
Developmental reinterpretation and readjustment to injury effects	Beginning of long-range planning, alteration of preinjury plans both for family members and the injured child

little to no context for this memory. Although the children who have been injured do not realize the severity of the injury at this stage, their families are extremely aware of it.

When a child experiences an acquired brain injury, the entire family feels its enormous impact, in terms of both the individual family members and family life in general. Because of the sudden and unexpected nature of the injury, parents often later describe the experience as dominated by overwhelming feelings of disbelief and shock (Williams, 1991). Initially, this sense of shock predominates over feelings of grief, fears of whether the child will survive and in what condition, anger at the cause of injury, and sometimes a wish for revenge. In addition, adult family members and older siblings often experience considerable guilt or feelings of responsibility for the child's injury. Sometimes this includes an immediate sense of responsibility, such as for driving the car that was involved in a motor vehicle accident or for not holding the hand of a young child who was hit in a crosswalk. Other times it is a less direct sense of responsibility, such as for not enforcing curfews for adolescents, for not restricting drinking and driving, and for not ensuring that school-age children wear bicycle helmets.

Trauma care has been described as feeling like grand larceny (J. Wasco, personal communication, November, 1990) to the family who has literally had their child stolen from them by the injury as well as by the emergency medical personnel and the hospital staff caring for their child. The family's sense of control over themselves and their child has been dramatically altered and reduced. The hospital and medical staff now have control over the child and, to a great degree, over the family members as well. For example, they dictate when the family is allowed to visit, how long the visits may last, and what the family is allowed to do for their child. There is a tendency, which is often well meant, for the hospital staff to take over a great deal of the typical tasks of parenting while the child is in the hospital. If hospitalization is prolonged, as with inpatient rehabilitation, the family can experience an overpowering need to take their child home to regain a sense of being in charge of their child and their lives again. In very practical terms, the experience of a brain injury extraordinarily disrupts family routines and family life; it shifts a family's focus to the hospital and the injured child and neglects basic daily activities, including cooking, laundry, work, and household chores. The impact of this disruption on all family members, including siblings who may get little attention or need to be cared for by extended family members, cannot be emphasized enough.

Beginning Response to Commands

The end of coma is often defined as occurring when a child can consistently respond to commands, such as moving a part of the body (e.g., move your leg, close your eyes). Motoric response can, and often does, emerge before the child is able to talk again. If a child has been in deep coma for a prolonged period of time, consistent response to commands can develop over a period of days or even weeks. Children, because of their familiarity and attachment to family members, may respond to commands given by parents, grandparents, or siblings before commands given by strangers, such as the nurses and therapists in the hospital. Family members are much better at knowing how and what to talk to their children about to elicit their best response. They can engage in specific routines that have a shared, special meaning, such as bedtime routines for a young child, or talk about favorite activities and special experiences with an older child.

The positive experience of having the child recognize and talk to family members can be exhilarating and spark a surge of hope that the child will actually recover from the injury. However, it can also increase tensions between family members and hospital staff. If a child's responses occur primarily during evening visiting hours with family members, hospital staff—especially those who work during the day—may be quite skeptical about responses they do not personally see during their care and treatment of the child. Hospital staff may give the impression or make statements that the family's hopefulness is unrealistic. Staff skepticism can often be laid to rest only when the child has improved enough to respond more consistently and to strangers as well as familiar people. In order for hospital staff and family members to work trustingly together at this stage, they need to be aware of the child's responses at different times of day and with different people. It is clearly important for hospital staff to observe the child's responses with family members before discounting their information as merely the wishful thinking of severely distressed families.

Agitation

After children emerge from deep, unresponsive coma, they are likely to enter a period of agitation. Although they are now able to do much more, a large amount of this increase appears to be in unfocused, nondirected movements and labile emotion. They may thrash around, moan and cry out, pull out feeding tubes and intravenous lines, hit out at caregiving staff, and generally react in a nonorganized way to their surroundings. If speech has emerged, it may consist of only perseverative words or statements, or even swearing. At this stage, children are not aware enough to engage safely or consistently in any typical adaptive behaviors or play activities. Day-to-day memory also is not yet recovered; children usually do not recall much—if anything—from this period.

The period of agitation may significantly challenge family members' hopefulness about their child's recovery. Although the children are more alert and responsive, they also appear uncomfortable and unhappy and are often very difficult to console for any length of time. Sometimes it is impossible for family members to visit their children's rooms without overstimulating them. Hospital staff often request that the family limit visitors to one at a time. However, this may be misperceived as being harmful and not in the child's best interest, especially when the stimulation provided by family visits was so important in the previous stages of coma recovery.

Early Cognitive Recovery

As agitation decreases and the children start to talk more and engage in basic daily activities, such as eating, going to the bathroom, and moving around more independently by either walking or using a wheelchair, it often becomes more apparent how confused they really are. This period of confusion can probably best be understood as a time of early cognitive recovery during which the children are beginning to process and react to more of what is going on around them. However, because of the cognitive effects of ABI, their perception and understanding are disorganized, distorted, and confused. For example, a boy may realize that he should not wet the bed but not be able to figure out what exactly to do about it; therefore, he may urinate in his water glass or on the floor. Confusion is also reflected in the children's accusations and misperceptions about the injury and hospitalization. For example, they may accuse people of hurting them who were not involved in the injury event or tell people that they are being held in jail. At this stage, the children have little understanding of the injury and often cannot remember and integrate what other people tell them about what happened.

As the children recover, their memory for daily events improves and posttraumatic amnesia begins to diminish. *Posttraumatic amnesia* is the inability to remember events that have occurred since the injury and is considered resolved when the child can recall events from one day to the next. As confusion fades, children enter a period that has been called *automatic functioning*. In this period, the children are able to go through the motions of daily life doing such routine things as eating, going appropriately to the bathroom, watching television, and carrying on a simple conversation. However, these are overlearned activities that children can do in a habitual way; their limitations become obvious when they are expected to plan, react to changes, or learn new things.

For families, this period of confusion can present a range of reactions from fearing that their child is going crazy to thinking that the child is being deliberately funny. However, the children's steady improvement in this period is usually very comforting, as they begin to do more and more of the basic activities they engaged in before the injury. If children have had severe injuries, it is typically at this stage that they leave the hospital. Although they are usually medically stable, no longer require hospital medical care, and are able to be at home, injured children during this period require very close supervision because of their reduced understanding, their somewhat unpredictable responses, and their limited judgment—all of which can lead to safety risks. Overt behavior problems are often not a major problem at this stage because of the children's limited responses and often persistent fatigue. Although children may begin to return to school during this period, they require close supervision and are seldom able to learn new skills. However, expectations both at home and at school are usually limited because the child is so clearly in early recovery and the memory of the injury for school personnel and neighbors is so recent.

Because it can be weeks or months before a child is discharged from the hospital, at least some of the family members have been expected to do their typical activities despite the major and minor daily disruptions caused by the injury and hospitalization. Siblings are expected to return to school, get their homework done, and participate in activities with their friends. At least one parent often has had to return to work to maintain income and medical insurance. Because they appear to have a grasp on typical activities, it can be difficult for other people to fully appreciate the daily stresses of trying to perform usual activities while visiting and planning for the return of their child with ABI. However, the family is all too aware that they are not living their typical lives. Siblings, in particular, may think that everything will be all right once their brother or sister returns home. Because this is rarely the case, their own reaction and anger at the changes they have experienced, their adjustment to the changes in their brother or sister, and their experiences of relative parental neglect can emerge into overt expressions of emotions and behavior. However, siblings also can provide considerable support and assistance both to their injured brother or sister and their parents, often in such practical ways as being able to help supervise and stimulate the child with ABI.

Continued Cognitive Recovery

Over the next several months—or sometimes next several years—the children with ABI continue to experience cognitive improvements and usually develop the ability to engage in purposeful actions that are more appropriate than during earlier recovery stages. However, the extent of cognitive and behavioral limitations can also become more apparent as children demonstrate their own pace and extent of recovery. Expectations for injured children also begin to increase with time. The discrepancy between what the child could do before injury and the difficulties he is having after injury can be more clearly and persistently seen from day-to-day living and learning at home and school. The child's friends and classmates without injuries also highlight the struggles of the injured child. Recovery continues to progress but is in some ways less visible and dramatic than it was during the acute stages; then, the child sometimes appeared to make major changes from one day to the next. The pace of change during recovery is also difficult to plan and adjust to. Although the rapidity has slowed, changes often continue swiftly enough to quickly outdate educational goals and expectations. With good recovery, the child also becomes capable of engaging in new learning again. However, this may be more effortful, fatiguing, and subject to memory loss.

For the family, some aspects of life begin to resemble preinjury typicality, routines resume with return to work and school. However, family members have less direct support from professionals and hospital staff during this period yet have the full burden of caring and planning for their child. The need for guidance and information about understanding and managing their child becomes more pressing and critical in terms of overall needs, but especially if significant behavior problems persist or emerge (Marks, Sliwinski, & Gordon, 1993). Also, the extent of the child's changes and limitations postinjury becomes more and more evident with emotional issues of dealing with the loss of their typical child. Although family members have sometimes been described as being in denial in terms of the severity of limitations exhibited by their injured child, this denial is usually a combination of the family's hopes for recovery along with their lack of experience in seeing the impact of limitations on their child's everyday functioning in the real-life settings of home and school. As family members resume daily living with the child with ABI, the reality of the injury and its effects become more apparent; still, their hopes for further improvement are reinforced and supported by recovery changes.

Social-Emotional Recovery

Cognitive improvements provide the capacity to think about and begin to understand the impact of the injury and its effects. The child with ABI can now, for the first time since the injury, realize what has happened to her and grieve, be depressed, or be angry about her losses. Because of the impact of brain injury on cognitive functioning, psychological understanding and emotional reaction to injury are delayed until sufficient cognitive recovery has occurred to allow the child to make comparisons between what he was like before and after the injury. When the initial reaction starts, the child may become quite emotional and depressed with lessened control. This reaction can seem like a regression in functioning to family members and school personnel. The often compliant child who they are used to from the earlier stages of cognitive recovery is often no longer as easy to manage.

The children's own grief, anger, and depression about injury circumstances and losses also reignite family members' traumatic emotions—just when they were beginning to feel somewhat resolved and less raw. Depending on the child's functioning, behavior changes and reduced emotional control may also alienate previous friends and siblings and lead to increasing social isolation. Because of the relatively long time since injury, other people's tolerance for behavior and cognitive changes wears thin; both the injured child and those around her often begin to strongly wish that the injury and its effects would simply "go away." Unfortunately, the effects usually do not go away, giving this period—which may last for several months to several years—a sense that things will never get better. However, if this period is anticipated and early intervention is provided for the child, family, and teachers, it can be a very productive, if painful, time. Although the injury will not go away and some effects may be permanent, this is a good time to work through problems and come to terms with the injury and the changes it has brought, without completely disrupting the life of the family or the future of the child.

Although the child has sustained an injury that has affected her in a potentially permanent way and altered her family unexpectedly, the development of the child and family continues. Developmental factors become very important in the latter stages of recovery, during the reconstitution of the child and family.

CHILD AND FAMILY DEVELOPMENTAL FACTORS

The stages of child development are well known; however, the final stage of the overall process, the interaction between typical child development and recovery from acquired brain injury sustained during different stages of development, are not. It is known that injury obviously affects the child's development from the point of injury. Therefore, the long-term effects of an injury sustained in infancy on a child reaching adolescence can be quite different from the effects of an injury sustained in late childhood.

Developmental Reinterpretation
and Readjustment to Injury Effects

When a child is injured in infancy or as a toddler, the psychological impact of injury is limited. As the child grows older, she begins to understand more about her injury and its effects—an understanding obviously affected by the child's cognitive abilities. This process is probably similar to the one that children with developmental disabilities go through as they realize that they are different from other children. The realization that they should have been typical people if it had not been for their injuries is often especially difficult and painful for children with acquired brain injury. Family stories of their childhood are often centered on before and after injury with family pictures and videotapes as visual documentation of the changes.

For children who were injured later in childhood and adolescence, this period of anger and mourning for their own loss of ability and sense of self occurs much sooner in the cognitive recovery process. Yet, they too undergo changes in their understanding of the impact of their injuries and its implications for their lives and capacities as they grow older. For these children, adjusting to the effects of injury requires a reunderstanding and readjustment with each developmental period and challenge.

Families develop and grow through the years, also. A young couple who have only recently gotten married and had their first baby are quite different from an older couple with several older children who are having their last baby. If these two infants sustained brain injuries, their stages of infant development would likely be quite similar. However, the stages of their family's development would be quite different. Not only are there other children in the family who would be affected by the infant's injury, but also the two sets of parents are very different ages with different sets of concerns. These differences in family development need to be taken into consideration when working with families who have a child with ABI. Acquired brain injury can also profoundly alter families with grown children who have lived on their own and now need to return to live with their aging parents for care after injury, or injured children who need to be raised by grandparents or other family members after their parents have been killed or seriously injured themselves.

GUIDELINES FOR WORKING WITH
FAMILIES USING THE PARALLEL PROCESSES MODEL

In institutional settings, such as hospitals or schools, it is tempting to consider a child as an individual without understanding him within the context of his family. However, professionals and staff must remember that the child will be returning to live with his family for the rest of his life after discharge from the hospital. Also, the family will fully resume primary responsibility for the child, both in terms of daily care and future planning. Part of the role of hospital and rehabilitation professionals is to better understand the families of the children they are working with as it is difficult to truly and effectively treat a child without considering his family.

Assessment of the family, as well as the child, is essential for effective treatment after a brain injury. If the specific family stresses, values, and concerns are not taken into account, they can severely undermine the efforts of medical and rehabilitation professionals despite all good intentions. Therefore, family evaluation should be made an essential component of treatment for a child with ABI.

The Rancho Scale—and other ways of conceptualizing the recovery process after ABI—were developed to help make a traumatic, sometimes overwhelming, experience more manageable and predictable for those professionals and families dealing directly with its impact (Waaland, 1990). Such conceptual models based in clinical realities have been, and continue to be, very useful in helping to define a child's current functioning level, predicting the next stage in recovery, and outlining what specific problems or challenges are likely to present next. However, the most practical application of the recovery models lies in their ability to function as a framework for communicating among family members, professionals, and eventually the child himself (Marks et al., 1993). Because recovery from acquired brain injury involves so many changes and potential for confusion in a climate of extraordinary stress and trauma, this clarification and way of communicating is basic to helping to plan interventions and preserving families.

Professionals who work with children with ABI may tend to develop a cognitive understanding of its recovery process. However, families and the injured children themselves must live through this process in a very immediate, personal, and emotionally charged way. Because the cognitive understanding of the stages can be learned relatively quickly and painlessly, professionals sometimes underestimate the difficulty of adaptation for families who gain their experience through the trauma of the injury and a lifetime of dealing with its effects.

By adopting the families' perspective, professionals can gain a much more practical and specific idea of what it means to actually live with an ABI. During a presentation by family members for professionals, one parent stated that it took 7 years for him to realize that his son was going to have permanent disabilities related to ABI. Another parent's response to listening to this was relief and some surprise, stating that it took her only 3 years. Interestingly, the first parent's child was injured at age 11 and the second parent's child at age 15. For these two parents, the natural changes and expectancies in the later teenage years provided the impetus for the development of an understanding of the impact of the ABI sequelae on their children's ability to become independent as young adults.

Perhaps by using a combined developmental and recovery model in their work with children and families after ABI, professionals will be able to acquire a long-term perspective even if they only work with the injured child and his family for a short time. Using such a model also can help professionals develop respect and patience in assisting families with their children in dealing with the issues and problems they are currently facing, as well as future issues and problems. It can also provide professionals with a practical tool in helping families regain control by 1) being able to anticipate the changes emerging in their injured child, and 2) preparing themselves to deal with them. After the experience of seemingly unpredictable changes and behaviors in their child after a brain injury, the sense that there is a pattern and there are successful approaches for the different stages can aid a family—sometimes meaning the difference between a family getting back in control or lurching from one crisis to another. This anticipatory guidance approach involves aspects of support, education, and family-centered intervention with the goal of helping the family develop the ability to anticipate upcoming challenges and acquire the knowledge of assistive resources.

REFERENCES

Hagan, C., Malkmus, D., & Durham, P. (1979). Levels of cognitive functioning. *Rehabilitation of the head injured adult: Comprehensive physical management* (pp. 5–9). Downey, CA: Professional Staff Association of Rancho Los Amigos Hospital, Inc.

Lehr, E. (1990). *Psychological management of traumatic brain injuries in children and adolescents*. Rockville, MD: Aspen Publishers, Inc.

Marks, M., Sliwinski, M., & Gordon, W.A. (1993). An examination of the needs of families with a brain-injured child. *NeuroRehabilitation, 3*(3), 1–12.

Waaland, P.K. (1990). Family response to childhood traumatic brain injury. In J.S. Kreutzer & P. Wehman (Eds.), *Community integration following traumatic brain injury* (pp. 225–248). Baltimore: Paul H. Brookes Publishing Co.

Williams, J.M. (1991). Family reaction to head injury. In J.M. Williams & T. Kay (Eds.), *Head injury: A family matter* (pp. 81–100). Baltimore: Paul H. Brookes Publishing Co.

4

The Roller Coaster

The Changing Roles of the Family in the Ongoing Recovery of Their Child

Ronald C. Savage and Karen J. Morales

The role of the family in the rehabilitation process of a child with acquired brain injury (ABI) is paramount to the child's continued recovery and changing needs. Professionals need to recognize the omnipotent role that families have as partners in the care of their children (Blosser & DePompei, 1989, 1992; Brooks, Campsie, Symington, Beattie, & McKinlay, 1986; DePompei & Blosser, 1994; DePompei & Zarski, 1989; Lash, 1991; Savage, 1991; Waaland, 1990; Williams & Kay, 1991; Ylvisaker, 1992). Families often describe themselves as therapists, information specialists, caregivers, service coordinators, advocates, and an array of other titles. From the very moment the child is injured, the family needs to be included, as much as they choose and are able to be, in the rehabilitation process of their son or daughter. From the emergency room, through the intensive care unit, into rehabilitation, back to their home and community, and through the continuing years, the multiple roles of the family shift, change, and evolve. Any attempt to understand the intricate role of the family in the rehabilitation process needs to address this "complex interface among the child with family members and their biopsychosocial system" (Waaland, 1990, p. 225); because, like a quilt, ABI involves an overall picture (i.e., what has happened) made up of numerous, intricate details (i.e., how to make sense out of everything). As the family reacts to the accident itself and experiences its ongoing repercussions, multiple roles and responses emerge (Williams & Kay, 1991). This chapter addresses the ways families modify, change, and revisit these multiple roles throughout the recovery process according to their child's concerns and degree of recovery.

My child is not what she was, nor will she be what she was to become. Neither am I. Neither is anyone else in my family. I never knew that a brain injury could be so devastating or so contagious—everyone in our family has been stricken. When you ask about my role in the rehabilitation process, I can only say that it is still evolving. As Janet's needs change, the roles change—even though it's been 5 years since her injury. Nothing has remained the same. My role has constantly shifted with her needs, her ups and downs, my own development, and our family's ability to redefine itself. My chief role, however, has been to know my daughter better than anyone else does—better than the doctors, the psychologists, the therapists—I need to know and love her the best. Otherwise this "rehab process," as you call it, just doesn't work.

A number of family recovery models have been developed. Unfortunately, many of these models were adopted from adult-centered models without integrating the unique needs of children. The seminal works of Kübler-Ross (1969) and Lezak (1988) proposed similarities between family recovery and terminal illness and family recovery and acquired brain injury. However, these studies did not necessarily address the circumstances and family reactions to childhood injury. DePompei and Blosser (1994), Waaland (1990), and Williams and Savage (1991) studied, in particular, the recovery of families with children with ABI and found that they have their own unique characteristics and recovery patterns. Issues regarding the child's premorbid history, the family's characteristics, the sociocultural environment, the school environment, the community resources, and the ongoing growth and development of the child all have significant impact on the family's reactions and recovery.

The work of the authors of this chapter has centered around the unique characteristics of families with children who have ABI, the families' reactions at various stages of rehabilitation, and the long-term needs of families as their children continue to develop and grow. The vignettes in this chapter are examples of various family reactions at six recovery milestones. Unlike the models of recovery for families with an adult who sustains ABI, these milestones do not follow a linear model of recovery; rather, they can best be described as a "roller coaster ride" through life. The families profiled consistently recounted the tremendous ups and downs experienced as their children progressed, or did not progress, after their brain injuries. Often, this recovery roller coaster mimics the child's degree of recovery and/or the developmental stages the child continues to experience. Children are still growing and developing after an acquired brain injury, and many of their problems do not show up until later, often exacerbated by the earlier injury. As children develop, life naturally becomes more challenging and complex. If areas of the brain have been compromised by an earlier injury, the child and his family may continually face new issues at every developmental stage. In some ways, brain injury to a child is more devastating than brain injury to an adult; it certainly creates different and unique issues for families.

FAMILY REACTIONS AT THE TIME OF INJURY

When I got to the emergency room I was panic-striken. A nurse took me in to see my son. I can barely remember her asking me if this was my child. I looked at the bloody face and almost lost everything. "I think that's his hair," I said. I could only recognize my son's long, black hair, but I knew it was Jamie. I just knew it. I remember sitting in a room off the ER. I was numb. Absolutely numb. All I wanted for my son was survival. Please, God, let him live. Let him live. I stayed through the night as the doctors worked on Jamie. After 2 days in the ICU his doctor told me things looked "good," whatever that meant. But the doctor also said that my son had a serious brain injury and might not come out of coma, and even if he did come out of coma he would never be the same. Never be the same! What in hell did that mean? Later that day a social worker tried to talk to me. I just sat there and shook my head. I was too overwhelmed. I don't remember a single thing she said. But I do remember overhearing her tell a nurse later on that I was in "denial." Denial? I was in "survival" not denial. I knew exactly what had happened to my son. I just wanted both of us to survive. I was his father, for Christ's sake. What other choice did I have?

A family's reactions to their child after the injury and in the first critical days of stabilization and recovery are filled with panic, shock, feeling overwhelmed or out of control, bewilderment, and a desire for survival. Often, information regarding a child's condition and prognosis comes from a variety of sources—physicians, nurses, social workers, and so forth. Families report that soon after the injury too many people gave them too much information in ways that were hard to comprehend and remember. "The doctors said this, the nurses said that, the social worker reported something totally different. It was so confusing. After a while, I stopped listening or believing anybody!" one parent reported. The vast amount of confusing information families receive can be overwhelming and many unanswered questions surface: What does it mean to evacuate a subdural hematoma? Don't you just wake up from coma and regain your senses? What are all these medications? What are all these wires and tubes for? Why can't anyone tell me something hopeful?

During this critical period, it is vitally important that the medical staff communicate with the family through one designated voice. Too many professionals speaking with the family and saying different things is daunting to say the least. If the medical professionals are able to work as a team and speak in one voice when giving families the important information in easily understood ways, the process will be much easier for family members. Periodic and regular status updates on their child, clear and concise information on acquired brain injury (verbal, written, or audio/video), and a designated professional (e.g., social worker, counselor) with whom to talk are all essential family recovery components in the early days after injury. Professionals need to build trust with the family, clarify confusing medical information, and temper hope without completely destroying it.

FAMILY REACTIONS TO STABILIZATION AND THE RETURN TO CONSCIOUSNESS

My wife and I were sitting in the day room down the hall when one of our daughter's nurses came to tell us that Maria had opened her eyes. We both ran down to her room, I guess expecting that everything the doctors had told us before was wrong. Maria just stared up like a doll, no not like a doll, like a person not really there. We had always talked to her while she was in coma and we asked her if she could see Mommy and Daddy. I guess I expected her to talk too. My wife started to cry. Over the next few days as we watched our Maria just stare into space, I realized it was not over by a long shot. I was more afraid for our daughter then than I had been in the beginning. What if she stayed like this forever? I didn't know how much more my wife and I could take, never realizing that it's now 3 years later and I still ask myself the same question.

Many families break from an almost robotic, protective cocoon once their child starts to regain consciousness. Their initial feelings of relief and the knowledge that their child is truly going to survive propel families on an upward roller coaster climb that can unfortunately plunge downward as they begin to understand the long road ahead of them. At this time, families report having been hit with two conflicting emotions: the tremendous relief that their child was coming out of coma and the horrific realization that the real recovery of their child was only just beginning. Unfortunately, television and movies portray awakening from unconsciousness as a miraculous experience, after which everything is just fine; children wake up, eat, talk, walk, and return home. In reality, the return to consciousness can be a painstakingly slow process that, once again, strips a family's hope as well as their ability to accept the seriousness of their child's injury. Professionals and family supporters at this stage of recovery need to help the family synthesize this juxtaposition of reactions as their child emerges from coma, offer educational and informational services regarding the early stages of regaining consciousness, and enable families to begin to address their fears of long-term recovery. As one mother stated, "I am afraid of the future. I wish I had a crystal ball to see what my son will do in 5 years, but no one has the answer."

For families whose children do not regain consciousness within the first few days or weeks, the pressure at times can become insurmountable. For other families whose children may never regain consciousness, a corresponding grief cycle begins to present itself.

After knowing that Petra might not come out of his coma for a long time, my husband had to go back to work. I stayed at the hospital every day and into the evening. I did not know what else to do. The counselor tried to get me out shopping or just for lunch, but my heart was aching so bad I thought it would break if I left Petra. After 3 months, my husband came by maybe only two evenings at the hospital and on Saturday. I knew we were growing apart. He would beg me to come home. "The other children need you, Alia. I need you!" he would tell me. I just could not move. I was frozen just like Petra. I see other families and their children come and go, but not us. "Why God?" I asked over and over. But no answer came until Petra died. His heart, the doctor said, had just stopped working. Later, I think, I can grieve for my Petra and grieve for my family.

For families whose children die from acquired brain injuries, the grief cycle and stages of recovery, although unique to each family, at least allow them to grieve the loss of their child. Losing a child has a tremendous impact on the family and can be unrecoverable. However, the loss can be dealt with as a reality; for those families whose children continue to linger in coma and/or in prolonged states of unresponsiveness, the recognized loss of their child and the grief they feel is never quite real, leaving them in a state of endless anticipation with no final resolution.

We were in the hospital for over 3 months with Johnnie, right through his third birthday. I felt stupid having a party for him, but everybody else was making a big deal out of it. His father showed up for the first time in weeks. Then right after that the social worker said they were going to discharge Johnnie to a skilled nursing place. "Why?" I asked, "How come he can't stay here in the hospital? You all know him. He could still come out of this. You even said so yourself." But we were sent—discharged, they called it—to a nursing home nearby. We've been here 6 months and still Johnnie is the same as before. He gets some therapy and stuff, but every time I think he looks more awake I realize he isn't. This is the way he is, probably for the rest of his life. Except the doctor said that adults can stay in coma for a long time, but it's harder for kids because their lungs and hearts are not as well developed. I don't know. What does this "persistent vegetative state" mean? Is my son's life over? Will he ever get better? Do I just go on like this in a state of limbo? What?

The issues of prolonged states of unconsciousness and persistent vegetative states for children are only sparsely researched. But families can become stagnant in their own recoveries if the child continues to be unresponsive. Some families will admit their children to facility after facility looking for the cure, the magical technique that will awaken their child. Despite their best efforts, social workers and counselors are not able to disengage families from this course until the family reaches a point of near-total collapse (e.g., marriages fall apart, homes are mortgaged to the hilt, siblings end up in trouble). Families who can continue to recover, despite the lingering state of their child, do so with tremendous guilt, anger, and depression; generally, they have extraordinary internal and external supports.

FAMILY REACTIONS DURING REHABILITATION

Families whose children are discharged to rehabilitation services often experience a sense of elation along with trepidation. Although advancing to a new stage of services brings optimism, leaving the caregivers at the hospital can create a great deal of anxiety. Many families will interpret rehabilitation as restoring their child to what she was like before the accident, which can create additional hope. Still, the fear of knowing that their child may never completely recover lurks in their thoughts.

———————

Walina was hit by a truck walking home from school. After almost 15 days in coma she started to respond. Her doctor recommended this rehabilitation center even though it was 3 hours from home. I was just happy we were going to rehab. When we got here the nurses and the therapists started Walina with 3 hours of therapy a day. In the next few weeks, I was amazed at how fast she was progressing. Pretty soon she was talking and understanding most everything said to her. But when she started to walk, I was ecstatic! As I look back now I guess I drove my case manager crazy with my demands—Why can't she have more physical therapy? Why can't she get that video test done so we can get her eating? Why aren't there more doctors here like at the hospital? Why? Why? Why? But it was exciting to see her improve. After 2 months, I began to see all the thinking problems Walina was going to have, especially in school. She always had special help in school before her accident and now she would need even more. One night after watching TV with her, I asked her about the show. She couldn't remember anything, not even the name of the show we watched just 5 minutes before. I cried, but I realized then that after her life was spared and she came out of coma, that her life was never going to be the same. With three other kids at home, all younger than Walina, I felt overwhelmed. She's only 13 years old. Will she still have friends? Will she ever marry? What will she do for work if she couldn't even remember for 5 minutes? On one hand, I was so happy with all her progress, she looked so good. But she wasn't herself. Would she ever be herself again? I grieved for the Walina I had lost.

———————

As many rehabilitation professionals know, families' reactions to their child's course of recovery are varied and quite unique. The inconsistency in their child's recovery sometimes leaves families with the never-ending question: As one father put it, "If my child is doing this well with this amount of therapy, what if we give him more and more? Won't my child recover quicker and better?" Families see their children doing amazingly well one day, only to have difficulty with the same task the next day. Performance and recovery in their child may seem sporadic and inconsistent, instead of following a predetermined progression as many ABI recovery scales portray. The counselors working with the family sometimes see the family's progress parallel similar progress in the child: If the child does well, the family does well. If the child proceeds slowly or has setbacks, often, so does the family. The family's roller coaster ride continues and can suddenly plunge or climb depending on the child's recovery, among other outside issues. The primary outside obstacle, according to parent after parent, is the uncertainty and anticipation. "If someone needs open-heart surgery or breaks a leg or an arm, it's something that can be fixed," commented a parent. "With something like this, you are in the dark. There are no guideposts to recovery. You just don't know what to expect."

As the acute inpatient rehabilitation stage ends, families are confronted once again with the concept of discharge. Although it is a much awaited and celebrated event, feelings of anxiety and trepidation about the future may surface. Questions regarding the readiness of the school district to meet their child's needs, the availability of support services, and the family's ability to adjust are a few of the more universal concerns. It is of critical importance that the family take an active role in the discharge-planning process. The duties of the case manager or discharge planner should not just involve setting up the appropriate services for the child and family but should also provide guidance and structure and encourage families to ask questions, make telephone calls, and network with other families and professionals to familiarize themselves with community resources and supports. As one family member stated, "I have to be my son's strongest advocate. I find talking to other families most helpful because they are going through it themselves. Whatever is out there, you can bet I'll find it." Ultimately, the family becomes their child's service coordinator as they are the ones who can best identify the needs and gaps in their child's life.

We were beginning to get excited. Manny's discharge date was all set. Only 3 more weeks. Not that we hated this place, but going home and resuming our lives after such a long ordeal was exciting. Finally we could get our lives back together again. The therapists had been to our house and to Manny's school. Everything was all set up. We moved his bedroom downstairs to make things easier at first. The school was all set and had an individualized education program (IEP) for him, plus all the teachers had received training. Even though he was still in a wheelchair, so what. He was doing so well otherwise. I guess the real scary part is the future, but when you have been living day-to-day for so long I guess you just hope that things will continue to work out. My wife and I are okay, our other kids are doing better, and I'm finally feeling that we can put all this behind us. I have my son back, that's all I care about.

FAMILY REACTIONS TO DISCHARGE AND
RETURN TO HOME, SCHOOL, AND COMMUNITY

Although returning home is one of the most exciting times for families, it can be one of the most stressful times. For many families, returning home is as stressful as the initial injury—this is the time in the family's life when reality comes full circle. Despite the supports that have been set up and the plans that have been made, the reality of returning home and leaving the medical community can create a false sense of security. Supports, plans, and best intentions can unravel within a few months after discharge and families are faced with a host of problems they may not be prepared to manage.

The entire community seemed to turn out when David returned home. We had a wonderful party. The cards, the flowers were everywhere. His friends from school and in the neighborhood all stopped by. But over the course of a few months, everything started to come apart. Slowly at first, but bit by bit, things were falling apart. David was no longer the Comeback Kid, as the newspapers had reported him after his injury and rehabilitation. His friends in school didn't invite him out. His behavioral outbursts and impulsivity got him in trouble in school. He was constantly picking on his sisters. His outpatient physical therapist and occupational therapist were inconsistent. Then he started to get real depressed. I think it was the first time he fully realized he wasn't the same 16-year-old as before his accident. No longer the star athlete and no longer Mr. Social with lots of friends. He started to call himself a retard and said he would have been better off dead. Despite all his memory problems, he still remembered what he was like before. His psychologist said that it would take David a long time to develop a new sense of self. I was so frightened for him. I was worried what he might do to himself or to someone else. I had been so happy in the beginning that he was home and alive that I just made myself believe that the hard part was over. The truth is, the hard part was just starting. I knew also that my hope to return to work and get on with my own life would also be put on a back burner once again. I didn't know where or even how to ask for help.

Families returning home with their child can again experience the roller coaster effect of initial elation and feelings of security that quickly crumble when the reality of plans and supports begins to falter. Many times the initial excitement of returning home and reestablishing the family unit are short-lived. After a few months, the critical issues that children and their families face begin to emerge. Redefining a new sense of self for the child and family and maintaining the supports and systems needed for success become a full-time job for families. The reality that the transition home is not a one-time event, but rather a series of new challenges, can send families into a downward spiral of confusion and hopelessness.

FAMILY REACTIONS 1 YEAR AFTER RETURNING HOME

The first year after the child's return to home, school, and community presents challenges that test the internal supports of the entire family unit. The cycle of good days and bad days often turns into good weeks and bad weeks as the family adjusts to the new demands presented by the injury. Some families will celebrate birthdays and holidays, take vacations, and reinvolve themselves as much as possible in their world as they did prior to their child's injury. Unfortunately, many families will become so overwhelmed by the changes that they will collapse into themselves and begin living isolated lives at home with little interaction with the outside community. The implosion that families may experience can leave them feeling helpless and alone or, one hopes, begin a tremendous healing process.

The best way to describe what happened to our family the first year after DeeDee came home is to call it a healing year. DeeDee certainly had to heal from her brain injury, but so did all the rest of us, even DeeDee's grandparents. Unless you've been through it, you can never know how contagious this brain injury stuff is. We all got sick, I guess you could say. My wife and I didn't eat right for a year. We rarely were intimate with each other. My other two sons, DeeDee's stepbrothers, tried to do so much to help out that they practically gave up everything else in their lives, especially sports. They made sure after school that she got to her outpatient therapies and on weekends, wherever they went, she went as well. I know that sounds great, but my sons became caregivers for DeeDee, not brothers. My wife's mother just about moved in and took over everything—cooking, cleaning, paying the bills. But in the end, I guess we've come through this year alright. At least we are all still together. I guess if I could do it all over again, I'd have stayed in counseling a lot longer. That will have to be a goal for next year, especially for me and my wife. As for DeeDee, she's doing well. Not great, mind you, but okay. School is getting better. She's still got a couple of good friends who have constantly stuck by her. I suppose our family is better off than others. I'm not really sure why. The thing that sticks in my mind is what our counselor told us at the rehabilitation hospital, "When you get home that's when the rubber hits the road. Give yourself time and give your family an opportunity to heal. Look at your strengths and what works for you and build on that." I still remember that—remember your strengths and what works for you. It saved us.

FAMILY REACTIONS 2 OR MORE YEARS AFTER RETURNING HOME

Although families who have the necessary internal and external supports fare better after leaving the rehabilitation setting, studies of families with children who are 2 or more years postdischarge are rare. Families do report that, as their child continues to grow, the child's next developmental milestones may create a new set of problems. Unlike adults with acquired brain injury, children's brains continue to develop after their injury and damage to their brain at an earlier age can have a significant impact on their continued development. In addition, despite all of the external supports available, the family ultimately becomes their child's long-term service coordinator—coordinating school meetings, friendships, social events, transitions to work and community, and a host of other services and systems.

Well, it's been 4 years now since Jacob's injury. He was in the hospital for over 6 months and has since had two other operations for his arm. He was 6 years old when he fell and got hurt. At the beginning, things went along quite well. School went well. His teachers took lots of time with him. He was slow in his reading, but last year he started to really pick up on that. His arm keeps him out of a lot of sports, but he had friends to play with and all. But ever since he turned 10 years, he has had some new problems. Mostly socially. It's like he's not maturing like everyone his own age. My 7-year-old, Mike, acts older than Jacob. Whenever we ask Jacob to do anything, he starts all this baby stuff. I know Mike gets real frustrated with him and so do the kids at school, Mike says. It's like he's still 6 years old at times. Like I said, his school work is better and better, but the way he acts and behaves isn't normal. You can't explain a thing to him or reason with him when he does something he shouldn't. My husband, Jacob's stepfather, gets real short-tempered with him. I mean, he would never hurt Jacob, but he's had to scold him real hard at times or Jacob won't get it. Otherwise, Jacob looks real good, except for his arm. I just hope that as he gets older his behavior will get better too. But I'm worried.

Many families find that as their child develops and new learning behaviors are expected in school and at home, she may experience tremendous frustrations. The difficulty in changing from a primary school to a middle school to a high school can be challenging for many children. For children who have sustained a brain injury, these developmental milestones may present even greater problems as regions of the brain are called upon that were previously injured. In other children, the onset of puberty and the hormonal changes of adolescence can trigger significant emotional and psychological problems that baffle families.

My wife and I are both medical professionals, but we were totally unprepared for the changes that Jenny would experience after her brain injury. The hospital and rehabilitation courses were fairly standard. She was in coma for only 3 days; she responded quickly and appropriately with no medical complications. In fact, we even didn't think that rehabilitation would be necessary in the beginning. Now that we are 6 years postinjury (Jenny was 7 years old when we were in the car accident), the residual limitations of the injury continue to emerge. After 6 excellent years following her injury—home was great, school went well, her peers were very supportive—all hell seems to have broken loose this past year. No longer is she the quiet, demure girl as before. Now she goes into these rages with no explanation. The first changes we saw in her were at the outset of her menstrual cycle. It was as if Jekyll and Hyde were living inside her. She now experiences panic attacks, cyclical mood swings, temper outbursts, and is inconsistent in her emotional feelings. My wife and I, quite frankly, are very frightened. We've had Jenny reevaluated by a psychiatrist who understands acquired brain injury; she has begun seeing her weekly. But like I said, my wife and I are totally torn apart. After surviving the most serious ordeal in our lives, our daughter's injury, and then seeing her return to her former self, now this. She is missing 2–3 days of school each week, her friends think she's crazy, and my wife and I are lost. What does all this mean for the rest of our daughter's life, her future, us?

As children reach new developmental milestones, new challenges emerge that families are often unprepared to understand. The long-term studies of children with acquired brain injury, who are now in their adult years, demonstrate that earlier injuries have an impact on their later development (Klonoff, Clark, & Klonoff, 1993). Problems associated with the increasing demands of new learning, organization, work, social interactions, and emotional reactions can persist and even worsen over time. For families, this creates an untold anxiety. As professionals become more aware of the long-term needs and supports of children and their families, systems to monitor and provide for these issues are being created.

CONCLUSION

Family recovery after childhood ABI does not necessarily follow a typical, linear course of recovery. Rather, family recovery tends to wind along a track—not unlike that of a roller coaster—parallel to the child's recovery and ongoing development. For families in the early stages of recovery, easily understandable information about their child and acquired brain injury through one consistent voice is important. As the child continues with specialized rehabilitation, it is necessary for professionals to recognize that families need to be an integral part of the planning process and that the entire family system needs a tremendous amount of supports. Once families and their children return home and reenter school and the community, the best-laid plans often fall apart within a few months; then, reality actually sets in and a whole new array of challenges emerge. Families who are many years postinjury begin to recognize that the injury to their child was not merely a one-time event. Their child may continually experience new challenges at various developmental and chronological milestones. Families with children who have sustained acquired brain injury have endured tremendous upheaval and losses. Professionals need to continue to develop family-centered services that enable families to meet, survive, and grow stronger from these experiences.

REFERENCES

Blosser, J.L., & DePompei, R. (1989, November). *Counseling family and friends of TBI survivors: The path less traveled.* Paper presented at American Speech-Language-Hearing Association National Convention, St. Louis, MO.

Blosser, J.L., & DePompei, R. (1992). A proactive model for treating communication disorders in children and adolescents with traumatic brain injury. *Clinics in Communicative Disorders, 2*(2), 52–65.

Brooks, N., Campsie, L., Symington, C., Beattie, A., & McKinlay, W. (1986). The five-year outcome of severe blunt head injury: A relatives' view. *Journal of Neurology, Neurosurgery, and Psychiatry, 49*, 764–770.

DePompei, R., & Blosser, J.L. (1994). The family as collaborator for effective school reintegration. In R.C. Savage & G.F. Wolcott (Eds.), *Educational dimensions of acquired brain injury* (pp. 489–506). Austin, TX: PRO-ED.

DePompei, R., & Zarski, J.J. (1989). Families, head injury, and cognitive-communicative impairments: Issues for family counseling. *Topics in Language Disorders, 9*(2), 78–89.

Klonoff, H., Clark, C., & Klonoff, P.S. (1993). Long-term outcome of head injuries: A 23-year follow-up study of children with head injuries. *Journal of Neurology, Neurosurgery, and Psychiatry, 56*(4), 410–415.

Kübler-Ross, E. (1969). *On death and dying.* New York: Macmillan.

Lash, M. (1991). *When your child is seriously injured: The emotional impact on families.* Brick, NJ: Exceptional Parent.

Lezak, M.D. (1988). Brain damage is a family affair. *Journal of Clinical and Experimental Neuropsychology, 10,* 111–123.

Savage, R.C. (1991). Pediatric brain injury and Public Law 101-476. *Neurodevelopments: Newsletter of the Pediatric Brain Injury Resource Center 1*(2), 3.

Waaland, P.K. (1990). Family response to childhood brain injury. In J. Kreutzer & P. Wehman (Eds.), *Community reintegration following traumatic brain injury* (pp. 225–248). Baltimore: Paul H. Brookes Publishing Co.

Williams, J.M., & Kay, T. (Eds.). (1991). *Head injury: A family matter.* Baltimore: Paul H. Brookes Publishing Co.

Williams, J.M., & Savage, R. (1991). Family, culture, and child development. In J.M. Williams & T. Kay (Eds.), *Head injury: A family matter* (pp. 219–238). Baltimore: Paul H. Brookes Publishing Co.

Ylvisaker, M. (1992). What families can expect from schools after TBI. *Neurodevelopments: Newsletter of the Pediatric Brain Injury Resource Center, 1*(3), 1.

5

Family-Centered Case Management

Preparing Parents to Become Service Coordinators for Children with ABI

Marilyn Lash

This chapter describes the roles and responsibilities of parents as service coordinators for their children with acquired brain injury (ABI). Using the term parent(s), rather than families, reflects the unique position of parents within the family unit; it is the parent who is legally, financially, and emotionally responsible for the care and well-being of the child. In this chapter, parents include biological, foster, step, and adoptive parents as well as legal guardians.

There are two major reasons for preparing parents to become knowledgeable and effective service coordinators for their children with ABI. First, parents who are effective service coordinators and professional case managers can work together as partners rather than adversaries. However, the differences between parents and professional case managers in knowledge, experience, accountability, authority, and financial resources must be acknowledged and respected in order for parents and professional case managers to develop an

---

The use of both the terms *case manager* and *service coordinator* throughout this chapter reflect the dichotomy between parents and professionals. Although professionals use the case manager title, it is inappropriate for parents. However, professionals may not identify with the service coordinator title, which is appropriate for parents and families.

effective partnership. The second reason for preparing parents to be effective service coordinators is that parents can be critical and effective resources for other parents. Although brain injuries in children result in distinctive functional, communicative, behavioral, and cognitive changes, some of their needs overlap with those of other children who have special health care needs, such as therapies for mobility, communication, or adaptive skills; special education; and vocational planning.

From a developmental perspective, children with brain injuries have much more in common with children with other health care conditions than they do with adults with brain injuries. As the work of clinicians and researchers with families of children with congenital conditions, ongoing health conditions, and acute medical conditions has a long history, the models and methods of service coordination used by families of children with special health care needs can likely be adapted to address the unique needs of children with brain injuries.

The philosophy of family-centered care has emerged from the efforts of parents and family members to be included and involved actively in the care and treatment of children with special health care needs. Extending services to families as well as the child with a disability is a principle of the family-centered early intervention programs for young children first authorized under the Education of the Handicapped Act Amendments of 1986, PL 99-457, and updated and amended in the Individuals with Disabilities Education Act (IDEA) of 1990, PL 101-476. Family-centered care is now a standard philosophy in many pediatric hospitals treating children with cancer, acute illnesses, and ongoing medical or congenital conditions (Shelton, Jeppson, & Johnson, 1989). The principles, methods, and models that have been developed and implemented for family-centered care with these populations need to be examined for their applicability to the treatment of children with ABI.

The Association for the Care of Children's Health lists the following eight fundamental components for family-centered care (Shelton et al., 1989):

1. The recognition that the family is the one constant in the child's life amidst changing systems and personnel
2. The facilitation of parent–professional collaboration at all levels of health care, including direct care, program development, and policy making
3. Having providers regularly and routinely share unbiased and complete information with parents about their child's care

4. The development of polices and programs that are comprehensive and provide emotional and financial support to meet the needs of families
5. Recognizing family strengths and individuality with respect for different methods of coping
6. Understanding the developmental needs of children of all ages and their families and incorporating them into health care delivery systems
7. The encouragement and facilitation of parent-to-parent support
8. The design of a health care delivery system that is flexible, accessible, and responsive to family needs

These principles have been developed and applied primarily within the health care delivery system. The model for family-centered service coordination described in this chapter extends these principles to a pediatric rehabilitation continuum that encompasses medical, educational, psychosocial, and prevocational services. Special emphasis is placed on applying the family-centered health care model to the education of children with ABI as school is a primary site and vehicle for the psychosocial and cognitive rehabilitation of children recovering from brain injuries.

DEFINING CASE MANAGEMENT

It is the parent who has the ultimate commitment and responsibility to the child. While staff and programs change, the parent remains a constant entity in the child's life. Consequently, it is the parent who ultimately becomes the child's case manager—a term that is contradictory to the vital role of parents. Families, which include parents and children, are not cases, but individuals; each family has a unique composition of members, characteristics, strengths, and difficulties. The word manager implies a relationship of primary authority and power over a secondary, and often dependent, party; families are not passive entities that need to be managed. Although parents may not be employed as case managers by a hospital, insurance company, or agency, they still have valuable skills, abilities, and knowledge that are essential to planning, coordinating, delivering, and evaluating services for their children. Parents are more accurately described as service coordinators within the family hub; here, parents are the inner core of the wheel, while services are the spokes that extend or radiate outward.

Families of children with ABI express a continuous need for case management. A Parent Task Force, composed of 42 parents caring for 35 children with disabilities, of which 71% had traumatic injuries at a mean age of 8 years, 9 months, identified the need to empower families and the need to prepare families to become service coordinators for their children as a critical task for meeting their children's long-term needs in the community. However, the fragmentation and scarcity of resources for children with ABI in the community have made it difficult to identify resources that could provide training and support to prepare families for the role of service coordinator (Lash & Wertlieb, 1993). Several studies of families with children with ABI have found that clear and understandable information and communication by professionals are high priorities for these families (Marks, Sliwinski, & Gordon, 1993; Waaland & Raines, 1991). In a survey of 67 families with children 1–3 years postinjury, 48% of the families reported that lack of information about community organizations and resources was a major concern (*Rehab Update*, 1993). Another study of families of children with multisystem trauma 1 year postinjury found a hidden morbidity of psychosocial consequences in family relationships, marital stress, sibling adjustment, and school performance, as well as changes in cognition, personality, and behavior (Harris, Schwaitzberg, Seman, & Hermann, 1989).

Commonly managed pediatric cases include infants at high risk for survival or multiple disabilities and children with acquired brain and spinal cord injuries, all cases that require long-term services to meet their complex needs (Henderson & Collard, 1988). However, medical and insurer models of case management, which usually place a physician, nurse, or social worker in the role of case manager, typically fail to address the long-term impact of a child's traumatic injury, particularly in the area of family adjustment, education, and vocational goals. The case management function provided by a hospital or inpatient rehabilitation program usually ends when the child is discharged. Similarly, the insurer's role as case manager may end when benefits are exhausted or services needed are nonmedical. Many state agencies employ case managers, but eligibility for these services usually requires meeting a complex array of financial and medical criteria.

The private insurer's case management plan typically has the following three components: 1) obtaining less expensive, but quality, care; 2) coordinating care among family members and providers; and 3) utilizing benefit coverage (Henderson & Collard, 1988). This model is now quite prevalent in hospitals, health maintenance organizations, preferred provider organizations, independent practice associations, primary care networks, and insurance companies. It has become a method to control costs, reduce inappropriate service utilization, and improve the quality of care (Like, 1988; Spitz & Abramson, 1987).

There are many models for case management; however, common functions include patient recruitment, assessment, care planning, coordination, patient referral, treatment, monitoring, evaluation, and patient advocacy (Like, 1988). The development of empowerment models that focus on the capabilities of families to become independent and self-sustaining, rather than dependent on a professional case manager who controls services and resources, is an outgrowth of the family-centered care approach to early intervention (Dunst & Trivette, 1989). The concepts of a family coordinator by Hutchins and MacPherson (1991) and family-directed care by Roberts, Wasik, Casto, and Ramey (1991) build on and support the strengths of families. Lash and Wertlieb (1993) have developed a six-step model that delineates parent and professional skills, then integrates them into specific roles and responsibilities for a family coordinator.

Entry Point of Families to Case Management

Parents of children who have been injured are at a distinct disadvantage in their initial role as service coordinators after hospital discharge. Data from the National Pediatric Trauma Registry (NPTR) show that the vast majority of children admitted to participating trauma centers with all types of injuries have no preexisting conditions, such as mental retardation, orthopedic difficulties, learning disabilities, ongoing health conditions, or congenital conditions (DiScala, 1994). These parents are likely to have no prior experience with the special needs system.

Whereas children with acute or ongoing health conditions or congenital disorders may be prepared for elective hospitalization or surgery, neither the child with ABI nor the parents can anticipate the trauma and subsequent hospitalization. With falls, motor vehicle collisions, bicycling, and sports injuries among the leading causes of brain injury in children, multiple body regions are frequently injured as well (Leschoier & DiScala, 1993). Parental reactions of fear, shock, and anxiety are complicated by feelings of guilt, anger, and blame as most injuries are preventable (Lash, 1991). Injuries are not necessarily isolated events; often, multiple parties are injured or killed, particularly in motor vehicle crashes. Consequently, parents may be dealing with the stresses of multiple losses and injuries to friends, spouses, or siblings as they cope with their child's injury and hospitalization.

It is during this initial crisis period that the parent typically first meets the professional case manager who may be a nurse, physician, or social worker employed by the provider or payer of services. The professional case manager functions as a critical link between the child and parent, provider of medical care, and the payer. The parent's initial reaction to the professional case manager often is relief and reliance. With the case manager taking responsibility for addressing the administrative aspects of care and coverage, parents are able to focus on their primary concerns—the survival and care of their child.

The case manager has a central role as the child's discharge approaches. Clinical needs for continuing care are assessed, and arrangements may include transfer to an inpatient rehabilitation program, follow-up by local outpatient programs, referrals for consultations with specialists, recommendations for special equipment, changes for home modifications, and altered routines for activity restrictions. There are also questions to be answered about when the child can return to school, if a home tutor is needed, whether special programs in school are needed, and if special testing needs to be done. How will this brain injury affect the child's ability to learn? Do previous plans and goals need to be changed? Will the local school staff know what to do? How will friends and classmates react? Will the child still be able to go to college? Or, fundamentally, how has life changed for our child and family?

The medical rehabilitation model that systematically includes opportunities for family meetings, support groups, training in caregiving, and preparation for discharge is commonly found in inpatient rehabilitation programs (Waaland & Raines, 1991). However, these programs are underdeveloped for children. The NPTR has found that more children with four or more impairments identified upon discharge from participating trauma centers go directly home in the care of their families than are transferred to inpatient rehabilitation programs (DiScala, 1994). This is significant because admission to a trauma center, rather than a local hospital, is an indicator of the potential severity of an injury. Families of children who go directly home from these trauma centers may not receive the professional case management services that are typically found within inpatient rehabilitation programs, which play a critical role in setting up linkages with schools and follow-up care.

Still struggling with the emotional aftermath of their child's injury and having little knowledge available about the long-term effects of ABI to guide them, parents are typically ill-prepared for the future. The relief that parents usually experience with the child's survival and discharge from the hospital is often later replaced by anxiety and concern as it becomes increasingly apparent that the child is now different. Just when parents need the knowledge of professional case managers about community resources and state and federal programs for children with disabilities, these services may no longer be available (e.g., after the child's discharge from the acute or rehabilitation hospital, when the child's needs become primarily educational or psychosocial rather than medical).

Skills Families Need as Service Coordinators

Children with ABI are likely to spend more time in school than with any other service provider. Therefore, establishing linkages with educational and vocational services is the next critical aspect of their rehabilitation. Consequently, if parents are to become effective service coordinators for their children, then the skills of family-centered service coordination must be implemented within these systems. This section describes the six essential skills needed by parents and demonstrates the application of these skills in educational settings (see also Chapter 8).

Any professional can help prepare parents to become service coordinators. It need not be the individual who carries the official title of case manager; it is the professional's recognition of the knowledge, skills, roles, and responsibilities of parents that is important. Thus, in the following section, the term *professional* is used to describe how professionals of multiple disciplines can be effective agents in assisting parents to become service coordinators. The suggestions provided under each skill are based on two pilot training programs in family-centered service coordination and the recommendations of a parent advisory group.

Skill #1: Assessment

- *Objective for parents—to identify how ABI has affected their child's ability to function at home and in school*
- *Objective for professionals—to determine clinical needs in order to develop effective treatment plans and appropriate resources for continuing care*

The family has a critical role in the assessment process. Parents have a lifetime knowledge of their child, intuitive recognition of subtle changes that may not appear on formal tests, and opportunities to observe the child in multiple settings under varying conditions. More objective observation and insights into injury-related changes can be provided by relatives such as grandparents, aunts and uncles, and former teachers—people who have the preinjury comparison of the child but less intense emotional involvement.

Parents may become aware of their child's needs for special help at school in many different ways. Some children may have obvious difficulties with speech, hearing, vision, or motor performance. Others may have less visible signs of change but have altered abilities to concentrate, control their impulses, and organize and complete their school work. Lower grades, complaints by teachers, punishments for disruptive or inappropriate behaviors in the classroom, and student reports of confusion and alienation from peers are warning signs of difficulties that may be caused by cognitive changes related to the child's brain injury.

In order to assess the difficulties that the child may be having in school, parents need to be educated by professionals about the range of possible cognitive and behavioral effects of ABI. These include the common sequelae of fatigue, impulsive behaviors, difficulties with social skills, memory loss, irritability, disorganization, shortened attention, and passivity. Parents need to be trained by professionals to develop and refine their observation skills in these areas. Professionals can collaborate with parents to identify existing and future possible sequelae of a child's ABI. It is important that parents understand that, although some changes may be immediately evident postinjury and upon the child's return home, other changes may not appear until later in the child's recovery and development. If parents are trained in observation and recording methods, they can provide professionals with clinical data on the child at various times of the day, when tired or rested, about solitary and group activities, and under various stimuli and distractions. Many families have designed notebooks to record this information. Professional case managers can assist families in setting up a notebook with sections that are relevant to the child's and family's needs.

Of special concern for parents is the delay between the injury and the identification of learning difficulties at school. In cases when the injured child is a preschooler, parents lack the preinjury baseline of school performance. Many express concern that if learning difficulties are identified later in the child's development, they will not know whether they were caused by the injury. Changes may be dramatic or subtle. For example, a 14-year-old junior high student was nonverbal after her brain injury; thus, her parents, rehabilitation staff, and teachers were immediately aware that she would need special educational services to help her communicate and learn. By contrast, the mother of another student who had survived a brain injury was frustrated by her daughter's inability to receive special education at school because her classroom performance and grades were within the average range of her peers. However, this average performance was a decline from her preinjury levels of high achievement and indicative of difficulties in cognitive functioning.

In addition to assessing the child, parents also need to assess the school's response to their child by asking critical questions of school personnel and by determining the appropriateness of methods used by school staff to evaluate their child's educational needs. A primary concern expressed by parents is the contrast in resources and expertise between hospital or rehabilitation settings and school programs. Local schools typically have far fewer resources and less experience with children who have ABI in comparison to medical and rehabilitation programs with specialized teams and treatment programs. Parents need to question school staff's experience with students with ABI, including teachers, guidance counselors, school psychologists, and special educators. When parents are concerned about limited experience and knowledge among school staff, they should assess the school's interest in acquiring more knowledge through such methods as in-service training, written materials, independent consultants, and meetings with rehabilitation staff.

A neuropsychological evaluation is an effective tool for assessing the student's educational needs; however, too often this is performed only as a baseline measure while the child is hospitalized or shortly before discharge. A common complaint by school staff is that hospital-based testing is so medically focused that findings are not interpreted in language that is useful to educators. If the examiner is not familiar with educational curricula for various grades and subjects, reports may lack practical recommendations for teachers and school staff. Once the child has left the hospital, the insurance may not cover payment for repeated testing. Also, the school may not see the need for neuropsychological testing if the child has scored within average limits on the standard intelligence tests.

The professional case manager needs to educate parents about the role of a neuropsychologist and current evaluation findings in developing the student's educational plan. Parents need to know when a neuropsychological evaluation should be requested, what kinds of information should be shared with the examiner about the student's educational strengths and difficulties, and how to form a request for an evaluation that will result in specific suggestions and techniques that address the student's unique needs and also respond to the resources and limitations of the school setting. Finally, parents need to determine who will pay for the neuropsychological assessment.

Skill #2: Gathering Information

- *Objectives for parents—to become informed about the laws of special education; to identify resources experienced in advocacy for special education for children with special needs; and to identify local, regional, state, and federal resources and a method for organizing this information*

- *Objective for professionals—to identify and convey relevant information to parents about available services, informed resources, and bureaucratic and eligibility procedures*

The process by which parents gather information is often thwarted by their lack of experience in the human services, rehabilitation, and special education fields. Unlike parents, professionals have an existing knowledge base via their clinical training and professional experience, as well as a collegial network and experience in managing bureaucracies. Too often, professionals provide information to parents but fail to teach them the process of gathering information. Although the content of the information will vary according to the changing needs of the child and family, the process of acquiring information will be repeated many times. The basic questions for parents are, "What information do I need?", "How do I get it?", and "How is this relevant to my child?"

Parents have identified the following two distinct needs for information: 1) the information about their child's present condition and current needs for services, and 2) the information needed to plan for their child's future. Continuing with the educational model, parents need to know what resources are available for their child's education and how to get them. Written materials on special education are available from each state's Department of Education and may also be found in many local schools. The rights of parents as well as the application and review process are clearly defined by each state. However, parents need to look beyond the current classroom, teacher, and school to gather information about long-range concerns such as vocational training, college, independent living, and special financial and medical benefits for children and adults with disabilities.

One parent involved in a parent advisory group described herself as being an "indiscriminate sponge" when gathering information. Experienced parents advocate collecting as much information as possible from a variety of resources. Too often, the uncertain path of recovery, the hopes of families, and the inability of experts to make prognostic predictions present barriers to collecting information. In addition, programs, services, or treatment are commonly limited to children with particular diagnoses. For example, parents may resist gathering information from agencies such as The Arc or United Cerebral Palsy Associations (UCP) because their child has an acquired brain injury, not a congenital disorder or retardation. However, many of these agencies have information that is applicable to all children with special needs. Such agencies usually have information about respite services, recreational programs, special education, vocational assessments, supported employment, augmentative communication, and independent living. Many conduct training programs for parents that are taught by parent advocates and have support groups led by parents of children with special needs. These parents can serve as skilled role models in the process of special education. Their experiences with application procedures, appeal processes, eligibility requirements, and review procedures can help parents anticipate bureaucratic procedures and barriers and apply strategies that have been demonstrated as effective.

Networking is critical to gathering information. Important sources cited by parents include support groups for parents of children with special needs, local agencies serving children with special needs, magazines for parents of children with special needs, conferences, visits to specialized programs, and rehabilitation experts. A strategy that has been especially effective is telephone networking; by asking each contact for the names of three other people, a network can be developed quickly. Professionals can facilitate information gathering and network development by preparing resource lists for parents in specific areas to serve as reference points.

Expectations that are too high or too low for a child with ABI can impede the provision of information to parents by professionals. When expectations are too high, the need for special services may not be recognized and parents may not be informed of available services or options. Similarly, when expectations are too low, professionals may not inform parents of all options. Professionals can facilitate parental information collection by providing written handouts and materials on local, regional, and state resources. Directories and resource manuals can be found in most professionals' offices and are used to identify resources, make contacts, and gather information; however, rarely do families have access to these materials. By making these materials accessible to parents, professionals can act as job coaches by teaching parents how to use them effectively and develop a method of information collection for future use and reference.

The process of gathering information is continuous. Experienced parents have organized resource boxes and files at home to collect information. Sharing this information with other parents seeking information, and even with professionals, has proven to be empowering for parents.

Skill #3: Referral

- *Objectives for parents—to determine when and why a referral is needed, to identify goals and possible outcomes of a referral, and to determine the effects of the referral process and recommendations on other family members*

- *Objective for professionals—to utilize referrals for special services based on identified needs for clinical expertise and consideration for special services or programs*

Data from the NPTR show that even though brain injury was the most frequent diagnosis, only 0.5% among the 32,754 children hospitalized in participating trauma centers were given referrals for special education services (DiScala, 1994). It is often the parent or local pediatrician who makes the referral. There are a number of reasons for delays in the referral process. First, if the child is hospitalized for only a short time or is not transferred to a rehabilitation setting, neither the parents nor the school staff may be advised of possible needs for special educational services. Second, because the application process for special education is defined by law and requires a lengthy assessment and documentation process, it typically does not happen quickly. Thus, many children return to school after ABI before the referral process for special education is completed. Third, some learning difficulties related to ABI may not be immediately apparent; thus, needs for special services may not be identified early in the child's recovery but will only become evident later as various brain processes are challenged by different educational tasks and increasingly complex school work.

Finally, the referral process may be delayed because making a referral for special education or to specialists to assess changes in a child's learning abilities is often complicated by differences between medical and educational services in funding sources and payment mechanisms. When referrals for consultation are made within the medical setting, the process is largely controlled by the physician and payment made by the insurer. The process is very different in the educational setting where parents play a much more critical role. Special education law gives parents considerable authority as parental approval is required before an educational plan can be implemented once the student has been determined eligible for special education. The law also has provisions about when independent evaluations can be requested by parents as part of the eligibility determination process. This means that parents potentially have a greater role in the determination, selection, and outcomes of referrals that are relevant to their child's education. Unfortunately, many families are typically not prepared for their role in negotiating the referral process.

Many parents prefer referrals to specialists who can explain procedures and results in terms that are understandable and applicable to their child's functioning at home and in school. Credentials do not necessarily indicate competence. Parents need to explicitly ask about a consultant's or specialist's experience with ABI among children and his or her experiences with the severity of the injuries and subsequent effects. It is also important for parents to ask about the specialist's or consultant's range of experience. Is it primarily in hospital settings or with schools, with formal testing or by classroom observation? How does the specialist determine what tests and measurements will be used? How does the child's age affect the selection of the instrument? How will the specialist make the information available to classroom teachers? Will the specialist review the findings with the parents as well as teachers? Who will receive written reports? What information will teachers receive from the testing to help the student learn in school and function at home?

Parents have found that observing how consultants or specialists interact with their child is important. For example, do they talk directly to the student or primarily through the parent or teacher? Is their focus on the child or the disability? Is the child's right to privacy and confidentiality respected during testing and reporting? How will the findings be presented and explained to the child? What are the child's rights for giving permission for the testing or choices about the manner in which testing will be done, and how the results will be used?

Selection of the professional who conducts the educational evaluation is often made by the school. The critical questions for parents to ask are, "What is the professional's experience with students with ABI?" and "How will my child's evaluation differ from that of a student with a learning disability, mental retardation, or congenital condition?" Often school-based psychologists are experienced primarily in congenital and emotional disorders and not with ABI. Consequently, routinely used tests and assessment batteries that measure intelligence and are conducted within the controlled testing environment may not be applicable to the student with ABI and his ability to function in the multisensory stimuli of the classroom environment. Families need to be actively engaged with school staff in determining when an evaluation for a neuropsychological assessment is indicated, what kind of information is sought, and how it is applied.

Parents have commented consistently on the resistance of educators and school-based staff to make referrals for specialists outside their system. Although cost is clearly a critical factor, many parents also feel that schools may perceive outside observation or evaluation as a threat to their competence and autonomy. Parents emphasize the importance of trusting their knowledge and intuition in determining when a referral is needed. At the same time, parents recognize the politics of the referral process and the importance of building a school-based team. Thus, parents stress the need to develop negotiating skills in order to interact effectively with professionals who are critical participants in the educational process. Separating personal preferences from the critical roles and responsibilities of professionals is essential to building an effective team.

Skill #4: Service Coordination

- *Objectives for parents—to plan and coordinate immediate and long-term needs and services, to identify funding and payment resources, to determine eligibility criteria, and to implement a family-based record of services*
- *Objective for professionals—to implement an integrated, cost-efficient plan to achieve clinical and programmatic goals*

The coordination of services as providers change, eligibility requirements overlap or conflict, and paperwork and billing multiplies is a major task. Whereas the coordination of services by professionals working for an agency, provider, or payer can relieve parents from these duties, these functions become the responsibility of parents when the professional manager is no longer available. Typically, professionals based in medical or insurance institutions become decreasingly involved as services shift to greater educational and vocational foci. However, the information gathered and the services provided during the medical aspect of treatment may provide a baseline of information for educational and vocational planning. It is therefore critical for professionals to mentor or coach families to prepare them for the ongoing coordination of services.

Professionals can assist families in identifying central service components from the time of injury to the present and into the future. Essential to this is the development of an effective record-keeping system—copies of billing, discharge summaries, evaluation reports, referrals, and consultations are essential for parents to track service providers and document the course of the child's treatment and recovery.

The coordination of information between educational and medical providers is a central aspect of this record keeping. Follow-up visits to medical and rehabilitation specialists can provide important information to educators and school-based therapists who are designing current programs and evaluating various modalities of instruction. Similarly, medical staff need to be continually advised of the child's progress in school, difficulties in class, relationships with teachers, and interaction with siblings and peers.

Parents are the critical link in this process. Only the parent is likely to have long-term communication and access to the various specialists, programs, and providers within rehabilitation, educational, prevocational, and school service systems. Parents can facilitate the transfer of information by carrying copies of written reports among specialists, personally communicating the effects and outcomes of treatment and interventions, comparing the efficacy of various programs and specialists, and determining where duplication and gaps in communication and service occur.

Too often, the aspect of service coordination that falls most heavily on parents is the struggle to maintain a balance among all family members. Not only do services need to be coordinated among professionals and providers, but they also need to be coordinated with the schedules and priorities of other family members. The time, energy, and costs (financial, physical, and emotional) associated with arranging and coordinating services, and then implementing recommendations, affect everyone in the family. Parents need to determine how many variables they can effectively coordinate to offset the negative aspects of multiple services with the potential gains to be achieved. Factors such as distance from home, travel, out-of-pocket costs, job demands, and child care arrangements are just some of those that parents consider in determining which services to use, how often, when, and why. Unfortunately, too many families are readily labeled as resistant when, in fact, the expectations and demands placed upon them by professionals are exclusively focused on the child with a disability and fail to recognize the needs of other family members as well.

Skill #5: Advocacy

- *Objectives for parents—to distinguish between effective and ineffective styles and methods of advocacy; to identify barriers to services, funding, and program development; and to promote programmatic and policy change*
- *Objective for professionals—to use their expertise and knowledge to develop service linkages and continuity of care for appropriate and effective services*

Parents bring unique roles and resources to the advocacy process as their primary allegiance is to their child, not an employer or insurer. A parent's perspective also includes immediate needs as well as the development of a vision for her child's life and future. As the focus shifts from medical care to education, the development and delivery of appropriate and effective educational services becomes a priority for parents. However, initial efforts at advocating for special educational services are frequently thwarted by parents' lack of experience with the special education system, educators' inexperience with students with acquired brain injury, and limited communication between medical and educational providers.

Parents have stressed the importance of identifying parent advocates and professional resources to understand and help negotiate the special education system. Two methods have been especially effective. The first technique is the identification of those resources within the local community or region that specialize in services for children with special needs. Many agencies conduct parent training programs and provide trained advocates to assist in negotiating educational plans. These resources are often located through agencies for children with developmental disabilities. The value of such programs is their expertise in the rights of parents and the development of skills in the planning and negotiation of special education services. The second technique is to form an alliance with a professional who can help educators understand how the consequences of acquired brain injuries differ from other conditions and who can assist in identifying the child's special needs for assessment and interventions. This can be done through written communication by professionals, participation in the negotiation of the educational plan, or through telephone communication. The emphasis is on developing alliances rather than adversaries.

Too often, advocacy by parents is perceived by professionals as adversarial, especially when parents and school staff disagree about educational goals, teaching strategies, or methods of evaluation. It is when costs associated with the educational plan are negotiated that conflict is very likely to occur. The model of family-centered service coordination approaches advocacy as a mechanism of support for the student, parent, teacher, or school.

Differences in funding mechanisms between school-based services and medical services can affect the commitment and perspective of professionals and institutions that will bear the expense. Advocacy by professionals may be influenced by who bears responsibility for the costs of services and the availability of funds. Parents need to be aware of the differences in funding mechanisms and their rights under the laws of education. However, parents also need to be trained in the pragmatic effects of advocacy. Although the federal and state laws of education ensure a child's right to special services when need has been demonstrated, the constraints of funding can affect the availability of services. By strategically identifying priorities for their child's education, parents can monitor services and differentiate between short- and long-term goals. Cost-sharing strategies between educational and medical funding sources, as well as identification of other charitable funds or special resources, are methods that parents have used to overcome financial limits of local schools.

The politics and pressures of advocacy can lead to alienation between parents and professionals and jeopardize the achievement of long-term objectives. Effective parent advocates are skilled at developing alliances with professionals not only in the process of negotiating for individual services, but in helping professionals advocate for larger systems change by testifying at public hearings, working with local representatives and congressional officials for legislative changes and funding appropriations, and by developing grass roots programs for community awareness.

Skill #6: Evaluation

- *Objectives for parents—to identify methods to evaluate the child's progress, to assess personal and financial costs of care and interventions, and to develop realistic and acceptable goals for all family members*
- *Objectives for professionals—to assess outcomes according to clinical criteria including the duration and intensity of services, to determine cost-effectiveness of services provided, and to determine the child's and family's satisfaction with providers and programs*

Professional measures to evaluate the efficacy of case management have largely focused on lengths of hospital stay, range and intensity of services provided, and the costs of care. The family, however, has a much broader perspective, as well as unique criteria, from which to evaluate their child's progress. Comparison of school grades, for example, is a common objective measure to compare overall performance pre- and postinjury. Parents may also evaluate school-based interventions by assessing the child's satisfaction with and performance among different teachers and subjects as well as interactions with peers. The family can evaluate the role of school within the broader context of the child's development and life goals. For example, placement of a child within a special classroom will affect that child's relationships with peers and his perception of being different from before the injury. Entry to a residential program may be considered necessary to achieve behavioral changes but may also result in emotional stress due to the separation from family members. Selection of a vocational or college tract has significant impact upon determining career goals for any student; this becomes even more critical for a student with acquired brain injury. Matching academic skills and functional abilities with vocational interests and gaining work experience are critical for evaluating future goals. The family must weigh the potential educational outcomes and vocational goals for their child with expected benefits and outcomes.

Methods cited by families to evaluate the effectiveness of educational programs include informal observations of the child's skills, the child's response to the program, and the program's relevance to the child's daily activities. Overall, parents stress the importance of evaluating whether the school program is designed to prepare the child for the many transitions to adulthood by assessing whether current learning is applicable and relevant to future goals that are consistent and realistic with the child's abilities and difficulties. Families stress that education needs to be a dynamic process that balances academic, functional, and real-life skills.

CONCLUSION

The role of parents as service coordinators over the long-term course of children's recovery from ABI needs to be acknowledged and respected by professionals through the creation of mechanisms to develop partnerships, mentor skills, and help parents bridge systems to prepare for the major transitions in needs and services as children approach adulthood. By recognizing the limits of their clinical expertise, the constraints of their professional roles, and the programmatic boundaries of institutions, professionals can work with parents to effectuate the transfer of responsibility in a supportive and graduated manner. Professionals have very specific and valuable skills in case management that can be adapted and modeled for parents to enable them to become effective service coordinators. Parents also have unique skills and expertise that are vital to the development of an effective service plan. Parents and professionals need to work as a team to build upon each other's strengths, compensate for weakness, and collaborate as partners for the development and effective management of services for children with very special needs due to ABI.

REFERENCES

DiScala, C. (1994, April). *National Pediatric Trauma Registry biannual report.* Boston, MA: Tufts University School of Medicine and New England Medical Center, Research and Training Center in Rehabilitation and Childhood Trauma.

Dunst, C., & Trivette, C. (1989). An enablement and empowerment perspective of case management. *Topics in Early Childhood and Special Education, 8,* 87–102.

Education of the Handicapped Act Amendments of 1986, PL 99-457. (October 8, 1986). Title 20, U.S.C. 1400 et seq: *U.S. Statutes at Large, 100,* 1145–1177.

Harris, B., Schwaitzberg, S., Seman, T., & Hermann, C. (1989). The hidden morbidity of pediatric trauma. *Journal of Pediatric Surgery, 24*(1), 103–106.

Henderson, M., & Collard, A. (1988). Measuring quality in medical case management programs. *Quarterly Review Bulletin, 14*(32), 33–39.

Hutchins, V., & MacPherson, M. (1991). National agenda for children with special health needs: Social policy for the 1990s through the 21st century. *American Psychologist, 46*(2), 141–143.

Individuals with Disabilities Education Act (IDEA) of 1990, PL 101-476. (October 30, 1990). Title 20, U.S.C. 1400 et seq: *U.S. Statutes at Large, 104* (Part 2), 1103–1151.

Lash, M. (1991). *When your child is seriously injured: The emotional impact on families.* Boston, MA: Tufts University School of Medicine and New England Medical Center.

Lash, M., & Wertlieb, D. (1993). A model for family-centered service coordination for children who are disabled by traumatic injuries. *Association for the Care of Children's Health Advocate, 1*(1), 19–27.

Lescohier, I., & DiScala, C. (1993). Blunt trauma in children: Causes and outcomes of head versus extracranial injury. *Pediatrics, 91*(4), 721–725.

Like, R. (1988). Primary care case management: A family physician's perspective. *Quality Review Bulletin, 14*(6), 174–178.

Marks, M., Sliwinski, M., & Gordon, W. (1993). An examination of the needs of families with a brain injured child. *NeuroRehabilitation, 3*(3), 1–12.

Rehab Update. (1993, Summer). Boston, MA: Tufts University School of Medicine and New England Medical Center, Research and Training Center in Rehabilitation and Childhood Trauma.

Roberts, R., Wasik, B., Casto, G., & Ramey, C. (1991). Family support in the home: Programs, policy, and social change. *American Psychologist, 46*(2), 131–137.

Shelton, T., Jeppson, E., & Johnson, B. (1989). *Family-centered care for children with special health care needs* (2nd ed.). Washington, DC: Association for the Care of Children's Health.

Spitz, B., & Abramson, J. (1987). Competition, capitation, and case management: Barriers to strategic reform. *The Milbank Quarterly, 65*(3), 348–367.

Waaland, P., & Raines, S. (1991). Families coping with childhood neurological disability: Clinical assessment and treatment. *NeuroRehabilitation, 1*(2), 19–27.

6

Comprehensive Family Support for Behavior Change in Children with ABI

Joseph M. Lucyshyn,
Charles Nixon,
Ann Glang, and Elizabeth Cooley

This chapter describes a comprehensive approach to intervention and support for families of children experiencing acquired brain injury (ABI) and behavior problems that aims to improve the behavior and lifestyle of the child with ABI, empower family members to effectively reintegrate the child into family life, and help the family regain the cohesion and stability that are often upset or lost after such an injury. This chapter also describes the need for child- and family-centered intervention approaches, discusses the theoretical basis and key fea-

Preparation of the chapter was supported in part by the U.S. Department of Education, Grant #H086P90023 from the Office of Special Education and Rehabilitative Services to the Oregon Research Institute, and Grant #H133B20004 from the National Institute on Disability and Rehabilitation Research to the Specialized Training Program. The views expressed herein do not necessarily reflect the position or policy of the U.S. Department of Education, and no official endorsement should be inferred.

tures of one particular approach, summarizes the steps in the support process, and presents a case study of one family's effort to support an 11-year-old boy experiencing acquired brain injury and subsequent severe behavior problems.

THE NEED FOR CHILD- AND FAMILY-CENTERED APPROACHES

A child's acquired brain injury traumatizes the whole family (Pieper & Singer, 1991; Williams & Kay, 1991). In one survey, 80% of parents of children with ABI reported symptoms that met the *Diagnostic and Statistical Manual of Mental Disorders* (DSM-IV) (American Psychiatric Association, 1994) criteria for posttraumatic stress disorder—a disorder usually experienced by war veterans and survivors of catastrophic events (Nixon, 1992). Just as children with ABI experience lifelong alterations, the families of these children also experience changes in the patterns of their daily lives, in their roles and caregiving responsibilities, and in their expectations and hopes for the future. Children often experience impairments in cognitive abilities such as memory, organizing, planning, decision making, and problem solving. Children who were formerly well-behaved, well-liked by peers, and successful in school may engage in behaviors that disrupt family life, friendships, and schooling. The confusion, grief, and disruption associated with these changes can overwhelm families. Family members may have difficulty maintaining or re-creating the structure, order, and predictability that characterized their lives together before the injury. As they proceed through the rehabilitation process, both children with ABI and their families experience the falling away of family and friends and the dwindling of their social support (Livingston, Brooks, & Bond, 1985; Williams & Kay, 1991). This loss of social support may make the family's effort to regain stability and hope even more arduous. Clearly, the effects of the child's brain injury have consequences for the entire family.

The child's and the family's experiences parallel and interact with one another. For example, many children with ABI have behavior problems such as inappropriate social behaviors, aggression, and destructive tantrums. Such problems may begin as child-centered difficulties directly related to the brain injury but often affect the family system. The family's reactions to the child's behavior can affect whether these behaviors are maintained or changed (Dadds, 1995; Florian & Katz, 1991; Patterson, 1982). If a child's behavior is going to change, both the child and the family must change. Effective interventions, therefore, must be both child- and family-centered. This notion that the rehabilitation of the child and the family are inseparable is becoming more predominant in the special education field (Turnbull & Turnbull, 1991c) and in the ABI rehabilitation field (McKinlay & Hickox, 1988).

Despite these conceptual developments, there remains very little intervention research with families of children with ABI. Although behavioral intervention in residential rehabilitation facilities has been shown to effectively reduce behavior problems and rebuild adaptive skills among adults with ABI (Burke, Wesolowski, & Lane, 1988; Davis, Turner, Rolider, & Cartwright, 1994; Peters, Gluck, & McCormick, 1992), to date, no comprehensive intervention approach has been developed and shown to be effective with children with ABI and their families. In the family intervention literature, a family network strategy has been anecdotally reported to be helpful to families of children with ABI, but no data have been gathered (Rogers, 1984). The family systems approach has been discussed in terms of its application to families and children with ABI (Turnbull & Turnbull, 1991c), but as yet there have been no attempts to empirically validate this approach with families of children with ABI; clearly, a definite need exists for the development and evaluation of comprehensive approaches to intervention aimed at addressing the challenges faced by children with ABI and their families.

Theoretical Basis and Key Features of Approach

The comprehensive approach to intervention with families of children with ABI discussed in this chapter is drawn from recommended practice in behavioral support to people with disabilities and behavior problems (Carr et al., 1994; Horner et al., 1990; Meyer & Evans, 1989; Wacker & Steege, 1993), behavioral parent training (O'Dell, 1985; Patterson, Reid, & Dishion, 1992; Sanders & Dadds, 1993), and ecological approaches to family assessment and support (Bernheimer, Gallimore, & Weisner, 1990; Singer & Powers, 1993). The following five key features characterize the approach:

1. A theory-guided understanding of child behavior problems and family ecology
2. The design of multicomponent, positive behavioral support plans
3. "Goodness-of-fit" between the support plan and family ecology
4. A focus on building successful family routines
5. The development of collaborative partnerships

A Theory-Guided Understanding of Child Behavior Problems and Family Ecology A central message in the literature on behavioral assessment and intervention is the importance of understanding the reasons for behavior problems and the ecology in which behavioral support will be implemented. This information is essential for the design of effective, acceptable, and feasible behavioral interventions (Dunlap, Kern-Dunlap, Clarke, & Robbins, 1991; Horner, 1994). Applied behavior analysis research and social learning theory (Patterson, 1982; Wacker, Cooper, Peck, Derby, & Berg, in press) indicate that child behavior problems serve a clear purpose or function and that behavior problems are developed and maintained within the moment-by-moment interactions between the child and parent.

For example, a child with ABI who has become impulsive may demand that his mother bake cookies for him just before bedtime. If his mother refuses and her son whines and hits her, she may relent and bake the cookies. The child might then stop his aggression and even help with baking. Although the mother may initially submit out of a sense of compassion for a son who has experienced so much trauma, her response also teaches an unintended lesson; the child learns that aggression is an effective way to get what he wants, when he wants it. The mother also learns something dysfunctional—that giving in to her son's unreasonable demands avoids or terminates aggressive behavior.

These coercive processes, once embedded in family interaction patterns, may be difficult to change without systematic intervention (Patterson et al., 1992). Via functional assessment of the child's behavior problems, the purposes of the child's behavior can be understood, and the consequences that maintain behavior problems and ineffective parenting strategies can be revealed. This knowledge then informs the design of child-centered interventions that will render behavior problems ineffective and rebuild family members' ability to effectively parent the child.

Ecocultural theory (Gallimore, Goldenberg, & Weisner, 1993; Gallimore, Weisner, Bernheimer, Guthrie, & Nihira, 1993) is a theory of child development in the family, derived from cross-cultural ethnographic studies of family life (Whiting & Edwards, 1988). It provides a useful framework for understanding ecological influences on child development in the home and for designing interventions that are individualized to the family. The theory supposes that families socially construct child activity settings (i.e., daily routines) to accommodate the needs of their children within the constraints and opportunities present in the family's environment. Gallimore and colleagues (see also Bernheimer et al., 1990) argue that the daily routine is the appropriate unit of analysis for understanding the ecology of a family and for designing family-centered interventions because ecological influences on the family are present and can be observed to operate in each family routine. According to ecocultural theory, daily routines comprise several elements:

- Time and place
- People present
- Material resources
- Goals, values, and beliefs about child raising and family life
- Tasks and how they are organized
- Motives and feelings
- Common scripts or patterns of interaction

Families proactively strive to construct routines that are meaningful given their values, congruent with their children's characteristics, and sustainable over time. The construct and concurrent validities of ecocultural theory were recently demonstrated by Nihira, Weisner, and Bernheimer (1994) in a longitudinal study of 102 families of children with developmental delays.

During assessment with families of children with ABI, an analysis of daily routines is particularly useful. When families discuss their efforts to parent their child with ABI, it is not uncommon for them to describe their successes or difficulties in rousing the child for school in the morning, orchestrating a pleasant dinner together, or helping the child prepare for bed. For many families of children with ABI, routines that once worked reasonably smoothly are now fraught with obstacles and problems, not the least of which are behavior problems. As the family describes the elements (e.g., goals, tasks, resources) of routines, many layers of the family's ecology are revealed, including family values, structure, functions, and interaction patterns.

Viewing the daily routine as a microcosm of family ecology can lead, in several ways, to the design of individualized and effective family interventions. First, it suggests that interventionists should view the family routine as the unit of analysis and intervention, as opposed to focusing solely on behavior problems and parenting skills. Second, it encourages interventionists to design child- and family-centered interventions that are effectively embedded in family routines. Third, if interventions support the success of valued routines, they are more likely to be accepted and implemented by the family.

The Design of Multicomponent, Positive Behavioral Support Plans The technology of positive behavioral support that has emerged largely from work with people with severe disabilities has much to offer children and families experiencing ABI. The approach emphasizes the design of individualized, multicomponent behavioral support plans. These plans are logically linked to functional assessment data and serve not only to ameliorate behavior problems but also to promote lifestyle improvement (Horner et al., 1990). Interventions are drawn from a growing body of empirically verified ecological/lifestyle, antecedent/proactive, educative, and consequent interventions, with an emphasis on prevention and education. Support plans are designed collaboratively with family members, educators, and other consumers of the support plan, and only those interventions judged to be acceptable and likely to be effective are included in the plan (Sprague & Horner, 1991). Positive behavioral interventions verified through applied research include improving activity patterns (Malette et al., 1992), offering choices (Dunlap et al., 1994), providing information to increase predictability (Flannery & Horner, 1994), teaching communication skills to replace behavior problems (Carr et al., 1994), teaching self-management skills (Kern Koegel, Koegel, Hurley, & Frea, 1992), and embedding preferred tasks within nonpreferred tasks (Horner, Day, Sprague, O'Brien, & Tuesday-Heathfield, 1991).

Two critical features of positive behavioral support—a focus on lifestyle change and the importance of multicomponent intervention plans—are particularly relevant to the needs of children with ABI. These children often experience dramatic setbacks in their lifestyle. A child may no longer be able to participate in favorite activities (e.g., sports) that require abilities that have been compromised due to the injury. Friendships may be lost and difficult to reestablish. Conversation with family members may be harder to start or maintain. This loss of valued experiences can alone be a source of behavior problems. Lifestyle interventions that emphasize the rebuilding of valued activities and social relationships may help to ameliorate behavior problems.

Children with ABI also experience behavior problems for a variety of reasons that are unlikely to be adequately addressed by only one or two behavioral interventions. In addition to lifestyle limitations, children with ABI may experience body function impairments, loss of impulse control and social skills, frustration with communication and academic performance, and interactions that inadvertently reinforce behavior problems. Also, for any particular child with ABI, behavior problems may serve different purposes, such as getting attention, avoiding aversive tasks, or protesting lost ability or opportunity. A comprehensive behavioral support plan must address all of the relevant conditions that trigger or maintain behavior problems and each of the purposes of the child's behavior (Horner, O'Neill, & Flannery, 1993).

For example, a child with ABI may cry and scream uncontrollably whenever she sees other children playing sports activities. This event may painfully remind her that, since her injury, she no longer participates in swim meets or gymnastics. She may also scream when her father talks with her brother but does not include her in the conversation. Although the behavior problems are the same in each example, the purposes of the behavior are quite different. In the former, the child screams to protest a lost opportunity; in the latter, she screams to get attention. Interventions need to address each separate purpose directly if the family hopes to reduce the screaming. Potential interventions logically linked to the functions of screaming might include creating opportunities to participate in sports activities geared toward her more limited abilities and teaching her to ask for attention and participate in conversation. Because behavior problems often serve multiple purposes, support plans will necessarily require multicomponent interventions.

"Goodness-of-Fit" Between the Support Plan and Family Ecology The effectiveness of a well-designed, positive behavioral support plan depends on the extent to which interventions are carried out. Effectiveness can also be judged by the degree to which interventions are implemented and maintained across all of the relevant settings in which behavior problems occur. Recently, behavior analysts and family interventionists have suggested that behavioral support plans are more likely to be implemented with fidelity and maintained over time if they fit well with the ecology of the family (Albin, Lucyshyn, Horner, & Flannery, 1995). Family variables relevant to "goodness-of-fit" include family goals, strengths, available formal and informal resources, and sources of stress. Behavioral interventions that fail to address family goals, ignore family strengths, or add significant stress are unlikely to be implemented or sustained.

For example, a parent may want to eliminate behavior problems and receive more help from other family members. If the support plan includes interventions aimed only at reducing behavior problems but provides no means to strengthen informal supports in the home, the plan may fail due to parental exhaustion or resentment. Interventionists need to listen to families and learn about their goals, strengths, resources, and stressors. They then need to collaborate with families and other stakeholders in the child's life (e.g., teacher, physical therapist) to design interventions that are not only technically accurate, but also contextually appropriate and feasible (Horner, 1994).

A Focus on Building Successful Family Routines A common subjective experience of families of children with ABI is to feel overwhelmed by the changes in their child's and family's lives. A multicomponent support plan should be designed to ameliorate, not add to, these feelings of helplessness. One strategy to make comprehensive support feel "doable" to the family is to implement interventions one routine at a time and tailor them to routines. This may make the plan appear more feasible and thus strengthen the family's perception that the plan will work. Intervening on the level of the routine may help the family cognitively reframe the challenges they face in supporting their child's rehabilitation (Turnbull et al., 1993). Rather than facing an insurmountable crisis, the family may see that they face the more manageable task of improving routines that are no longer working.

Another benefit of tailoring interventions to fit family routines relates to the family's interpretation of a stressor such as a pediatric brain injury; the impact of a stressor is mediated by an individual's interpretation of it (Lazarus & Folkman, 1984). Therefore, the impact of a child's brain injury on the family is affected by the family's perception of stress (Chwalisz, 1992). One family may find their child's personality change to be the greatest stressor, while another family may experience the loss of social support as the most stressful outcome. The brain injury to a child should be understood in terms of the subjective experience of the family, and interventions should be tailored to that. For example, interventions designed to improve a bedtime routine in which one parent is stressed by exhaustion and feelings of isolation are likely to include skilled respite care at other times of the day and a weekly schedule of help during the routine negotiated with other family members.

The importance of routines to family coping is supported by research on everyday stressors and hassles (Kanner, Coyne, Schaefer, & Lazarus, 1981). Some researchers have found daily hassles (i.e., disruptions in daily routines) to be a better predictor of family stress and coping than major life events (Delongis, Coyne, Dakof, & Folkman, 1982). The implication of this finding for interventions with children with ABI and their families is clear: The impact of the brain injury on a family is, to an extent, mediated by disruptions in daily routines. It follows, then, that the negative effect of the brain injury on the child and the family can be ameliorated by making family routines more effective and hassle-free.

A final advantage in intervening at the level of the routine is that generalization and maintenance of treatment effects may be more likely because behavioral interventions are embedded within the ecology of routines (e.g., goals and values, tasks, resources) (Albin et al., 1995; O'Donnell & Tharp, 1990). Families who succeed in promoting behavior change in two or three routines may find it easier to apply interventions in other routines that share similar properties. For instance, if a mother successfully motivates her son to go to bed cooperatively by reviewing behavioral expectations and negotiating a reward natural to the routine (e.g., reading a story to him after completing the routine), she may use similar practices to motivate him to behave properly at the dinner table. Also, behavioral improvement may endure over a long period of time because the interventions were specifically tailored to fit the ecology of the routine, including the social supports necessary for maintenance. For instance, if both parents equally shared the task of supporting their son in the bedtime routine, both parents may get the rest they need to continue using the support plan.

The Development of Collaborative Partnerships The values and practices in the family support approach are designed to empower family members and build strong collaborative relationships among the consultant, the family, and the other team members (Dunst, Trivette, Gordon, & Starnes, 1993). Family knowledge is respected and collaboration with the consultant and other team members is encouraged throughout assessment and intervention. Families of children with ABI are the ultimate experts on their child's strengths and behavior problems as well as their family's ecology. Although the family may feel overwhelmed as a result of the trauma to their child and the disruption to their lives, they still possess many strengths and resources that can contribute to the success of a support plan.

It is, therefore, essential that family members collaborate in the design and selection of behavioral interventions, the selection of routines in which to intervene, and the choice of implementation support activities. Family members also should evaluate the acceptability and effectiveness of plan goals, interventions, and outcomes and recommend revisions in interventions or support activities that are not working well. The consultant should encourage collaborative relationships between the family and key stakeholders—such as the child's teacher or skilled respite care providers—via team meetings, coordination of implementation across home and school, and development of formal supports to the family (e.g., skilled respite care). These values and practices contribute to the development of a strong therapeutic alliance between the family and the consultant (Kanfer & Grimm, 1980) and to the development of a community of support around the child and the family; such an alliance and community can help to overcome the trauma of ABI and rebuild the child's and family's life together.

Steps in the Comprehensive Family Support Process

The key features of the support approach have been organized into a seven-step behavioral consultation process:

1. Referral
2. Comprehensive assessment

3. Preliminary plan design
4. Team meetings and plan finalization
5. Implementation support
6. Continuous evaluation and plan revision
7. Follow-up support

The process, described in detail by Lucyshyn and Albin (1993), is briefly summarized below emphasizing the way in which each step in the process is relevant to children with ABI and their families.

Referral   The referral interview has several purposes. First, during the initial interview, the consultant assesses for extreme situations, such as life-threatening behavior or suicidal tendencies, which would require immediate action. During the referral interview, the consultant also obtains informed consent. The consultant informs family members of what will be involved in the development and implementation of a comprehensive family support plan, emphasizing that the plan will be developed cooperatively with the family.

Another purpose of the referral interview is to identify the stakeholders whose participation could contribute to improving the child's behavior and lifestyle. In addition to the child's parent(s), stakeholders may include siblings, friends, education professionals, and community service representatives (e.g., scouting, respite services staff). Potential stakeholders nominated by the family are invited to participate in assessment and plan design activities as members of a family support team.

The referral interview also provides an occasion to reframe the family's problems in a more positive light. The consultant stresses that, as the child's family, they possess most of the information needed to design a support plan, the support effort will be guided by their values, and the plan will build on their strengths. The consultant also notes that intervention will occur in the context of family routines and that the family will participate in the selection of routines, interventions, and support activities. Finally, the consultant also shares with the family success stories about prior interventions with other families similar to themselves. The goal of the reframing process is to help the parents believe that they are powerful, in control, and capable of effecting change.

Comprehensive Assessment   The synthesis of child- and family-centered approaches to intervention is reflected in the second step of the support process. The assessment consists of a functional assessment of behavior problems and a family ecology assessment. The goal of the functional assessment is to provide information necessary for the design of an individualized behavioral support plan for the child. The goals of the family ecology assessment are to provide information necessary for the design of family-centered interventions and for the creation of a "goodness-of-fit" between the behavioral support plan and the family's ecology.

The functional assessment uses the assessment protocol designed by O'Neill and associates (O'Neill, Horner, Albin, Storey, & Sprague, 1990). Information gathered during the assessment includes the following:

- A specific description of behavior problems
- Ecological factors associated with those problems (e.g., medical problems, activity patterns)
- Educational factors (e.g., skill impairments in language)
- Common predictors (e.g., interruptions, difficult tasks, transitions)
- Possible functions of the behaviors and their maintaining contingencies

Assessment activities consist of interviews and observations in home, school, and other relevant settings as appropriate. In addition to family participants, interviews and observations typically include other team members such as the child's teacher or physical therapist. Interviews are casual, jargon-free, and respectful of the knowledge and expertise of each team member. The consultant also may ask parents or teachers to complete observations in the home or school using a functional analysis observation form (O'Neill et al., 1990). From these interviews and observations, the consultant develops hypotheses about the functions of behavior problems and about the promotion of desirable behavior.

The family ecology assessment consists of two interviews. During the first interview, the family replies to open-ended questions about family goals, strengths, resources and social supports, and sources of stress (Summers, Behr, & Turnbull, 1989; Turnbull & Turnbull, 1991a). During the second interview, the family describes the daily routines in which their child participates. After enumerating all current routines, the family identifies three or four routines in which they would like intervention and then describes what each routine would look like if it were successful.

In addition to gaining information necessary for the design of a comprehensive family support plan, the assessment process gives the family critical information about their child and family. When families conduct functional analysis observations, they discover the types of interactions or events that trigger behavior problems and the purposes that these behaviors serve. Behavior problems are cognitively reframed from willful acts of noncompliance to inappropriate attempts to satisfy important wants and needs. The family ecology assessment has a similar awareness-building function. For instance, when families talk about their strengths, they are reminded that despite the trauma of ABI, they still possess many qualities of an effective family: Both parents may recognize that they remain loving and forgiving in their relationship with their children; a mother may see that her ability to coordinate family activities remains intact; a father may realize that he continues to effectively support his children. Acknowledging strengths and resources helps families regain the sense of hope that may have been lost through grief and the struggle to cope.

Preliminary Plan Design During and immediately after the comprehensive assessment, the consultant engages the team members in a dialogue about the content of a preliminary positive behavioral support plan and an implementation plan. Guided by the hypotheses generated during the functional assessment, they discuss together interventions that may render behavior problems irrelevant, ineffective, and inefficient in achieving their purpose. Five categories of intervention are considered:

1. Ecological/lifestyle interventions
2. Antecedent/proactive interventions
3. Interventions to teach new behaviors or skills
4. Effective consequences
5. Emergency procedures

Effective consequences typically include positive reinforcement strategies to strengthen adaptive behavior and de-escalation procedures to weaken behavior problems. Emergency procedures may be proposed if necessary to prevent physical injury or property destruction.

Information from the family ecology assessment is used to select child- and family-centered interventions that advance family goals, build on family strengths, use resources and social supports available to the family, and diminish sources of stress. For example, family goals may include helping their child with ABI make new friends and finding ways for the parents to get more rest from caregiving responsibilities. Interventions may include enrolling the child in the local chapter of Girl Scouts or developing a small group of skilled respite care providers. Information about family routines helps with the design of child- and family-centered interventions that are effectively embedded in the routines. For example, during a dinner routine an affectionate older sibling may be willing to praise her brother with ABI for appropriate behavior during the meal.

The family and the consultant also discuss potential implementation support activities. The family and consultant collaboratively decide on the routines in which to intervene as well as the activities that will support implementation and long-term maintenance. Potential activities include home meetings, behavioral rehearsal, and coaching in the actual routine. The result of this dialogue is a preliminary implementation plan that includes recommendations for support activities, roles, and a time line.

Team Meetings and Plan Finalization The purposes of the team meeting are to finalize the behavioral support and implementation plans and build collaborative relationships among team members. In preparation for the team meeting, the consultant summarizes functional assessment data and preliminary plans on flip charts. During the meeting, the consultant highlights the results of the assessment, reviews hypotheses, and guides a discussion of potential behavioral interventions and implementation activities. During the review and discussion, team member input is solicited. Plans are presented tentatively, and team members are encouraged to change, add, or delete any part(s). When disagreements arise, they are negotiated until there is consensus.

Effective team meetings achieve consensus on every level. Consensus about hypotheses, goals, interventions, and implementation activities will allow the finalized plans to be supported by all team members. Consensus also may strengthen collaborative relationships and commitment to improving the behavior and lifestyle of the child and family. Finally, consensus creates a context in which the family can be supported in the implementation of interventions, responsibilities can be delegated, and accomplishments acknowledged.

Implementation Support During the implementation phase, the family, consultant, and other key stakeholders implement the behavioral support plan. Support activities defined in the implementation plan, such as behavioral rehearsal and home meetings, are used to 1) build or strengthen the family's capacity to support the child, 2) help enact lifestyle changes, and 3) sustain collaborative relationships. Most support activities take place in the family's home or neighborhood as that is where problems occur. Changes in the behavior of a child with ABI can be made at a residential or rehabilitation facility, but these changes are unlikely to be maintained when the child returns home if the reinforcement and interactional patterns of the family as a whole have not been changed (Willer & Corrigan, 1994).

When implementation begins, the consultant initiates support activities tentatively and flexibly. Some families may like a particular support activity (e.g., role playing), while other families find the same activity stressful. Thus, support activities need to be undertaken with flexibility until the right mix of effective and acceptable activities for a family is discovered.

Support activities commonly used during implementation support include the following: 1) written procedures that succinctly describe interventions and provide examples and nonexamples of appropriate use; 2) implementation checklists that parents use to self-evaluate and self-monitor implementation fidelity; 3) behavioral rehearsal (role play) in which parents and the consultant practice how to implement interventions; 4) coaching in the natural performance setting, involving instruction, modeling, and feedback; 5) home meetings where progress is reviewed, accomplishments acknowledged, and new or recurring problems solved; and 6) telephone consultation.

Continuous Evaluation and Plan Revision Multiple methods of evaluation are used to assess the outcomes of the comprehensive family support effort. These methods are designed to answer four central questions:

1. Has the plan promoted meaningful and durable behavior change for the child?
2. Has the plan improved the lifestyle of the child and family?
3. Do parents and stakeholders use interventions effectively?
4. Do family members perceive plan goals, interventions, and outcomes as acceptable and effective?

Potential evaluation methods include direct observation, implementation checklists, social validity questionnaires, and qualitative interviews with key informants (e.g., parents, siblings, teachers). Methods of evaluation are selected during the team meeting and used continuously during implementation support. Information gained from evaluation data guides changes in implementation support activities and revisions in child- and family-centered interventions. When the data from multiple methods converge to indicate that the central aims of the support effort are being achieved, the consultant begins to fade his support, and the family and consultant confirm a date to terminate the consultant's regular participation in support activities.

Follow-Up Support Although interventions may prove effective and the support effort evaluated a success, the endurance of these positive changes cannot be assumed. For the child to continue her progress, the family will need to continue implementing interventions with fidelity, solve new problems as they arise, and respond deftly to life cycle developments in the child and family. A variety of stressors are likely to impinge on the family and may hinder the parents' on-going ability to support their child. Although behavior problems may have been reduced to near-zero levels, they rarely disappear. The potential for regression is, thus, ever present.

For these reasons, families often need follow-up support. At the conclusion of implementation support, families are encouraged to call the consultant when problems reemerge or new issues arise. Sometimes these problems can be resolved through a series of telephone consultations. At other times a home meeting may be required. In some cases where skills have eroded or interventions have been neglected, a series of coaching sessions in the home may be necessary.

Case Study: Michael

Michael was 11 years old at the time of the study and lived at home with his mother and father, Peggy and Alan, and four siblings: two older sisters, 14 and 17; and two younger brothers, 5 and 8. The family lived in a four-bedroom house in a middle-class neighborhood of a Pacific Northwest community of approximately 100,000 people. Both parents worked outside of the home.

When Michael was 8 years old, he ran across a street and was hit by a car. In the accident, Michael experienced severe brain injury with brain stem contusion and was comatose for approximately 4 months. Michael's initial hospitalization was agonizing for his family because they did not know if he would come out of the coma, or whether he would live or die. They believed that if he awoke, Michael would be himself again. His parents described the experience as "unreal." They reported that after he awoke and they realized his loss of ability, they experienced a shock from which they have not yet recovered.

After 4 months, Michael was transferred to a rehabilitation unit where he remained for 3 months before coming home. During those 7 months in the hospital, Peggy devoted almost all of her time to Michael at the hospital and was not available for the other four children. Only one of the siblings, Michael's 14-year-old sister, visited him at the hospital.

Outpatient rehabilitation occurred for 2 months; then the family moved to another state, where rehabilitation continued. The parents reported that immediately following the accident, their family received much social support from their friends at church, but the subsequent move separated them from their social support network. The family had difficulty building a new social network in their new community; at the time of the study, Michael did not have any friends.

Prior to the accident, Michael had been in a gifted and talented educational program, performing at a grade and a half above his age level. Neuropsychological testing approximately 1 year postinjury revealed a significant visual-spatial problem, poor fine motor control, and slow and dysarthric speech. He scored in the low-average range on a measure of intelligence and two to three grade levels below his expected grade level on academic measures. As a result of this loss of ability, Michael was placed in a self-contained special education classroom in his neighborhood school.

Michael's parents reported that, before the accident, he was a soccer player and star athlete. At the time of the study, the right side of his body was weak, the right side of his face drooped, and his right hand shook. Because of the weakness in his right leg, he walked with a limp, was very unsteady, and often fell. He used his left hand to feed and dress himself. He wasn't able to write with his left hand and so wrote using a computer and keyboard.

Michael's personality and behavior also changed after the accident. He developed a temper that was much more difficult for him or others to control. He screamed, hit, bit, and threw things in flashes of intense anger never seen before the accident. Once he escalated into high-intensity behavior problems, it was difficult for him to regain his composure. Like many children with ABI, he also lost many of his social skills. He asked strangers unsuitable questions, said whatever popped into his mind no matter how inappropriate, and acted immaturely in interactions with his peers.

Referral   At the time of referral, Michael's family was desperate about their inability to control his angry outbursts and destructive behavior. They had seriously considered placing Michael in an inpatient program for children with ABI at a cost of $20,000 per month. Michael's mother had participated in several support programs (e.g., stress and behavior management classes, a parent support group) for families of children with ABI, but her participation was episodic and the services were not intensive enough to overcome Michael's behavior problems and related family problems.

Peggy learned about the availability of the comprehensive family support process during individual counseling at a center that served families of children with disabilities. During the referral interview, the family counselor described the comprehensive family support process and emphasized the approach's home-based and collaborative features. Peggy expressed a strong interest in participating; her husband Alan, although skeptical about the chances for success, was willing to try. The family consented to participate for a nominal fee and also agreed to take part in research activities to evaluate child and family outcomes.

Comprehensive Assessment

Functional Assessment The consultant completed functional assessment activities with Michael's parents, his elementary school teacher, his sisters, and a volunteer respite care provider who had established a positive relationship with Michael. Assessment activities included functional analysis interviews, functional analysis observations in the home and school, and discussions about the purposes of behavior problems and about interventions that might strengthen desirable behavior or diminish behavior problems. Assessment activities were completed across a 5-week period and required approximately 15 hours (total).

The functional assessment indicated that Michael primarily engaged in behavior problems in the home or community in the presence of family members. At school, Michael was in a highly structured program that included many functional and preferred activities, and the teacher was highly skilled in curriculum design and behavior management. Michael engaged in three types of behavior problems:

1. Aggressive behaviors, including slapping, hitting, kicking, and throwing things
2. Property destruction, such as knocking objects off tables and ripping clothing and furniture
3. Whining and screaming

These behaviors sometimes occurred in an escalating sequence beginning with whining and screaming and ending with aggression or property destruction.

In the home, several ecological conditions appeared to set the stage for behavior problems. Michael spent much time with his mother after school and had few opportunities to leave the house and visit friends or engage in favorite sports activities. His mother often felt exhausted from her job, taking care of a large family, and being the primary caregiver for Michael. Michael's father sometimes engaged in roughhouse play with the boys, including Michael, that involved playful slapping and punching. Siblings often avoided Michael because of fear of being slapped or hit. Several features of home routines appeared to provoke behavior problems, including competition among brothers at dinnertime, difficult tasks during homework, unstructured leisure time in the middle evening, and an early bedtime in a room next to a noisy family room.

Many of Michael's skill limitations were associated with his behavior problems. He had difficulty remembering social rules and controlling feelings of embarrassment, frustration, or anger. His memory and communication problems made it harder for him to ask for help or negotiate compromises. He also had difficulty structuring free time and remembering scheduled events. In addition, his loss of motor skills seriously limited his opportunities to participate in previously enjoyed sports activities.

Several types of interactions and events appeared to contribute to and maintain his behavior problems. These included task demands, adults failing to fulfill promises, delays in having requests fulfilled, and seeing peers engaged in sports that he could no longer do. A typical pattern was for Michael to make a request for an item or activity followed by his mother saying "no" or asking him to wait until another time or day. Michael would then escalate into behavior problems ranging from low (whine) to high (hit) intensity until his mother gave in to his demands. Peggy, through this form of coercive training by the child (Patterson, 1982), began to fulfill unreasonable demands at earlier stages in the escalating sequence of interactions. Another common pattern occurred when Michael refused to engage in tasks he didn't like, such as getting ready for bed. He would whine, scream, or hit a parent until the parent withdrew the task demand, delayed the nonpreferred event (e.g., going to bed), or escalated into shouts, physical prompts, or corporal punishment.

Four hypotheses about the functions of Michael's behavior problems emerged from the assessment:

1. Michael whined, screamed, or hit to get attention or assistance.
2. Michael whined, screamed, became aggressive, or engaged in destructive behavior to get an item or activity.
3. Michael whined, screamed, became aggressive, or destroyed to avoid a nonpreferred task, activity, or person.
4. Michael became aggressive and destroyed to protest a loss of ability or opportunity.

These hypotheses served as the foundation for the design of a multicomponent positive behavioral support plan that addressed each purpose of Michael's problem behavior.

Family Ecology Assessment Peggy was the primary participant in the interviews about the family's ecology, with Alan confirming information and describing his own experiences and perspective. Interviews about family characteristics and routines were completed across four meetings in the home. In the first two meetings, Peggy and Alan described their goals, strengths, resources and social supports, and stressors. During subsequent meetings, Michael's parents identified four family routines they wanted to improve, described the current structure of each routine, and generated a vision of what the routines would look like if they were successful.

The family assessment revealed that despite the presence of many stressors, the family had clear goals, possessed many strengths, and benefited from several resources and social supports. For example, the family wanted Michael to learn to manage his own personal needs and free time and better tolerate errors, mistakes, and disappointments. His mother wanted other family members to share child care and household chores more equitably. The family had strong Christian values that encouraged family members to continue caring for each other despite the many difficulties they faced. On his own, Michael's father naturally used several effective strategies (e.g., telling Michael what to expect, offering calm reassurance) to help his son remain calm and cooperative. Informal resources used by the mother included help with child care and household chores from her husband and daughters. Effective formal resources included Michael's teacher, who maintained excellent communication with Peggy. The family also received money from an insurance settlement that helped defray the costs that had been incurred since Michael's accident.

These positive characteristics provided a counterbalance to the stressors felt by family members: Michael's behavior problems, Peggy's exhaustion and frustration with the unequal distribution of child care tasks in the home, and Alan's sense of powerlessness in the family. Prior to the interview, Peggy and Alan thought their family had become totally dysfunctional; afterward, they began to reframe their concept of their family as a healthy one struggling to overcome challenging, yet definable, obstacles.

During the discussion of family routines, Peggy and Alan decided to promote change in four routines that were not working well:

1. An early evening dinner routine in which family members sat together and ate in the dining room
2. A homework routine in which Michael's parents helped him complete his homework
3. A middle evening leisure routine in which Michael attempted to entertain himself and interact with other family members
4. A bedtime routine in which Michael's parents helped Michael get ready for bed

Peggy first described each routine in terms of the elements of activity settings (e.g., goals, tasks, resources) (O'Donnell & Tharp, 1990). Following her description, she then envisioned what each routine would look like if it were successful. During this exercise, the consultant encouraged Peggy to reconstruct the routine in her mind so that it was consistent with Michael's strengths and limitations, congruent with family goals and values, and sustainable over a long period of time. A description of the family's current and envisioned bedtime routine illustrates the process.

Peggy usually started the bedtime routine for Michael earlier than his two younger brothers (around 8 P.M.). Michael's bedroom is adjoined to his parents' bedroom and the living room where his younger brothers continued to watch television or play together. The main resource to Peggy during the routine was Alan, who usually took over the routine when Michael began to hassle his mother. Meanwhile, her daughters were usually upstairs watching television or in the dining room talking or snacking; they typically did not offer to help. Michael's tasks in the routine were (with prompting from a parent) to go to his room, get his pajamas on, use the toilet if needed, brush his teeth and wash his face, and go to bed. Once in bed, Michael's father sometimes read him a story. Peggy's goals and values included Michael going to bed early; the children going to bed clean, peaceful, and happy; and Michael staying in his bedroom. Her motives and feelings included worrying about how Michael would behave, wanting to get Michael out of the way so that she could get some rest, feelings of exhaustion, and resentment at the lack of help from other family members. Patterns of interaction during the routine were predominantly negative: parent demands followed by child whining and aggression and Peggy asking Alan for help after behavior problems escalated.

Having gained some insight into the family's current bedtime experience, the mother and consultant discussed what a successful routine would look like. Peggy envisioned a routine in which most elements were changed or expanded. Alan would help more proactively and more often. Her two daughters would help put the younger boys to bed. Goals would include a fair and predictable sharing of child care tasks, and Peggy taking time after the routine to relax or talk with her daughters. Michael would complete routine tasks more independently and without behavior problems. Positive patterns of interaction would include the family quieting down and cooperatively preparing for bed and family members helping each other.

After a vision was generated for each targeted routine, the content and structure of each were discussed with other family members; members then agreed to support efforts to achieve the vision. The consultant concluded the assessment by explaining how the information gained would drive the design of a behavioral support plan that would fit well with the family's lifestyle and help them move toward their vision of family life.

Preliminary Plan Design Based on assessment information, the consultant—in continued dialogue with the family—designed a preliminary positive behavioral support plan and an implementation plan that described how interventions would be put into place. The consultant used the plan design guidelines described by Horner et al. (1993) to select behavioral interventions and used the guidelines described by Albin et al. (1995) to ensure that interventions fit well with the characteristics and ecology of the family. Following is an abridged description of this process.

Positive Behavioral Support Plan Design For each function of the child's behavior problems, ecological, antecedent, skill-building, and consequent interventions were proposed that would make behavior problems irrelevant, ineffective, or inefficient for achieving their purposes. For example, Michael often engaged in behavior problems to obtain a preferred item or activity. Proposed interventions logically related to this hypothesis included 1) making Michael's life more predictable by giving him information about when he can get preferred items and about when he can do preferred activities; 2) giving Michael a personal written schedule that lists his responsibilities and rewards for completing them; 3) teaching Michael verbal negotiation skills, including how to make reasonable requests, compromise, and accept limits; 4) using effective positive contingency contracts and praising attempts to use negotiation skills; 5) de-escalating behavior problems at an early stage (e.g., when he whined rather than when he became aggressive); and 6) firmly telling him, after he became aggressive, that he cannot get what he wants by using this behavior and making sure that he does not get the desired item or activity for the rest of the day.

Goodness-of-fit was established by first ensuring that interventions advanced family goals, incorporated family knowledge and strengths, used resources available to the family, and appeared likely to diminish stressors. Peggy's goals included getting more free time away from child care duties and having Michael become more independent during family routines. To accommodate the family-centered goal, the weekly use of skilled respite care was proposed so that Peggy could relax and pursue other interests on a regular basis. To accommodate the child-centered goal, a personal schedule was proposed to help Michael self-manage his bedtime routine.

Strengths of the family included the family's devotion to the Bible as a source of inspiration and wisdom and the father's knowledge of several positive strategies for supporting Michael's participation in game activities, chores, and community outings. With the family's Christian values in mind, the consultant asked the family to identify quotes from the Bible that appeared consistent with the emerging support plan and to use these quotes to fortify and inspire them in their effort to promote change. One quote Peggy found helpful was, "Pleasant words are as a honeycomb, sweet to the soul and healing to the bones" (Proverbs 16:24, *The Layman's Parallel Bible*, 1977). When Peggy praised Michael's independent performance, she perceived her actions as not only technically correct but also as inherently meaningful. The consultant also reflected on the father's use of effective precorrections during difficult tasks as well as his use of calm reassurance and redirection when Michael began to grow agitated. These parenting skills became important features of teaching strategies and de-escalation procedures in the support plan.

Implementation Support Plan Design   Based on assessment information and discussions with Michael's parents and teacher, a preliminary implementation plan was designed that emphasized direct training support in the home, weekly telephone consultation, family team meetings to discuss and role play interventions and solve new problems, and continued counseling support. The family decided to first implement interventions in the bedtime routine, and then work on improving the leisure, homework, and dinner routines.

Team Meetings and Plan Finalization   Two team meetings were convened to review assessment information and finalize the preliminary positive behavioral support and implementation plans. The meetings were completed in $3\frac{1}{2}$ hours. Meeting participants included Peggy and Alan, Michael's older sisters, his elementary school teacher, a middle school teacher who might assist with his transition to middle school, an ABI consultant to the family, and the family consultants. Michael did not attend the meeting because his family judged that his behavior would be disruptive and make meeting tasks difficult to complete.

The consultant summarized assessment and plan information on flip charts. Meeting participants first reviewed the functional assessment information and the hypotheses about behavior problems. After achieving a consensus on the reasons for Michael's behavior problems, the team reviewed and discussed the interventions in the proposed behavioral support plan and the support activities and roles described in the proposed implementation plan.

During the reviews and discussions, the consultant answered team members' questions and concerns, encouraged suggestions for modifications, and acknowledged team members' contributions. Michael's parents and other team members agreed with the hypotheses about behavior problems and with most of the recommended interventions and support activities; they also suggested some improvements. Michael's elementary school teacher recommended that behavioral consultation meetings be held with middle school teachers and administrators before the start of the next school year to ensure a smooth transition. With team member recommendations incorporated, the plans were finalized. Soon after the meeting, the consultant wrote up the finalized plans and distributed them to team members. Summaries of the positive behavioral support plan and implementation plan are presented in Tables 1 and 2.

Implementation Support During implementation, the consultant helped the family put the plan into place. Over a period of 3 months, the consultant and the family first intervened in the bedtime routine and then initiated intervention in the leisure routine. Coaching during home routines and telephone consultations typically occurred once per week. Coaching sessions lasted $1-1\frac{1}{2}$ hours, while telephone consultations lasted 15–30 minutes. Approximately once a month, a team meeting was held with family members to discuss progress and role-play interventions. Support activities used during implementation support are summarized below.

Embedding Interventions in Envisioned Routines The first task of implementation support was to identify relevant interventions from the support plan and effectively embed them in the first targeted routine—going to bed. Toward this end, the consultant designed a brief, routine-specific plan that described interventions in terms of the content and structure of the bedtime routine. For example, one goal was for Michael to go to bed independently. Tasks included putting on his pajamas, completing hygiene tasks, and getting into bed.

Behavioral interventions were embedded into the routine by teaching Michael to use a personalized self-management notebook that listed the tasks in the bedtime routine and the reinforcers (e.g., bedtime story, dictate story for journal) available for going to bed cooperatively. The parents were also encouraged to praise Michael whenever he attempted to complete routine steps independently. To ensure that the routine included more frequent and predictable help from other family members, the family negotiated a weekly schedule of helpers and posted the schedule in the kitchen. To achieve the calmer atmosphere envisioned, Michael and his brothers began to go to bed at the same time (between 8:30 P.M. and 9 P.M.), and other family members agreed to keep activities in the living room quiet after 8 P.M.

Coaching During the first few coaching sessions for the bedtime routine, the consultant and family negotiated a style of coaching that was most comfortable for Michael and his parents. At the start of a session, the consultant asked Michael and his parents for their in-

Table 1. Michael's multicomponent positive behavioral support plan

Family-centered interventions

1. Plan for skilled respite care at least once a week.
2. Share child care and housecleaning tasks fairly and predictably so that each family member can rest.

Child-centered interventions

Lifestyle/ecological

1. Help Michael feel important (e.g., offer choices and honor reasonable preferences, patiently listen to him, let him do things on his own without unwanted assistance).
2. Support Michael in the development of friendships with peers without disabilities.
3. During major transitions (e.g., back to school after a holiday), increase choice and reinforcement.

Antecedent/proactive

1. Have Michael use a self-management schedule that reminds him of tasks, social rules, and available reinforcers during routines at home and during classes at school.
2. Provide precorrections before he makes social errors or acts impulsively in the community.
3. Support Michael when he does homework by helping him in a quiet room, by interspersing easy and fun tasks with new and difficult tasks, and by using humor to keep the atmosphere lighthearted.

Teaching new behaviors and skills

1. Teach Michael to self-manage his schedule of tasks and activities.
2. Teach Michael to negotiate choices and accept compromises and limits.
3. Teach Michael to control his anger by teaching him to say "No big deal" when he makes a mistake, to do deep breathing if he feels upset, and to find an adult to talk to about the problem.

Positive reinforcement

1. Praise Michael often for trying, displaying independence, and showing self-restraint.
2. Use effective positive contingency contracts and follow through consistently.

De-escalation strategies

1. Before Michael's disruptive behavior escalates, assess the reason for his agitation and use a support strategy that matches the reason, remind him to use his skills instead of his behaviors, prompt or model the use of the appropriate skills, praise remaining calm and trying to use skills, redirect him back to task or activity, and praise re-initiating task or activity.
2. If Michael's behavior escalates to get an item or activity, calmly but firmly say, "No," redirect him to a dissimilar task or activity, remain calm and firm, but sympathetic and do not negotiate.
3. If Michael's behavior escalates to get attention, calmly but firmly say, "No," walk away for 1 to 2 minutes, return and remind him of rule, tell him when you can give him attention, and redirect him to an activity he can do independently.

Table 2. Michael's implementation plan

Support activities (5-month time line)
1. Written positive behavioral support plan
2. Routine specific plan with implementation checklist
3. Coaching in targeted routines, one at a time (1 time per week)
4. Telephone consultation (1 time per week)
5. Family team meeting to discuss and role play interventions (1 time per 4–6 weeks)
6. Counseling support
7. Friendship development support
8. Transition support to middle school

Roles and responsibilities
1. Parents: Primary implementors of interventions
2. Daughters: Informed participants, secondary implementors
3. Behavioral consultant: Primary implementation support person, respite care support and development, support for transition to middle school
4. Family counselor: Supervisor of clinical support effort, support for lifestyle changes, counseling support
5. School teachers: Support for transition to middle school, implementation and adaptation of interventions in the school
6. ABI consultant: Life-planning support, long-term social support

formed consent and then met briefly with the parents to talk through the use of interventions. Also during the first few sessions, the consultant modeled the interventions with Michael while his parents observed. During subsequent sessions, the parents implemented interventions while the consultant observed or waited in another room until the routine was completed. After Michael went to bed, the consultant and parents briefly reviewed the session, emphasizing parent skillfulness and child progress.

Telephone Consultation and Use of Implementation Checklist During telephone consultation, the consultant and the parents discussed progress in implementing interventions during the previous few days. An implementation checklist was used to structure the discussion. The checklist evaluated Michael's completion of routine steps, the parents' use of interventions, behavior problems, and the acceptability of the support effort (see Figure 1). The parents described their successes, continued problems, and feelings or frustrations related to Michael and the support effort. The consultant commended the parents' achievements, helped solve new or recurring problems, and provided emotional support when a parent expressed grief over the child's accident or frustration with recurring behaviors.

Family Counseling During natural opportunities that arose in coaching sessions, telephone consultations, and family meetings, the consultants helped family members reframe their views of themselves,

Six steps to a harmonious bedtime routine	Unable to do this		Did this very well		
1. I reviewed schedule and rules with Michael.	1	2	3	4	5
2. I offered choice of reward for independence and cooperation.	1	2	3	4	5
3. I provided help only if needed.	1	2	3	4	5
4. I praised independence and following rules.	1	2	3	4	5
5. If Michael calmly went to bed, I fulfilled the deal.	1	2	3	4	5
6. If Michael hit, kicked, or threw things, I did not fulfill the deal.	1	2	3	4	5

How Michael did during routine	Much help		By self		
1. He completed the routine with little help.	1	2	3	4	5
2. He calmly said goodnight and prepared to sleep.	1	2	3	4	5
3. He whined/screamed (number of times).	0	1	2–5	6–10	10+
4. He hit, kicked, or threw something (number of times).	0	1	2–5	6–10	10+

How I feel about the bedtime routine	Disagree		Agree		
1. The routine was stressful.	1	2	3	4	5
2. The steps to success were difficult to implement.	1	2	3	4	5
3. All children went to bed happy.	1	2	3	4	5
4. I got some relaxation time.	1	2	3	4	5

Figure 1.   Michael's implementation checklist for bedtime routine.

each other, and Michael. Peggy was encouraged to see herself as a person who proactively solved problems before they happened rather than one who worried about problems until they occurred. Through modeling and dialogue, the consultants helped family members see Alan as a competent leader in teaching Michael new ways to behave, rather than as a powerless father. Similarly, the family was encouraged to view Michael not as a damaged person but rather as a young boy striving to overcome obstacles to his development that frustrated and confused him.

Coordination of Lifestyle Goals and Transition to Middle School
Concurrent with direct and indirect support for family routines, the consultants and family collaborated to implement lifestyle interventions, such as increasing Michael's friendships and getting skilled respite care into the home on a regular basis. The consultants, for example, collaborated with Peggy to enroll Michael in a summer church camp for children without disabilities and provided consultation support to the camp counselors. Michael also became a participant in a project to help children with ABI develop friendships. During implementation support, the consultants facilitated meetings between Peggy and the director of a respite care program and participated in discussions about the development of skilled respite care for Michael.

At the start of the new school year, the consultants met with school personnel at the middle school, discussed the family's progress, gave the receiving teacher a copy of the behavioral support plan, and discussed interventions that would be relevant to the school setting. In all conversations with school personnel, the consultants emphasized the parents' expertise in supporting Michael and encouraged administrators and teachers to view Michael's family as a valuable resource to the school and able collaborators in the coordination of support between the home and school.

Termination of Implementation Support and Follow-Up
Following 7 weeks of implementation support in the bedtime routine (involving approximately 17 hours of direct and indirect support) and 5 weeks of implementation support for the leisure routine (involving approximately 12 hours of primarily indirect support), the family chose to terminate their participation in implementation activities, except for continued telephone consultation on an as-needed basis. Their reasons for terminating most implementation support included improvements in Michael's behavior across all routines; family confidence that they could continue supporting Michael without intensive, direct intervention in the home; and Peggy starting a new job and wanting to simplify her life. The consultants supported the family's decision to terminate implementation support, contacted the family by telephone approximately once a month to assess the maintenance of behavioral improvement in Michael, and completed follow-up measures 2, 3, and 5 months after implementation support ended.

Evaluation Methods Four methods of evaluation were used to assess child and family outcomes:

1. A single-case research design to summarize direct observations of behavior problems in four family routines

2. Implementation checklists to assess parent fidelity in use of interventions
3. A social validity measure to evaluate the acceptability of plan goals, procedures, and outcomes
4. Qualitative interviews to provide an interpretation of the family's subjective experience of the support effort

Evaluation methods are summarized below.

Single-Case Research Design A single baseline, time-series research design (Barlow & Hersen, 1984) was employed to assess the correlation between implementation of the behavioral support plan and improvement in child behavior in the dinner, homework, leisure, and bedtime routines. The quasi-experimental design had three phases: baseline, intervention, and follow-up. Direct observation of child behavior across the four routines was completed by trained observers during each observation session. Three behaviors were operationally defined: 1) aggression, including hitting, kicking, and biting; 2) destructive behaviors, including throwing objects, knocking objects off tables or counters, and breaking objects; and 3) screaming, involving high-intensity shrieking or shouting. An interval-recording method of observation was used and observations in each routine lasted for 15 minutes. During an observation session, the observer used a clipboard with an earphone attached that emitted a beep every 30 seconds. Following each interval, the observer recorded whether behavior problems occurred during the interval.

Observers participated in 10 hours of training, including discussion of definitions and procedures and pilot observations in targeted routines, until interobserver agreement scores of 85% or better were achieved. Interobserver agreement was measured in 6 of the 17 (35%) observation sessions, and agreement measures were distributed across the three phases of the study. Average interobserver agreement for behavior problems was 88% (range, 79%–99%).

Implementation Fidelity During telephone consultations about intervention in the bedtime routine, the consultant used an implementation checklist to guide an interview with Michael's parents about the use of interventions. The family evaluated fidelity using a 5-point Likert scale (1 = not able to use, 5 = used very well). Michael's parents completed this interview on four occasions.

Social Validity The social validity of the support effort was evaluated during intervention in the bedtime routine and after follow-up measurement. During the parents' self-evaluation of the bedtime routine, they also rated statements about the acceptability of the routine (e.g., family members helped, all children went to bed happy) using a 5-point Likert scale (see Figure 1). Two months after the last follow-up observation, Michael's mother evaluated the social validity of the overall support effort using a 10-item questionnaire with a 6-point Likert scale (1 = disagree, 6 = agree). The items addressed issues related to the acceptability of support plans goals, procedures, and outcomes.

Qualitative Interviews Once during implementation support and once again during follow-up, Michael's parents were interviewed about their perceptions of the support effort. The consultant asked three open-ended questions:

1. How has Michael's behavior and lifestyle improved since the support effort began, if at all?
2. How has the family's lifestyle improved since the support effort began, if at all?
3. What problems continue to occur?

The first interview took 45 minutes, while the second interview lasted 1 hour. The interviews were tape recorded and transcribed. These data then were analyzed for descriptive themes using qualitative methods of analysis (Gilgun, Daly, & Handel, 1992). Themes that emerged from the data were summarized into a brief interpretation of the family's experience.

Results

Behavior Problems Data collected across the four routines were combined into a composite percentage of intervals of behavior problems (see Figure 2). Overall, the data indicate significant improvement

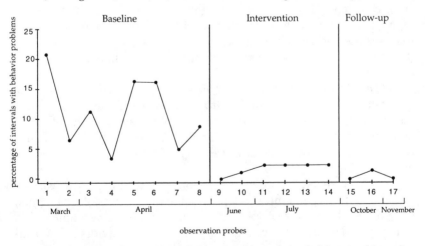

Figure 2.   Percentage of intervals with behavior problems during four home routines: dinner, homework, leisure, and bedtime.

in the level, trend, and stability of behavior problems across the four targeted routines after the positive behavioral support plan was implemented in the bedtime routine, and subsequently—albeit briefly—in the leisure routine. Baseline data show high variability, an increasing trend (split-middle method of trend analysis [Tawney & Gast, 1984]), and an average percentage of 10.6 of total intervals evidencing behavior problems. During implementation support, behavior problems fell to a stable average of 1.5% of total intervals observed; further improvement (0.5%) was evidenced 2 and 3 months after implementation support was concluded. Because the data represent a composite percentage across four routines, an interpretation of behavior change in any one routine cannot be made. Also, because of limitations inherent in the research design, these changes suggest only a correlation between implementation of the positive behavioral support plan and improvements in child behavior across the four routines. A causal relationship cannot be inferred.

Implementation Fidelity Across four ratings (1 = unable to do; 5 = did very well) during implementation support in the bedtime routine, the parents evaluated themselves as increasingly able to implement interventions. During the first self-evaluation the average rating was 3.3; this improved to 4.2 by the last evaluation. These data suggest that the parents perceived themselves as becoming more capable of using interventions effectively in the bedtime routine.

Social Validity Across four ratings (1 = disagree; 5 = agree) of the bedtime routine, Michael's parents indicated that the routine was not so stressful (2.6), interventions were not difficult to implement (1.5), children went to bed fairly happy (3.8), and they had time to relax (4.2). The parents' evaluation of the comprehensive support effort is presented in Tables 3 and 4. These data suggest that, overall, the family was very satisfied with support goals, interventions, and outcomes.

The Parents' Experience: "He Fits into the Family Better" The qualitative findings served to confirm and further illuminate improvements in Michael's behavior, parental use of behavioral interventions, and overall improvements in the family's lifestyle. The findings also revealed areas where little progress was made and where family problems remained.

Michael's parents consistently reported that Michael was calmer, more cooperative, and more independent in many areas of his life than he had been before the support effort. His parents viewed him as less whiny and less apt to escalate into aggressive behaviors. They estimated that major behavioral incidents had decreased from about once a week to once or twice a month and that behaviors during an incident were less intense.

Table 3. Social validity evaluation: Ratings

Social validity category	Rating
1. Goals were appropriate.	5
2. Goals were consistent with my family's values.	5
3. Interventions were difficult to carry out.	3
4. Interventions were effective in improving child's behavior.	5
5. Outcomes were beneficial to my child.	5
6. Outcomes were beneficial to my family as a whole.	4
7. The plan caused unanticipated problems in my family.	1
8. Training activities were well organized and helpful.	5
9. The consultants showed respect for our values.	5
10. Overall, the support effort strengthened my family.	5

Note: 1 = Disagree, 5 = Agree.

Michael's parents partly attributed his gains in independence to changes they had made in themselves. They saw themselves as more patient with him, not expecting him to complete tasks as quickly as he did before the accident. They also noted that they were giving Michael more opportunities to do things for himself. For Michael's part, they perceived a renewed willingness and ability to do things independently. Peggy explained what she meant by independence:

It means he doesn't need our help as much. He's able to know what he has to do and do it while I can help other members of the family. It means he can take care of himself as far as getting dressed. He's not as demanding or whiny. I don't have to drive him to do things like get ready for bed. He's just more confident about the fact that he can do things and that he's part of the family.

Peggy and Alan also experienced Michael as more willing and able to negotiate wants and to accept compromises or limits. He was viewed as listening more, reasoning better, and trying to understand why he wasn't allowed to do certain things.

Both parents reported that Michael was doing well in middle school, liked his middle school teacher, and had begun to make friends at school. They viewed his teacher as very dedicated and skilled. Although Michael was perceived as having friends at school, his parents reported that he still did not have after-school friends. A remaining

Table 4. Social validity evaluation: Parent comments

We have been successfully taught how to look for and recognize the signs of potential problems that could escalate into inappropriate behavior in our child and how to redirect him in a more positive manner.

We are sometimes lulled into forgetting the strategies because Michael behaves so well for longer periods of time; when he—or we—have a bad day, it takes some quick thinking and attitude adjustments on both parts.

Michael is much more cooperative, independent, calm, and pleasant to have around.

Living with the pressures and demands of a brain-injured child along with four other siblings will always be stressful, but this support has been essential in helping us as parents cope and alleviate a major part of that stress.

source of frustration and anger for Michael was seeing his younger brother having friends over or leaving the house to visit friends.

Michael's parents viewed themselves as much more effective at parenting Michael. They found themselves using praise, positive contingencies, and precorrections to build cooperation and independence. Peggy described how she often praised him for doing things independently around the house: "I'll say, 'It really helps me when you have the table all set—all I have to do is get the milk.'" His parents also said they were better at de-escalating problems by remaining calm themselves; not worrying so much about Michael "losing it"; and providing information, reassurance, or redirection before he escalated. Finally, his parents observed that they had become consistent about not giving in to Michael when he tries to use behavior problems to enforce his will.

Alan and Peggy described a few improvements in the quality of the family's life together since the start of the support effort. They believed that their relationship had improved and that they were more supportive of each other. Peggy said she was able to get more rest because Michael's behavior was more predictable and he was better able to manage his free time. Alan said he was able to take Michael on outings with the other boys successfully because he always told Michael what to expect and made sure he rewarded the boys for cooperating together. Unsolved problems in the family include Michael's relationship with his 8-year-old brother, which remains competitive and contentious, and the continued isolation of the two older daughters from Michael and the rest of the family.

CONCLUSION

This chapter describes a comprehensive approach to intervention with families of children with ABI and behavior problems that combines recommended practice in positive behavioral support, family support, and behavioral parent training. Implementation of the approach was associated with clinically significant improvements in child behavior that maintained during follow-up measures 3 and 4 months post-intervention.

Four contributions of the family support approach to the ABI rehabilitation field bear emphasis. First, the approach synthesizes a behavior-analytic understanding of child behavior problems with an ethnographic view of family ecology and culture. This synthesis contributes to the design of multicomponent, positive behavioral support plans that are both effective and contextually appropriate for children with ABI and their families.

Second, functional assessment with children experiencing ABI, while acknowledging the influence of trauma on the development of behavior problems, suggests that additional factors influence the development and maintenance of problem behaviors (O'Neill et al., 1990; Wacker et al., in press). These factors include the child's skill limitations, changes in parent–child interaction patterns that inadvertently strengthen behavior problems, and reductions in the child's quality of life. The benefit of this expanded view of factors related to problem behaviors is that each skill limitation, detrimental social interaction pattern, or lifestyle loss can be linked to an intervention that may reduce problem behaviors and rebuild adaptive behavior.

Families of children with ABI can take heart in a functional perspective on problem behaviors (Carr, Robinson, & Palumbo, 1990). Through this perspective, parents may see that 1) their child's behavior problems often serve a clear purpose (e.g., escape demand, get help); 2) problem behaviors are typically triggered by observable events in the environment; and 3) the trauma to the child need not be a solid barrier to behavioral rehabilitation. Empowered by this perspective, families can collaborate with interventionists to design acceptable and effective interventions that address each purpose of the child's problem behaviors.

Third, the collaborative approach to assessment of family ecology naturally encourages professionals to listen to families as this is the only efficient way to gain an in-depth understanding of family characteristics (e.g., goals, strengths, stressors) and routines (Gallimore, Weisner, et al., 1993; Summers et al., 1989). Thus, the assessment process inherently honors the family. Several benefits accrue from an assessment approach that may be experienced by families as empowering (Turnbull & Turnbull, 1991b): The development of a therapeutic alliance may be facilitated. A dialogue about family strengths may rekindle the family's sense of hope and self-confidence. An understanding of family routines may lay the groundwork for the design of behavioral interventions that are specially tailored to fit well with the features of the routines.

A final contribution is viewing the family routine as the unit of analysis and intervention (O'Donnell & Tharp, 1990). Because family routines include many of the relevant features of the child's problem behaviors and the family's ecology, intervening within a routine can be a highly efficient and effective means for promoting initial change that the family can see, understand, and attribute to their own effort. For example, when Michael's family successfully intervened in the bedtime routine, they not only improved their son's problem behaviors and their parenting practices—they also improved several other relevant features of family ecology (e.g., equity between mother and father, mother's need for free time, Michael's status among younger brothers). Equally important, the focus and continuity that intervention in one routine provided allowed Michael's parents to recognize their new-found ability to transform a failed routine into a successful one.

Research design and outcome limitations suggest the need for caution when interpreting results: The case study design does not permit certainty about attributing behavioral improvement to the support process. Other factors occurring at the same time as the intervention may also account for improvements in Michael's behavior. Also, although 3- and 4-month follow-up data are encouraging, these data are not sufficient to comment on the long-term durability of the support effort. A technology of positive behavioral support and the design of contextually appropriate support plans should promote meaningful change that endures for many years.

A related caution is that the positive behavioral support approach did not cure Michael of problem behaviors. His continued success at home will depend on the extent to which family members continue to support him effectively. Because threats to maintenance are numerous in family settings (e.g., fatigue, illness, marital distress) (Griest & Forehand, 1982), interventionists will do well to consider ways to support the long-term maintenance of positive outcomes. One approach that may have promise is to build periodic follow-up support into a long-term model of support to families (e.g., once every 6 months for 3–5 years). In addition, future research should replicate the support approach with other families of children with ABI to better demonstrate the efficacy of the approach and to demonstrate its utility across a diversity of families.

In conclusion, the results, although requiring some caution in their interpretation, nevertheless suggest the comprehensive family support approach's promise for ameliorating behavior problems in children with ABI, for helping families reintegrate their child with ABI into valued family routines, and for rebuilding the stability and cohesion that typically characterizes families before the trauma to the child and family.

REFERENCES

Albin, R.W., Lucyshyn, J.M., Horner, R.H., & Flannery, K.B. (1995). Contextual fit for behavior support plans: A model for "goodness-of-fit." In L. Kern Koegel & R. Koegel (Eds.), *Community, school, family, and social inclusion through positive behavioral support.* Baltimore: Paul H. Brookes Publishing Co.

American Psychiatric Association. (1994). *Diagnostic and statistical manual of mental disorders* (4th ed., pp. 424–429). Washington, DC: Author.

Barlow, D.H., & Hersen, M. (1984). *Single case experimental designs: Strategies for studying behavior change.* Elmsford, NY: Pergamon.

Bernheimer, L.P., Gallimore, R., & Weisner, T.S. (1990). Ecocultural theory as a context for the individual family service plan. *Journal of Early Intervention, 14,* 219–233.

Burke, W.H., Wesolowski, M.D., & Lane, I.M. (1988). A positive approach to the treatment of aggressive brain-injured clients. *International Journal of Rehabilitation Research, 11,* 235–241.

Carr, E.G., Levin, L., McConnachie, G., Carlson, J.I., Kemp, D.C., & Smith, C.E. (1994). *Communication-based intervention for problem behavior: A user's guide for producing positive change.* Baltimore: Paul H. Brookes Publishing Co.

Carr, E.G., Robinson, S., & Palumbo, L.W. (1990). The wrong issue: Aversive versus nonaversive treatment; The right issue: Functional versus nonfunctional treatment. In A. Repp & N. Singh (Eds.), *Perspectives on the use of nonaversive and aversive interventions for persons with developmental disabilities* (pp. 361–379). DeKalb, IL: Sycamore Press.

Chwalisz, K. (1992). Perceived stress and caregiver burden after brain injury: A theoretical integration. *Rehabilitation Psychology, 37,* 189–203.

Dadds, M.R. (1995). *Families, children, and the development of dysfunction.* Beverly Hills: Sage Publications.

Davis, J.R., Turner, W., Rolider, A., & Cartwright, T. (1994). Natural and structured baselines in the treatment of aggression following brain injury. *Brain Injury, 8,* 589–598.

Delongis, A., Coyne, J.C., Dakof, G., & Folkman, S. (1982). The relationship of hassles, uplifts, and major life events to health status. *Health Psychology, 1,* 119–136.

Dunlap, G., dePerczel, M., Clarke, S., Wilson, D., Wright, S., White, R., & Gomez, A. (1994). Choice making to promote adaptive behavior for students with emotional and behavioral challenges. *Journal of Applied Behavior Analysis, 27,* 505–518.

Dunlap, G., Kern Koegel, L., Clarke, S., & Robbins, F.R. (1991). Functional assessment, curricular revision, and severe behavior problems. *Journal of Applied Behavior Analysis, 24,* 387–397.

Dunst, C.J., Trivette, C.M., Gordon, N.J., & Starnes, A.L. (1993). Family-centered case management practices: Characteristics and consequences. In G.H.S. Singer & L.E. Powers (Eds.), *Families, disability, and empowerment:*

Active coping skills and strategies for family interventions (pp. 89–118). Baltimore: Paul H. Brookes Publishing Co.

Flannery, K.B., & Horner, R.H. (1994). The relationship between predictability and problem behaviors for students with severe disabilities. *Journal of Behavioral Education, 4,* 157–176.

Florian, V., & Katz, S. (1991). The other victims of traumatic brain injury: Consequences for family members. *Neuropsychology, 5,* 267–279.

Gallimore, R., Goldenberg, C.N., & Weisner, T.S. (1993). The social construction and subjective reality of activity settings: Implications for community psychology. *American Journal of Community Psychology, 21,* 537–559.

Gallimore, R., Weisner, T.S., Bernheimer, L.P., Guthrie, D., & Nihira, K. (1993). Family responses to young children with developmental delays: Accommodation activity in ecological and cultural contexts. *American Journal on Mental Retardation, 98,* 185–206.

Gilgun, J.F., Daly, K., & Handel, G. (Eds.). (1992). *Qualitative methods in family research.* Beverly Hills: Sage Publications.

Griest, D.L., & Forehand, K.C. (1982). How can I get any parent training done with all these other problems going on? The role of family variables in child behavior therapy. *Child and Family Behavior Therapy, 14,* 37–53.

Horner, R.H. (1994). Functional assessment: Contributions and future directions. *Journal of Applied Behavior Analysis, 27,* 401–404.

Horner, R.H., Day, M., Sprague, J.R., O'Brien, M., & Tuesday-Heathfield, L. (1991). Interspersed requests: A nonaversive procedure for reducing aggression and self-injury during instruction. *Journal of Applied Behavior Analysis, 24,* 265–278.

Horner, R.H., Dunlap, G., Koegel, R.L., Carr, E.G., Sailor, W., Anderson, J., Albin, R.W., & O'Neill, R.E. (1990). Toward a technology of "nonaversive" behavioral support. *Journal of The Association for Persons with Severe Handicaps, 15,* 125–132.

Horner, R.H., O'Neill, R.E., & Flannery, K.B. (1993). Building effective behavior support plans from functional assessment information. In M. Snell (Ed.), *Systematic instruction of persons with severe handicaps* (4th ed., pp. 184–214). Columbus, OH: Charles E. Merrill.

Kanfer, F.H., & Grimm, L.G. (1980). Managing clinical change: A process model of therapy. *Behavior Modification, 4,* 419–444.

Kanner, A.D., Coyne, J.C., Schaefer, C., & Lazarus, R.S. (1981). Comparison of two modes of stress measurement: Daily hassles and uplifts versus major life events. *Journal of Behavioral Medicine, 4,* 1–39.

Kern Koegel, L., Koegel, R.L., Hurley, C., & Frea, W.D. (1992). Improving social skills and disruptive behavior in children with autism through self-management. *Journal of Applied Behavior Analysis, 25,* 341–354.

Lazarus, R.S., & Folkman, S. (1984). *Stress, appraisal, and coping.* New York: Springer-Verlag.

Livingston, M.G., Brooks, D.N., & Bond, M.R. (1985). Patient outcome in the year following severe head injury and relatives' psychiatric and social functioning. *Journal of Neurology, Neurosurgery, and Psychiatry, 48,* 876–881.

Lucyshyn, J.M., & Albin, R.W. (1993). Comprehensive support to families of children with disabilities and behavior problems: Keeping it "friendly." In G.H.S. Singer & L.E. Powers (Eds.), *Families, disability, and empowerment: Active coping skills and strategies for family interventions* (pp. 365–408). Baltimore: Paul H. Brookes Publishing Co.

Malette, P., Mirenda, P., Kandborg, T., Jones, P., Bunz, T., & Rogow, S. (1992). Application of a lifestyle development process for persons with severe intellectual disabilities: A case study report. *Journal of The Association for Persons with Severe Handicaps, 17*, 179–191.

McKinlay, W.W., & Hickox, A. (1988). How can families help in the rehabilitation of the head-injured? *Journal of Head Trauma Rehabilitation, 3*, 64–72.

Meyer, L.H., & Evans, I.M. (1989). *Nonaversive intervention for behavior problems: A manual for home and community.* Baltimore: Paul H. Brookes Publishing Co.

Nihira, K., Weisner, T.S., & Bernheimer, L.P. (1994). Ecocultural assessment in families of children with developmental delays: Construct and concurrent validities. *American Journal on Mental Retardation, 98*, 551–566.

Nixon, C.D. (1992). *Posttraumatic stress disorder in parents of children with traumatic brain injury.* Unpublished manuscript, Oregon Research Institute, Eugene.

O'Dell, S. (1985). Progress in parent training. In M. Hersen, R.M. Eisler, & P.M. Miller (Eds.), *Progress in behavior modification* (Vol. 9, pp. 57–108). New York: Academic Press.

O'Donnell, C.R., & Tharp, R.G. (1990). Community intervention guided by theoretical development. In A.S. Bellack, M. Hersen, & A.E. Kazdin (Eds.), *International handbook of behavior modification and therapy* (2nd ed., pp. 251–266). New York: Plenum.

O'Neill, R.E., Horner, R.H., Albin, R.W., Storey, K., & Sprague, J.R. (1990). *Functional analysis of problem behavior: A practical assessment guide.* Sycamore, IL: Sycamore Publishing Co.

Patterson, G.R. (1982). *Coercive family process.* Eugene, OR: Castalia Publishing Co.

Patterson, G.R., Reid, J.B., & Dishion, T.J. (1992). *Antisocial boys.* Eugene, OR: Castalia Publishing Co.

Peters, M.D., Gluck, M., & McCormick, M. (1992). Behavior rehabilitation of the challenging client in less restrictive settings. *Brain Injury, 6*, 299–314.

Pieper, B.S., & Singer, G.H.S. (1991). *Model family–professional partnerships for interventions in children with traumatic brain injury.* Albany: New York Head Injury Foundation.

Rogers, D. (1984). Family crises following head injury: A network intervention strategy. *Journal of Neurosurgical Nursing, 16*, 343–346.

Sanders, M.R., & Dadds, M.R. (1993). *Behavioral family intervention.* Newton, MA: Allyn & Bacon.

Singer, G.H.S., & Powers, L.E. (Eds.). (1993). *Families, disability, and empowerment: Active coping skills and strategies for family interventions.* Baltimore: Paul H. Brookes Publishing Co.

Sprague, J.R., & Horner, R.H. (1991). Determining the acceptability of behavior support plans. In M. Wang, H. Walberg, & M. Reynolds (Eds.), *Handbook of special education* (pp. 125–142). Elmsford, NY: Pergamon.

Summers, J.A., Behr, S.K., & Turnbull, A.P. (1989). Positive adaptation and coping strengths of families who have children with disabilities. In G.H.S. Singer & L.K. Irvin (Eds.), *Support for caregiving families: Enabling positive adaptation to disability* (pp. 27–40). Baltimore: Paul H. Brookes Publishing Co.

Tawney, J.W., & Gast, D.L. (1984). *Single subject research in special education.* Columbus, OH: Charles E. Merrill.

The layman's parallel bible (8th ed.). (1977). Grand Rapids, MI: The Zondervan Corporation.

Turnbull, A.P., Patterson, J.M., Behr, S.K., Murphy, D.L., Marquis, J.G., & Blue-Banning, M.J. (Eds.). (1993). *Cognitive coping, families, and disability.* Baltimore: Paul H. Brookes Publishing Co.

Turnbull, A.P., & Turnbull, H.R., III. (1991a). *Families, professionals, and exceptionality: A special partnership.* Columbus, OH: Charles E. Merrill.

Turnbull, A.P., & Turnbull, H.R., III. (1991b). Family assessment and family empowerment: An ethical analysis. In L.H. Meyer, C.A. Peck, & L. Brown (Eds.), *Criticial issues in the lives of people with severe disabilities* (pp. 485–488). Baltimore: Paul H. Brookes Publishing Co.

Turnbull, A.P., & Turnbull, H.R., III. (1991c). Understanding families from a systems perspective. In J.M. Williams & T. Kay (Eds.), *Head injury: A family matter* (pp. 37–61). Baltimore: Paul H. Brookes Publishing Co.

Wacker, D.P., Cooper, L.J., Peck, S., Derby, K.M., & Berg, W. (in press). Family-performed functional assessment. In A.C. Repp & R.H. Horner (Eds.), *Functional analysis of problem behaviors: From effective assessment to effective support.* Pacific Grove, CA: Brookes/Cole.

Wacker, D.P., & Steege, M.W. (1993). Providing out-clinic services: Evaluating treatment and social validity. In R. Van Houton & S. Axelrod (Eds.), *Behavior analysis and treatment* (pp. 297–319). New York: Plenum.

Whiting, B., & Edwards, C. (1988). *Children of different worlds: The formation of social behavior.* Cambridge, MA: Harvard University Press.

Willer, B., & Corrigan, J.D. (1994). Whatever it takes: A model for community-based services. *Brain Injury, 8,* 647–659.

Williams, J.M., & Kay, T. (Eds.). (1991). *Head injury: A family matter.* Baltimore: Paul H. Brookes Publishing Co.

ACKNOWLEDGMENTS

The authors gratefully acknowledge the contributions of several colleagues to the development and refinement of the family support approach, to the conduct of the study, and for editorial assistance in preparing the manuscript. For the development of the initial process of support we thank Richard Albin, Robert Horner, Philip Ferguson, Robert O'Neill, Brigid Flannery, and Roz Slovic from the University of Oregon. Other contributors who we thank include George Singer at Dartmouth University, Jacqui Lichtenstein at Direction Service Counseling Center, Nancy Hawkins at the Eugene Clinic, Ali Erickson at the Lane Education Service District, Glen Dunlap at the University of South Florida, and Ann Turnbull at the Beach Center on Families and Disability. For improvements to the support process we thank John Reid and his colleagues from the Oregon Social Learning Center. We also thank Larry Irvin from Teaching Research, Eugene, for his help with planning the study; Tuck Stevens, Kelly Woods, and Charlie MacKnee for their assistance with data collection; and Jane Bell for preparing the manuscript for publication. Special thanks to Robert Horner for his editorial recommendations. Finally, we are indebted to the family for their collaboration in the research process and their many contributions to our knowledge.

7

Providing Support to Siblings of Children with ABI

Sally Kneipp

Although it is widely recognized that acquired brain injury (ABI) is a family matter (Williams & Kay, 1991), scant attention has been paid to the particular issues faced by the siblings of ABI survivors. Kreutzer, Marwitz, and Kepler (1992) have provided a chronological review of the literature on family response and outcome following acquired brain injury since 1972. Their detailed accounting, however, revealed no studies that examined the effects that children with ABI had on their siblings. They pointed out that the data have primarily been collected from wives and mothers and that very little is known about the reactions of fathers, brothers and sisters, or children of individuals with ABI. They stated, "Unfortunately, least is known about the families of children with ABI" (p. 777).

REVIEW OF THE LITERATURE

Although there is a growing body of literature describing the impact of having a brother or sister with a congenital disability, an ongoing health condition, or a terminal illness (Powell & Gallagher, 1993; Singer & Powers, 1993; Stoneman & Berman, 1993), there is very little available about the impact of having a sibling with ABI. And yet, the sudden changes in the family that result from acquired brain injury can be particularly stressful for siblings.

In virtually the only research study specifically addressing siblings, Orsillo, McCaffrey, and Fisher (1993) focused on the stress associated with having a sibling with ABI. They found that siblings of individuals with severe brain injuries "experienced significant psychological distress as long as 5 years postinjury" (p. 110). Their study suggested that the siblings' cognitive and behavioral styles contributed to their level of psychological distress. Orsillo et al. believe that knowing siblings' cognitive–behavioral style may help to predict if they will have prolonged adjustment difficulties. Although worthwhile, this study had the following methodological limitations that make it necessary to interpret the results cautiously:

1. The sample size was small—only 13 siblings—and suggests that replicating the study with a much larger sample size may be beneficial. The demographic questionnaire and the instruments were mailed to 20 people, 13 of whom responded.
2. There was no control group and several of the findings were inconsistent.
3. In retrospect, the study seems unable to pinpoint whether the maladaptive cognitive and behavioral styles were a result of premorbid characteristics or a reaction to the sibling's ABI.

Orsillo et al. recommended future studies to examine "the relationship between cognitive–behavioral style and psychological distress in relatives of individuals with ABI, while controlling for premorbid functioning and other life events" (p. 114).

Livingston and Brooks (1988) discuss the concept and measurement of burden, noting that burden is easier to appreciate than define. They state the following:

> [Burden] depends greatly on the perception of the caregiver and his or her capacity to cope. It is bound to reflect not only the effect one individual, the patient with brain injury, has on another, the caregiver, but also the nature of the interaction between these individuals and other family members. (p. 8)

The concept of burden is relevant to siblings of children with ABI, as many are thrust into the role of caregiver on an intermittent, temporary, or permanent basis. However, the burden on siblings has not been given the attention that would seem indicated, given the frequency of occurrence.

Gervasio (1993) discusses the role of caregivers following the acquired brain injury of a family member and cites some of the demands on children who become caregivers for a parent with ABI. However, the caregiving role assumed by siblings, in relation to a brother or sister with ABI, was not addressed. And yet, "The loss of friendship is one of the most frustrating and saddening interpersonal changes that survivors of traumatic brain injury can experience" (Gervasio,

1993, p. 3). Given that brothers and sisters are frequently lifelong friends, it is perplexing that the changes in their relationships are not given more attention.

Chwalisz (1992) provides a theoretical framework for examining the burden of caregiving for people with ABI by summarizing the literature pertaining to studies of burden, which have almost exclusively investigated the burden experienced by spouses of individuals with ABI. Although focusing on the caregiver burden of spouses, Chwalisz states that a "main outcome of the current review of the caregiver burden literature is the emergence of the need to view caregiver burden as a process that evolves over time" (p. 199). Because the relationships between siblings are lifelong, and because brothers and sisters usually outlive the parents of individuals with acquired brain injury, it would be useful to examine longitudinally the impact of ABI on brothers and sisters.

Allen, Linn, Gutierrez, and Willer (1994) have also investigated the burden following acquired brain injury, but they limited their investigation to the burden of 60 spouses and 71 parents regarded as primary caregivers. They pose the following three specific research questions:

1. Do spouses experience (or report) greater levels of burden than parents?
2. Are the areas of impairment specific to acquired brain injury (i.e., cognitive and/or behavior problems) associated with the presence of burden to a higher degree than other factors, such as initial injury severity and extent of physical disability?
3. Does the association among cognitive, behavior, and physical problems and burden vary by the type of burden being considered?

Although the authors report an interest in comparing the responses of spouses and parents to stress and burden following acquired brain injury with the stress and burden experienced by spouses and parents of people with other disabilities, no recommendation was made to investigate the stress and burden experienced by siblings of children with ABI.

Hall et al. (1994) conducted a 2-year follow-up that examined the effects of ABI on caregivers. As with the other reported studies, the caregivers were primarily the spouse (43%) or parent (45%). Hall et al. reported that 6% were "other relatives" but did not specify their relationship to the individual. Their findings did not address the burden of children with ABI on siblings.

First-person accounts and personal communication with siblings of children with ABI support the hypothesis that stress and/or psychological distress are still present many years postinjury. Kneipp (1993) moderated a panel presentation for the annual seminar of the New Jersey Brain Injury Association, Inc., in which three individuals discussed the impact of having a brother or sister with ABI. Based on additional personal communication, Kneipp and Rubovitz (1994) described, at a national brain injury conference, the impact of a brother's or sister's ABI at various points following the injury: immediately following the injury; during emergency or acute care; during inpatient rehabilitation; when the brother or sister has returned home from the hospital; and ongoing, long-term issues.

DePompei and Blosser (1994) discuss the reactions of siblings and peers at the time of the injury, during the rehabilitation process, and in relation to their expectations for the future. Nodell (1990) emphasizes, "Sibling bonds are strong even if parents see only rivalry and competition for attention" (p. 6).

SITUATIONS FACING SIBLINGS

One way to examine the impact of having a brother or sister with an acquired brain injury is to examine the situation temporally, which makes it easier to anticipate the kind of family education, supportive services, or interventions that may be needed, and to ensure that they are available in a timely manner.

During Emergency and Acute Care

The responses of siblings at this stage will understandably be affected by such variables as their ages, the age of the brother or sister with ABI, the parents' and siblings' usual patterns of familial communication, previous exposure to children with serious illnesses or disabilities, the policies and procedures of the hospital (e.g., regarding visitors), and the availability and willingness of the hospital personnel to share information as it becomes known. Siblings, in retrospect, will often acknowledge feeling fearful and anxious at the time of hospitalization, even if they did not express it then. In cases of severe or profound brain injury, siblings are understandably fearful that their sister or brother may die or seem like a very different person if he or she survives. Siblings have also described feeling extreme anxiety in reaction to their parents' state of panic and fear, particularly in homes where the parents' demeanor is a source of stability for the children—seeing their parents out of control can be especially upsetting.

Although the siblings may be quite aware of the parents' need to devote time and energy to their brother or sister, the loss of—or limited—attention from their parents can be very stressful. Feelings of abandonment are common and frequently complicated by concurrent feelings of guilt once the siblings recognize their parents' need to spend large amounts of time at the hospital. Some siblings are attended to by close relatives, friends, or neighbors, but others end up responsible for themselves for the first time. In essence, these siblings become latchkey kids, without any preparation, while the parents constantly remain at the hospital during their brother's or sister's coma. Siblings report feeling out of the loop during this time, and the absence of communication contributes to the stress and anxiety they feel.

The feelings during this period were poignantly stated by Maurer (1991), an identical twin brother of an individual who sustained an acquired brain injury: "Siblings, I think, even in the first days of trauma, undergo sweeping changes...And one begins to live moment by moment—taking baby steps to avoid shattering altogether" (p. 30).

During this period, information that could help reduce the anxiety is often not available to siblings. Siblings have reported being terrified at the sight of the awesome devices and apparatus needed to sustain their brother or sister. Understanding what is taking place, and why, can assist the siblings to cope more effectively with the changes that surround them. Siblings reported feeling ignored or demeaned by what seemed to be conscious efforts on the part of their parents or the treatment team to protect them by not giving them the answers to questions they asked or wished to ask. Receiving information, even when it was discouraging, helped them to feel more in control of themselves.

During Inpatient Rehabilitation

Siblings report that, after their initial shock, fear, and anxiety subsided, other emotions began to surface. In particular, after they were certain their brother or sister was going to survive, they felt less able to understand or accept the limited attention they were receiving from their parents. Feelings of resentment and jealousy emerged, especially after a new routine had developed, centered around the needs of their injured brother or sister. Siblings report having had little understanding of the changes to expect in the individual with ABI or of the prognosis for recovery. DePompei and Blosser (1994) remarked, "None of the siblings stated that they understood, at this time in the rehabilitative process, that their sibling may have lifetime problems" (p. 5). In the absence of information, siblings often expect a full recovery, as they have seen occur on television or in the movies. To facilitate the process of recovery as they envision it, most siblings want to help. Siblings acknowledge frustration and anger over not having been allowed to help in the way they believed they could and not understanding why they were forbidden to assist.

Gans, Mann, and Ylvisaker (1990) emphasize, "Particular attention should be paid to the siblings and their reactions during the discharge planning process. Family life has been significantly disrupted during the inpatient phase of recovery" (p. 609). They further point out that siblings may evidence behavior problems and that attending to their emotional needs may lead to a more successful transition when the brother or sister with ABI returns home. Waaland and Kreutzer (1988) caution, "Reactions of siblings who are placed in the caregiver role may vary from depression, anxiety, and withdrawal to anger and resentment toward the injured child. Siblings of all ages may display academic declines, delinquency, and related psychosocial problems" (p. 59).

Following the Return Home

In American society, a discharge from a hospital is almost always a sign of good recovery; for the siblings of children with ABI, their brother's or sister's discharge home is sufficient to stimulate expectations of a return to typical life—life as it was prior to the injury. However, siblings quickly begin to experience their brother's or sister's challenging behavior and the ongoing disruption it causes in family routines. Usually without all the information needed to make a sound decision, siblings begin to consider the part they will play, or be expected to play, in their sibling's continuing recuperation from an acquired brain injury.

Conflicting emotions arise when, for example, parents tell the siblings that their help is needed and place them in a caregiving role at a personally inopportune time (e.g., on the evening of a junior prom). In addition, feelings of rejection are promulgated when siblings want to help but are not allowed to and are told that there are certain ways to help that only specially trained people are qualified to perform. Siblings must also learn that family activities will now revolve around the brother or sister with ABI and that they will have to delay expression of their own needs or desires for an unspecified period of time. Siblings notice that friends who visited their brother or sister in the hospital have stopped visiting now that he or she is home and wonder if that always happens and if it could happen to them as well.

Ongoing, Long-Term Issues

Many siblings express satisfaction in having learned how to handle the intra- and interpersonal dynamics of living with a brother or sister with ABI; others report continuing to struggle with how best to handle common situations. They frequently report feeling hurt by comments made about their brother or sister, feeling confused by conflicting bits of information and advice offered by well-meaning people, feeling embarrassed by the brother's or sister's behavior, and then feeling guilty about being embarrassed.

Over time, it becomes apparent to the sibling that the physical, cognitive–communication, behavioral, and emotional sequelae of their brother's or sister's ABI are likely to be permanent. This awareness naturally leads to questions, often unasked, about their own future. Siblings may wonder what happens if the parents die—will they become responsible for their brother or sister with ABI? Very often siblings report a lack of knowledge about who pays for the services their brother or sister receives (e.g., home health aides) and how the services get arranged. Of great concern is wanting to socialize and develop one's own relationships without worrying about where the brother or sister fits into the equation. Siblings question whether a sustained intimate relationship and/or marriage will be possible if they are responsible for their brother or sister.

Maurer (1991) sums up these issues when he says, "This, I find, is the great sibling conundrum: How much is enough (in rehabilitation, communication, intervention), and when do you simply embrace what is and live?" (p. 32).

RECOMMENDATIONS FOR SIBLINGS DEALING WITH ABI

The ages and educational levels of all siblings involved will be major determinants of how best to assist them following the injury. This is particularly so as any information to be shared will need to be presented in language and terms easily understood by the siblings. Other factors to be taken into account include the following:

- The number of siblings and birth order (in terms of the possibilities for support as well as the sharing of experiences and responsibilities)
- The family system and how it functions (e.g., whether it is a single-parent household, whether both parents work outside the home)
- Religious orientation
- Usual pattern of interacting with extended family members
- Available community support
- Personality dynamics and coping styles of the various family members
- Having access to information
- Concepts and perceptions of illness and disability
- Past experience with traumatic life events (particularly serious illness or disability)

- The health status of other family members
- The etiology of the brain injury
- Peer group reactions
- Complicating factors such as substance abuse

In families where a single accident has resulted in brain injury or significant disability to more than one family member, the level of stress on the family and the demand on its resources are extreme. This particular scenario, while not the focus of this chapter, is an all-too-common occurrence that needs further examination with respect to its impact on the family system.

The variables affecting a sibling's response to ABI are numerous and complex. Each situation must be assessed carefully and individually. Some general recommendations are offered as follows because of their reported usefulness:

1. Suggest to the parents that, before the siblings see their brother or sister in the hospital, they prepare them for what they will see (e.g., describe the equipment and its purpose). Enlist the assistance of hospital staff to provide this information, if necessary. In addition, request booklets, handbooks, and family guides that may be available and useful. This information is usually available at rehabilitation hospitals or facilities and through the Brain Injury Association, Inc.[1] and its state associations.
2. Provide education about acquired brain injury to the siblings and help them to understand their parents' reactions as well as their own.
3. Encourage the parents to permit and normalize the siblings' expressions of fear, anxiety, vulnerability, jealousy, resentment, anger, sadness, guilt, or any other emotion they may be experiencing.
4. Encourage the parents to include the siblings in any way possible (e.g., providing stimulation during coma) and to receive training to assist with more complex tasks if they are able to be of assistance (e.g., wheelchair transfers). Gans et al. (1990) suggest that older siblings (adolescents) might do volunteer work in the hospital.
5. Sensitize parents to siblings' needs—help to arrange brief periods of respite (later, these periods can be longer) so that the parents can attend to the siblings' needs. Help them problem-solve to meet the needs of all their children.

---

[1]Brain Injury Association, Inc., 1776 Massachusetts Avenue, NW, Suite 100, Washington, D.C. 20036-1904; telephone: (202) 296-6443; FAX: (202) 296-8850.

6. Include the siblings in the discharge planning process; before the injured child returns home, ask for their suggestions and find out what is important to them during this transitional phase.

7. Encourage the siblings to participate in any family or team meetings the rehabilitation team may hold during the postacute stage. If the individual with the brain injury is involved in a nonresidential community reentry program, schedule meetings at the individual's home to increase the likelihood that siblings will participate.

8. If one does not exist, form a siblings support group; this can even consist of just a few siblings. Siblings groups provide siblings with support to address issues and problems, such as peers ridiculing the injured brother or sister or how to react or respond when it is clear that the parents are struggling emotionally and not coping well. The state Brain Injury Association may be a valuable resource in forming a siblings support group, in addition to collaboration with other service providers.

   Highly recommended for siblings are Sibshops, originally created for siblings of children with developmental disabilities ages 8–13. The Sibshop model was developed as part of The Sibling Support Project funded by the Office of Special Education Programs, U.S. Department of Education. The Sibshop model is highly applicable to siblings of children with acquired brain injury and can easily be adapted to meet the concerns of younger or older children. In their workbook on Sibshops, Meyer and Vadasy (1994) provide the necessary information to organize and run a Sibshop.

9. Provide, or make a referral for, individual counseling, if needed; consider joint sessions to include both the injured and noninjured sibling. Guided role plays can help ease the interaction strain that frequently results following disability and can improve communication.

10. Talk with school guidance personnel and alert them to signs of stress, depression, or anxiety in the sibling(s); this is particularly necessary to prevent deterioration in school performance.

11. Make sure the siblings are involved in meetings with lawyers, financial advisors, and so on, if decisions to be made affect them in any way.

12. Provide the siblings with written information about such pertinent issues as insurance policies or funding for services—including contact names and telephone numbers.

13. Arrange family counseling or therapy, if needed. In determining the level of family intervention, Rosenthal and Young (1988) recommend the PLISSIT model, initially proposed by Annon

(1974) for purposes of sexual counseling. As noted by Rosenthal and Young (1988), PLISSIT is an acronym for four levels of intervention: 1) P—Permission, 2) LI—Limited Information, 3) SS—Specific Suggestions, and 4) IT—Intensive Therapy. Rosenthal and Young explain PLISSIT as follows:

At the *permission stage,* the family members are encouraged to express their hopes and fears regarding future recovery to a staff member, who simply listens in a supportive, uncritical manner. Specific questions are referred to the appropriate member of the team.

At the *limited information level,* basic information about brain injury is provided through brochures, articles, lectures, or the media.

In the *specific suggestions stage,* families are provided with concrete, detailed responses to questions.

Finally, at the *intensive therapy stage,* families are often experiencing a great deal of confusion, uncertainty, and emotional distress and need to receive psychological counseling to help them adapt and cope. (p. 43)

CONCLUSION

The concerns of siblings of children with acquired brain injury have received very little attention, particularly considering the multiple, complex situations they face from the time of the injury, throughout the course of their lifetime. A review of the literature on family responses and outcomes revealed several studies that focused on the concerns of caregivers; however, the caregivers were generally considered to be parents or spouses, even though siblings often assume a caregiving role. And although they may not be the primary caregivers, their roles as caregivers may be accompanied by stress and other reactive emotions. The concerns of siblings at various points following the injury were described and recommendations made to increase awareness of these concerns and ways to address them during their brother's or sister's emergency care, acute rehabilitation, as well as following their return home and at later stages postinjury.

REFERENCES

Allen, K., Linn, R.T., Gutierrez, H., & Willer, B.S. (1994). Family burden following traumatic brain injury. *Rehabilitation Psychology, 39*(1), 29–48.

Annon, J.S. (1974). *The behavioral treatment of sexual problems* (Vol. 1). Honolulu, HI: Enabling Systems.

Chwalisz, K. (1992). Perceived stress and caregiver burden after brain injury: A theoretical integration. *Rehabilitation Psychology, 37*(3), 189–203.

DePompei, R., & Blosser, J.C. (1994). Siblings and peers of youth with TBI: In need of our attention. *The Newsletter of the Society for Cognitive Rehabilitation, Inc., 2,* 4–6.

Gans, B.M., Mann, N.R., & Ylvisaker, M. (1990). Rehabilitation management approaches. In M. Rosenthal, E.R. Griffith, M.R. Bond, & J.D. Miller (Eds.),

Rehabilitation of the adult and child with traumatic brain injury (pp. 593–615). Philadelphia: F.A. Davis.

Gervasio, A.H. (1993). How TBI affects the family. *TBI Transmit, 9*(1), 1–3.

Hall, K.M., Kazmark, P., Stevens, M., Englander, J., O'Hare, P., & Wright, J. (1994). Family stressors in traumatic brain injury: A two-year follow-up. *Archives of Physical Medicine and Rehabilitation, 75*, 876–884.

Kneipp, S. (1993, May). *The impact of traumatic brain injury on siblings: Struggles and solutions.* Panel presentation at the eleventh annual seminar of the New Jersey Head Injury Association, Inc., Eatontown.

Kneipp, S., & Rubovitz, K. (1994, June). *The impact of traumatic brain injury on siblings: Struggles and solutions.* Paper presented at the eighteenth annual postgraduate course on Rehabilitation of the Brain-Injured Adult and Child sponsored by the Medical College of Virginia, Virginia Commonwealth University, Williamsburg.

Kreutzer, J., Marwitz, J.H., & Kepler, M. (1992). Traumatic brain injury: Family response and outcome. *Archives of Physical Medicine and Rehabilitation, 73*, 771–778.

Livingston, M.G., & Brooks, D.N. (1988). The burden on families of the brain injured: A review. *Journal of Head Trauma Rehabilitation, 3*(4), 6–15.

Maurer, J. (1991). Special issues for a sibling. In J.M. Williams & T. Kay (Eds.), *Head injury: A family matter* (pp. 29–33). Baltimore: Paul H. Brookes Publishing Co.

Meyer, D.J., & Vadasy, P.F. (1994). *Sibshops: Workshops for siblings of children with special needs.* Baltimore: Paul H. Brookes Publishing Co.

Nodell, S. (1990). The forgotten feeling, fears, and family: Sibling issues from a parent's perspective. *Cognitive Rehabilitation, 8*(2), 6–7.

Orsillo, S.M., McCaffrey, R.J., & Fisher, J.M. (1993). Siblings of head-injured individuals: A population at risk. *Journal of Head Trauma Rehabilitation, 8*(1), 102–115.

Powell, T.H., & Gallagher, P.A. (1993). *Brothers and sisters: A special part of exceptional families* (2nd ed.). Baltimore: Paul H. Brookes Publishing Co.

Rosenthal, M., & Young, T. (1988). Effective family intervention after traumatic brain injury: Theory and practice. *Journal of Head Trauma Rehabilitation, 3*(4), 42–50.

Singer, G.H.S., & Powers, L.E. (Eds.). (1993). *Families, disability, and empowerment: Active coping skills and strategies for family interventions.* Baltimore: Paul H. Brookes Publishing Co.

Stoneman, Z., & Berman, P.W. (Eds.). (1993). *The effects of mental retardation, disability, and illness on sibling relationships: Research issues and challenges.* Baltimore: Paul H. Brookes Publishing Co.

Waaland, P.K., & Kreutzer, J.S. (1988). Family response to childhood traumatic brain injury. *Journal of Head Trauma Rehabilitation, 3*(4), 51–63.

Williams, J.M., & Kay, T. (Eds.). (1991). *Head injury: A family matter.* Baltimore: Paul H. Brookes Publishing Co.

8

Helping Parents Negotiate the School System

Ann Glang, Bonnie Todis, McKay Moore Sohlberg, and Penny R. Reed

Once a child returns to school following acquired brain injury (ABI), the educational system becomes the primary service provider for that child (Ylvisaker, Hartwick, & Stevens, 1991). Because most children and adolescents make excellent physical recoveries after brain injuries, it has been assumed that their return to school will be relatively smooth (Lehr, 1990) and that their educational needs can be addressed by existing general and special education practices. It is only recently that medical and school personnel have realized that many students experience a range of unique challenges upon their return to school.

Since 1990, an increasing number of articles has been devoted to effective educational programming for students with ABI. Authors have offered detailed guidelines in the following areas:

Preparation of this chapter was supported in part by Grants #H086D10008 and #H086R30029 from the U.S. Department of Education. The views expressed in this chapter do not necessarily reflect those of the funding agency. The authors would like to thank Dr. Elizabeth Cooley for her assistance with conducting the educator survey and for her feedback and support in their early work with schools and families, and Kay Sample for her comments in reviewing the manuscript.

1. Evaluation (Begali, 1994; Savage & Carter, 1991)
2. Placement (Cooley & Singer, 1991; Savage & Carter, 1991)
3. Transition from hospital to school (Lehr, 1990; Savage, 1991; Savage & Carter 1991; Ylvisaker et al., 1991)
4. Modifying educational environments (Blosser & DePompei, 1994; Cohen, 1991; Cohen, Joyce, Rhoades, & Welks, 1985)
5. Specific instructional and behavioral strategies (Blosser & DePompei, 1994; Cohen, 1991; Deaton, 1994; Glang, Singer, Cooley, & Tish, 1992; Light et al., 1987; Savage & Wolcott, 1988)
6. Transition to post–high school education and employment (Condeluci, 1994; Nordlund, 1994)

For most children, a successful school experience may depend not only on the strategies employed in the school setting, but also on the advocacy skills of their parents. Parents who are knowledgeable about the types of services and approaches that can help their child and who can effectively advocate for them will be more satisfied with their child's educational program (see Chapter 5), as one mother explains in the following testimony:

I don't know if my son's school ever had students with acquired brain injury. Because I was an educator, because I am an advocate for my child, I think I forced them to look at the issue. But, most people wouldn't go through what we went through. We became the clanging bell—the parents that they could never please.

This chapter presents an analysis of educational services for students with ABI from the perspective of those who have the most at stake in the success of these services: children, parents, and educators. It presents results from several pilot surveys that asked parents and educators to identify the strengths and weaknesses of current educational services for students. Information gathered from qualitative interviews and participant observation expands on the survey results. Guidelines for addressing some of the key challenges identified and helping parents effectively negotiate the school system to achieve successful school experiences for their children are also offered.

THE CHALLENGE OF ABI: CHILD, PARENT, AND EDUCATOR PERSPECTIVES

Developing an effective educational program for a student with ABI presents a challenge for everyone involved, especially for the child who returns to school as a different person with changes in nearly every aspect of her life. Each child experiences differing cognitive, behavioral, physical, and emotional alterations as a result of a brain injury—the effects of which produce lifelong changes in the child's development and self-concept. For example, some adolescents report that the injury affected their career plans. Almost all children and adolescents also notice dramatic shifts in their social support networks (see Chapter 2; Thomsen, 1974; Willer, Allen, Durnan, & Ferry, 1990).

I've always known I was going to go to college. I didn't know what I was going to do. After my brain injury, a lot of my problem-solving and cognitive [abilities]—for English and spelling and that basic core curriculum—were a lot harder for me, so I didn't enjoy it anymore. So that kind of eliminated that area of career choice but one thing that wasn't really hampered was creative ability. That's what I was left with, so I kept working with it and now I love it, so that's why I'm planning on going into it.

It's like my life had changed after my brain injury; it was real hard to deal with people who were used to me being a different way than I was. And, there were things that they expected that I couldn't do. I wasn't in a wheelchair and I didn't have scars on my head, [so] they couldn't see that I had some real disabilities.

Social isolation can become more extreme over time. Students with ABI may experience organically based behavior problems and miss out on opportunities to learn age-appropriate social skills. Both factors can contribute to students with ABI engaging in social behaviors that their peers find bizarre or offensive. The following description from a series of participant observations illustrates this problem:

At age 13, 6 years after his brain injury, Mike became interested in girls. At first his interest was manifested by staring intently at certain girls in classrooms and between classes. Later, observing the behavior of his peers, Mike started making sexually suggestive comments as girls walked by. However, unlike his peers' comments, Mike's comments were audible to the girls. Mike also repeatedly sent friends to tell a girl that he wanted to go out with her, much to the girl's embarrassment. In one class, he continually whispered to the girl sitting in front of him, "Let's do it! Want to do it with me? When can we do it?" The girl found his remarks threatening and offensive and complained in tears to the teacher about Mike's behavior.

As children cope with the many changes resulting from injury, they must also negotiate the overall process of child development. The dual-pronged nature of the rehabilitation process can be particularly problematic for adolescents. The cognitive, behavioral, and social challenges they face are exacerbated by the increased demands of secondary settings (Ewing-Cobbs, Fletcher, & Levin, 1985; Rosen & Gerring, 1986). Students must operate in larger schools with more complex scheduling, more difficult logistical demands, and more peers to interact with—at a time when all students face the dramatic developmental changes and insecurities of adolescence. Most important, students with ABI are expected to function more independently in these new and complex environments. As students make the transition to middle and high school settings, they must not only manage the complicated details of these demanding environments, they also must demonstrate that they are developing skills necessary for adulthood, such as learning to solve problems independently, making appropriate choices, and handling the frustrations of this difficult time with decreasing assistance from adults.

Educators' Perspective

For the educator, the student with ABI presents a complex constellation of needs. Most educators have not received training in teaching children with acquired brain injury (Savage, 1985) and feel unprepared to meet these students' needs (Cooley & Glang, 1994; Savage & Carter, 1991). Furthermore, the heterogeneity of the ABI population makes these students particularly challenging for general educators—no one approach, strategy, or curriculum is appropriate for all students in this group (Cooley & Singer, 1991). Reflecting on her year-long experiences with a particularly challenging student, one teacher said, "He's the only identified child with ABI we had and we didn't know what to do with him."

Lack of awareness of the range of effects of ABI and how these might be manifested in student behavior also contributes to educators' difficulty in meeting student needs, as a teacher who struggled with the severe behavior problems of one of her students reported:

I called his mother recently. As it turns out, he had a severe brain injury 5 years ago and maybe that has something to do with it, I don't know. His mother explained that these episodes are usually set off by stress and a warning sign that he's going to have a tantrum is that he gets a severe headache. Well, I never put any stress on him. I have the same expectations for him that I have for all my other students. Besides, once he said he had a headache, but when I sent him to the nurse, boom, within 2 minutes he was playing with another boy who was down there. I'm not buying the brain injury aspect; I think he's just trying to get out of doing his work.

Parents' Response

Parents encounter an ongoing source of stress when their child returns to school. In addition to the financial and emotional burdens involved with coping with ABI, parents now face the added challenge of working with school professionals (who may or may not be knowledgeable about brain injury) to gain access to needed educational services for their child. Because, prior to the injury, most children with ABI progressed typically through school, parents may be unfamiliar with their rights under the Individuals with Disabilities Education Act (IDEA) of 1990, PL 101-476; many find the system unwieldy. In addition, parents may find that schools provide a much lower level of services than rehabilitation settings, particularly in the areas of physical, occupational, and speech-language therapies (Lash & Scarpino, 1993). As a result, parents may make what appear to be unrealistic demands for services, which can cause a defensive response by school personnel and set an adversarial tone for parent–professional interactions.

Unfortunately, parents are forced to become advocates for their children at a point when they are overloaded and ill-prepared for involvement in such a complicated process (Savage & Carter, 1991). As one parent reports, her first encounters with the educational system came at a very stressful time, "All of our efforts had been in trying to keep the rest of the family healthy, trying to keep our marriage alive." Another parent began her role as advocate following a car accident in which her husband was killed, both of her children sustained brain injuries, and she herself was injured.

The stresses parents must cope with do not diminish once their child has successfully made the transition to school. At the beginning of each new school year (and in many cases, the beginning of each new school term), children and parents must learn how to negotiate a new schedule, become familiar with new teachers' classroom systems, and learn to work collaboratively with a new group of professionals. In reality, then, the transition to school does not fully end until the child has completed school. Each new setting brings new challenges and the stresses associated with them.

Parents who are strong advocates for particular services for their children are sometimes labeled by school personnel as being "in denial" about the severity of their child's cognitive disabilities or inappropriate behaviors. When asked how she handled such negative perceptions, one mother who had adopted 10 children with brain injuries

said, "I begin every meeting with a new school representative by saying, 'Everything you've heard about me is true: I'm in denial, I'm a
crazy lady, I'm unrealistic. Now, let's get down to business.' " Another
mother who felt responsible for the accident that caused her daughter's brain injury said, "I finally sat all the school people down and
said, 'Look, I'm motivated by guilt, and you should know that, because of that, I'm not going to stop hounding you until you give my
daughter the services she needs.' "

PILOT SURVEYS

A range of problems with the way schools serve students with ABI
has been identified in the literature (Cooley & Singer, 1991). In an
attempt to ascertain parent and teacher perspectives of current educational services, two pilot surveys were conducted as well as a series
of focus groups and qualitative interviews.

Parent Survey

In the fall of 1993, 31 parents throughout the northwest completed a
questionnaire about their children's educational experiences. All but
two of the parents had a child who had survived an acquired brain
injury more than 2 years prior to completing the survey; the children
of the remaining two parents were more recently injured. The children
ranged in age from 5 to 21. Six of the children were currently served
in inclusive settings with peers without disabilities, 15 were placed in
self-contained or pull-out programs, and the remaining students were
no longer attending public school.

All of the parents believed that the brain injury had significantly
affected their child's educational experiences. The parents identified
problems with organization and planning, memory, behavior, and social isolation as barriers to successful experiences. Most of the parents
were dissatisfied with how the schools addressed their children's educational needs. Table 1 shows how parents rated their children's
schools in six domains. Making the school physically accessible was
the only domain in which parents felt schools were doing a satisfactory job. In all five of the other domains, parents rated schools as
doing a below-average to poor job.

The respondents identified two key reasons for the school's un-
satisfactory performance—limited staff knowledge of ABI and its related effects (46%), and limited resources (24%). When asked what
they might recommend to their children's schools to improve services
for students with ABI, 15 of the parents recommended more training
for teachers and related services staff. A number of the parents sug-

Table 1. Parents' ratings of school's performance in six educational domains

Educational domain	Mean rating	Standard deviation
Making the school physically accessible	4.15	.89
Training teachers to understand ABI	1.89	1.14
Dealing with social and behavior problems	2.16	1.27
Dealing with memory and learning problems	2.4	1.2
Helping child or adolescent become independent	2.8	1.2
Communicating with family about coping with ABI	1.92	1.14

$N = 26$.

Key: 1 = School does a poor job; 2 = School does a below-average job; 3 = School does an average job; 4 = School does an above-average job; 5 = School does a great job.

gested that schools improve communication with parents, saying that educators would be more successful in designing educational programs if they worked more closely with parents. For example, one parent wrote, "[Schools should] communicate more with the child's parents, and consider the parents to be the child's key link between the child and the educational experience. [They should] listen to parents, they do know their children."

Focus Groups

To further explore parent perspectives, a focus group was conducted with a sample of parents who had responded to the survey. In the focus group, parents consistently reported feeling frustrated with their children's school experiences. This frustration occurred despite wide diversity in their children's ages, etiologies, levels of functioning, and time postinjury. As described by the parents, the obstacles to successful school experiences could be classified into the following four categories:

1. Educational barriers produced by the child's memory and organizational impairments
2. Problems due to the student's poor social integration
3. Difficulties produced by teachers' misperceptions about brain injury
4. Frustrations related to the schools' inability to adjust their regimen to the needs of the student

Several parents made comments about a particular teacher or administrator who demonstrated a caring attitude; however, there were virtually no descriptions of positive actions taken by a school or classroom teacher that resulted in more effective educational experiences. The parents themselves had generated and shared with teachers many helpful strategies; but, for the most part, these were not implemented in the school settings. For example, one parent described the importance of her son taking a short break when he felt overwhelmed by too much information. This strategy had been effective during her son's therapy sessions in the medical setting. When this idea was posed to her son's teacher, it was rejected as the teacher felt it might set an undesirable precedent for other students. Other representative comments from parents include the following:

His teachers tended to only focus on the fact that he had previous behavior problems and didn't recognize the contribution of the brain injury.

Every day is different for my child depending upon his fatigue, stress, and so on. When he performs differently in different classes they think he isn't trying.

The principal said the general classroom teachers in the sixth grade did not want to do the extra stuff for my son, and we should wait till the seventh grade where there are some teachers who are more supportive of kids with disabilities.

Educator Surveys

The results from the parent survey are consistent with earlier educator surveys in which educators reported that they were not knowledgeable about ABI and did not feel prepared to manage the range of problems experienced by those students (Cooley & Glang, 1994). In a statewide survey of 183 educators designed to ascertain educators' knowledge and perceptions of students with ABI, respondents scored moderately low on a measure of knowledge (mean score = 71%). When these same educators were asked to rate how prepared they felt to meet the needs of students with ABI (on a scale of 1–5, 1 = not at all prepared, 5 = very prepared), the average rating was between 2.9 and 3.3, or somewhat prepared. Ratings were consistent across behavioral, academic, social, and cognitive domains. As a group, general educators consistently rated themselves as feeling less competent than did special educators and other consulting and administrative professionals. An interesting finding showed that, for all those completing the survey, knowledge and perceived competence were negatively correlated: Those professionals who scored highest on the knowledge quiz reported feeling the least competent.

A second educator survey was conducted in the spring of 1993 in conjunction with a regional workshop on ABI. Thirty-four educators who had experience with students with ABI completed a questionnaire about their perceptions of the challenges of serving this population. Like the parents surveyed, these educators listed many of the same cognitive impairments identified in the literature as obstacles to success in school for children with ABI. On a scale of 1–5 (1 = not descriptive, 5 = very descriptive), respondents rated problems with memory (4.0), attention (4.0), generalization (3.87), problem solving (3.82), and learning rate (3.76) as barriers to successful school experiences.

Educators' lack of awareness of the effects of ABI can interfere with effective delivery of services for students (Rosen & Gerring, 1986; Todis & Glang, 1994). The following field notes from classroom observations of two students provide an example:

Jose is fully integrated into general middle school classes, receiving support from special education staff. A recent assignment for English, creating a brochure "All About Me," was one that the special education teacher felt was perfect for Jose, given his artistic ability. He had ample time to work on the brochure in class over a 2-week period, and special education assistants and teachers checked with him daily, asking how his project was coming. They were stunned when the day before the project was due, Jose asked one of them, "What are we supposed to do on this project thing?" The special education teacher expressed her dismay: "I had been told that students with brain injuries sometimes have trouble with initiation, but I guess I didn't understand that meant that he literally would not be able to get going on this without very direct support. Also, when we check in with him, I guess we have to do a lot more than ask, 'How's it going, Jose?' Because he always says 'Fine,' and maybe he really thinks everything is fine. But we need to actually see his work, see what he's done."

A mother of a fourth-grade girl reported that she had asked her child's teacher why her daughter was still adding only single-digit figures at school, when at home she had demonstrated more advanced math skills using the computer. The teacher explained that the hospital representative who had conducted a 1-hour in-service for the staff to ease the girl's transition from hospital to school had told the teacher that it was important for Jane to experience success in her schoolwork. The teacher had interpreted this to mean that Jane should be given only tasks that she already knew how to do. As a result, Jane had received no new instruction in the 2 years since her return to school.

Results from surveys, focus groups, and qualitative observations suggest that neither educators nor parents are satisfied with the ways students with ABI are served in schools today. Efforts to improve services must include changes on the parts of both educators and parents.

IMPROVING EDUCATIONAL SERVICES: WHAT EDUCATORS AND PARENTS CAN DO

Few educators have an understanding of the complex and unique issues faced by the growing population of students with ABI (Blosser & DePompei, 1991; Lash & Scarpino, 1993; Ylvisaker et al., 1991). Acquired brain injury is an underaddressed topic in university teacher training programs; *only 8% of graduate programs in special education provide training in ABI* (Savage, 1985). Clearly, educators can benefit from learning about ABI's effects on the school experience and specific strategies for addressing these students' academic, social, and behavioral needs. An increasing number of resources are available to educators to guide staff development efforts in ABI education (Begali, 1994; Blosser & DePompei, 1994; Savage & Wolcott, 1988; Siantz-Tyler, 1990). In some areas, statewide training efforts are being undertaken to increase knowledge and awareness of ABI in school settings (Lash & Scarpino, 1993; Pearson, 1994; Todis & Glang, 1994; Tyler, 1994).

In addition to gaining knowledge about working with students with ABI, educators may benefit from skill development in working collaboratively with the variety of disciplines represented on the school-based team (e.g., families, related services providers, administrators) to provide educational services in general education settings. Training in creating effective parent–professional partnerships may be especially helpful. Unfortunately, parent–professional relationships can easily become adversarial because of the many stressors both families and school staff face in designing educational programs for students with ABI (Lash & Scarpino, 1993). Educators may perceive parents as demanding and overbearing and parents may feel their child's unique needs are not being addressed—thereby creating roadblocks to effective service delivery. As Walker (1989) writes:

> A serious failure occurs in service delivery when the two most influential agents for change in the child's learning experience—parents and teachers—do not collaborate successfully in the planning and monitoring of the child's educational program. When this happens, the essential connection between home and school is lost. Unresolved conflict often leads to severed communication or adversarial encounters, and produces a great deal of stress for many parents and teachers. Ultimately, both parties may feel ineffective in their efforts on the child's behalf, and the student is cheated of the benefit of a coordinated learning experience. (p. 103)

The most effective approach to creating a successful transition back to school and an effective educational program will involve cooperative problem solving with the education and rehabilitation teams, family, and student.

Parents' Role

Parents will be most successful in gaining access to effective educational services for their child when they 1) are knowledgeable about their child's needs and the types of services that will benefit their child, 2) work collaboratively with school personnel to incorporate these services into the educational program, and 3) take time for themselves so that they can take on the time-consuming and stressful role of being their child's advocate. Following are guidelines designed to help parents work with school personnel to create educational programs that meet their children's needs:

   Parent Skill #1: Get Informed About Services and Your Rights to Them   Because most educators lack training in ABI, parents may be the most knowledgeable source of information about the effects of ABI and strategies for assisting students to be successful in school settings (DePompei & Blosser, 1994). Through their experiences in rehabilitation settings, networking with other parents, and dealing with a variety of professionals in the brain injury field, most parents learn a great deal about their child's needs and approaches that can be helpful. Parents may also have access to written materials and resources via state Brain Injury Associations, conferences, and other parent groups. Parents are also the most obvious sources of information specific to their child's needs (DePompei & Blosser, 1994). They can provide suggestions for behavioral, social, and cognitive interventions that are invaluable to the educational team.

   Before a child returns to school following a brain injury, parents should ensure that an in-service training session on ABI is provided to all staff (including noneducational staff such as janitors, coaches, and bus drivers). Possible sources for presenters include a neighboring district that has worked with students with ABI, a rehabilitation unit, the state Department of Education, or an intermediate education unit or agency. Parents and the student may also want to participate in the in-service training session to discuss specifics about the student's injury and needs. As part of the in-service training session, parents should suggest that their child's school acquire print and video resources about ABI for ideas and assistance.

Jane's mother was closely involved in her daughter's hospital rehabilitation program and was impressed with Jane's ability to process new information when presented on a personal computer. When their small community asked how they could help after Jane was released from the hospital, her mother indicated that she would need a computer to do her homework. The community held a fund-raiser and purchased a computer and software for Jane. When school personnel expressed reservations about Jane's ability to use the computer and about the value of giving sophisticated equipment to a low-functioning third grader, Jane's mother invited several teachers to her home to see how Jane used the computer to practice math and reading.

One of the most important duties for parents in developing their child's individualized education program (IEP) is sharing information about ABI with those responsible for providing the education. It is therefore critical for parents to become knowledgeable about the IEP process and other school procedures that must be followed when gaining access to special education services. Parents should familiarize themselves with their rights and responsibilities under IDEA by contacting the special education division of their state's Department of Education. Most states also have a parent education group about which the special education division should be knowledgeable; these groups have different names in each state, but their role is the same—to assist parents of students with disabilities in gaining access to educational services that address each student's individual needs. In addition, because of the rapid changes associated with ABI, it is important that parents request frequent updates for their child's IEP.

Many parents suggest that written communication can streamline the IEP process (Glang, Fielder, Fielding, Sample, & Turner, 1994). For example, parents can submit a written agenda to the school team prior to the IEP meeting so that parents and teachers come to the IEP meeting with ideas and strategies. Keeping written records of important decisions, meeting notes, and communication with school professionals can also help prevent misunderstandings. Unless parents participate fully in the IEP process, important strategies may not be included in the educational program.

A mother received notice that her daughter's IEP meeting was scheduled for a date 2 weeks away. Noting that only 20 minutes were allotted for the meeting, she asked whether she could reschedule when more time was available as she would like to talk in-depth about her daughter's goals, perhaps through a MAPs (a team-based, problem-solving process) planning session (Forest & Pearpoint, 1992). The school staff responded that, ideally, they would hold such meetings for every special education student, but time did not permit this; the staff would have the goals written prior to the meeting, and the mother could just sign off as she had in previous years. The mother sought the advice of a parent advocacy group and learned that parents are entitled to be involved in goal setting, the meeting must be scheduled at a time that is convenient for parents, and parents are not obligated to sign an IEP just because the school staff are on a tight schedule.

Parent Skill #2: Establish a Collaborative Relationship
Although becoming knowledgeable about effective strategies and services and the mechanisms for incorporating them into the IEP is necessary, it does not guarantee that the desired student outcomes will be achieved. Parents must also advocate effectively and work collaboratively with the education team. For many parents, this is a difficult task.

There are a number of reasons why parent–professional relationships become unproductive. Turnbull and Turnbull (1986) list the following factors as contributing to adversarial relationships between parents of children with disabilities and educators: 1) poor communication skills, 2) unfavorable attitudes, 3) parental disinterest and lack of experience in dealing with medical and educational systems, 4) lack of coordination among various professionals and agencies working with families, 5) lack of professional training for dealing effectively with parent concerns and emotions, and 6) logistical problems in arranging contacts between parents and educators.

Improving parent–professional relationships may be less difficult than it seems. Walker (1989) offers three simple skills parents can use to foster collaboration between parents and professionals:

1. Take the perspective of the educator: Understand the position taken by another and appreciate the good intentions that motivate behavior. It is especially important for parents to acknowledge that teachers and other school staff are already frustrated with the lack of time and resources to accomplish all they need to do.
2. Appreciate the steps taken that are helpful to parents and children: Express appreciation for behaviors in others that are helpful.
3. Maintain frequent contact: Sustain communication between home and school through notes, telephone calls, and personal visits. Parents may want to find a key person at the school with whom they can communicate regularly. This might be a teacher, counselor, or nurse. Many parents also find it helpful to set up a daily journal in which they and their child's teachers can communicate back and forth from home and school and to establish a regularly

scheduled time to visit with their child's teacher about their child's progress (e.g., a weekly telephone call on Friday afternoons, coffee together every other Wednesday morning).

Walker (1989) found that when parents and teachers both used these skills, there were increases in the number and length of parent–professional contacts and the frequency with which individualized contacts occurred. Parent–professional contacts were also rated as more positive in tone, and there was an increase in positive perceptions toward collaboration in planning services for children.

Parent Skill #3: Remember to Take Care of Yourself It is important for parents to remember to take care of themselves as they deal with the stresses of working with educators to plan services for their child. If parents do not monitor their own stress and take steps to nurture themselves, they will be less effective advocates for their child (see Chapter 13). For some parents, this may involve seeking the counsel of friends or a minister; for others it may mean sticking to an exercise regimen. For still other parents, taking the time for a shopping trip and lunch out may be helpful. It may also be important for parents to occasionally take a break from being an advocate to step back and regroup before beginning to advocate anew.

Sometimes parents are frustrated when they attempt to work collaboratively with school personnel and find that the school is unwilling to view them as partners or team members. Parents may sense that school staff devalue their perceptions of their children's abilities and consider the parents' attempts to give input on school decisions and practices as interference.

Some parents respond by giving up and keeping quiet about their ideas for improving their child's educational program. Other parents develop personal and practical skills for becoming effective advocates for their children. One mother tells how this process unfolded for her:

———

I came from an alcoholic, abusive family. Before I was forced to begin advocating for my children 11 years ago, I had a high school education. I lacked the self-confidence to confront people in authority about getting the services my children were entitled to. I gradually became more empowered. But I've never done any of this alone. I've always taken a support person with me to meetings: a friend, my mother, and later, my attorney. My children have great school programs now, and I'm a different person. I'm starting law school next year.

———

CONCLUSION

According to those with the most invested in successful school experiences for students with ABI—parents, educators, and students—the current educational service system is not meeting the complex needs of this group of students. To improve the way educational services are designed and implemented, educators and parents must work together to create innovative ways to serve children.

This chapter has focused primarily on what parents can do to improve their child's educational program—become knowledgeable about ABI and learn to work collaboratively with school personnel so that they can effectively advocate for their children. The most compelling reason for parents to become effective advocates is the effect of positive parent–professional relationships on the child's school experiences; when teachers and parents work collaboratively, the child benefits.

To sustain themselves in the hard work of advocacy, parents need to know that their efforts are worthwhile. Perhaps the best encouragement comes from those receiving the benefits of advocacy—students with ABI:

Following his severe brain injury, Max, a high school senior, was determined to carry on as if nothing had happened. Although he experienced severe headaches and fatigue, he insisted on trying to maintain a full academic schedule. When he became exhausted and frustrated, he started cutting classes. In an interview several years following his injury, Max talked about how he needed his mother to be a strong advocate because he was seen by school personnel as lacking credibility: "When you are by yourself, you can't prove yourself; that's why I needed my mom so much. You know, she came in and said 'Look, this is what's going on: He's not skipping class because he's a slacker. He's skipping class because he doesn't understand, because he can't understand. And because he is overwhelmed and it has snowballed and you need to give him some leeway on that.' After my head injury, advocating for myself was really really hard."

REFERENCES

Begali, V. (1994). The role of the school psychologist. In R. Savage & G. Wolcott (Eds.), *Educational dimensions of acquired brain injury* (pp. 453–474). Austin, TX: PRO-ED.

Blosser, J., & DePompei, R. (1991). Preparing education professionals for meeting the needs of students with traumatic brain injury. *Journal of Head Trauma Rehabilitation, 6*(1), 73–82.

Blosser, J., & DePompei, R. (1994). Creating an effective classroom environment. In R. Savage & G. Wolcott (Eds.), *Educational dimensions of acquired brain injury* (pp. 413–452). Austin, TX: PRO-ED.

Cohen, S.B. (1991). Adapting educational programs for students with head injuries. *Journal of Head Trauma Rehabilitation, 6*(1), 56–63.

Cohen, S.B., Joyce, C., Rhoades, K., & Welks, D. (1985). Educational programming for head-injured students. In M. Ylvisaker (Ed.), *Head injury rehabilitation: Children and adolescents* (pp. 383–410). Austin, TX: PRO-ED.

Condeluci, A. (1994). Transition to employment. In R. Savage & G. Wolcott (Eds.), *Educational dimensions of acquired brain injury* (pp. 519–542). Austin, TX: PRO-ED.

Cooley, E., & Glang, A. (1994, April). *From isolation to integration: Facilitating school reentry and inclusion of students with traumatic brain injury.* Paper presented at the meeting of the Council for Exceptional Children, Denver, CO.

Cooley, E., & Singer, G.H.S. (1991). On serving students with head injuries: Are we reinventing a wheel that doesn't roll? *Journal of Head Trauma Rehabilitation, 6*(1), 47–55.

Deaton, A. (1994) Changing the behaviors of students with acquired brain injuries. In R. Savage & G. Wolcott (Eds.), *Educational dimensions of acquired brain injury* (pp. 257–276). Austin, TX: PRO-ED.

DePompei, R., & Blosser, J. (1994). *The family as collaborator for effective school reintegration.* In R. Savage & G. Wolcott (Eds.), *Educational dimensions of acquired brain injury* (pp. 489–506). Austin, TX: PRO-ED.

Ewing-Cobbs, L., Fletcher, J.M., & Levin, H.S. (1985). Neuropsychological sequelae following pediatric head injury. In M. Ylvisaker (Ed.), *Head injury rehabilitation: Children and adolescents* (pp. 71–89). Austin, TX: PRO-ED.

Forest, M., & Pearpoint, J. (1992). Putting all kids on the MAP. *Educational Leadership, 50*(2), 26–30.

Glang, A.E., Fielder, K., Fielding, J., Sample, K., & Turner, A. (1994). *What's going on in Oregon's schools for students with TBI.* Salem: Oregon Head Injury Foundation.

Glang, A.E., Singer, G.H.S., Cooley, E.A., & Tish, N. (1992). Tailoring direct instruction techniques for use with students with brain injury. *Journal of Head Trauma Rehabilitation, 7*(4), 93–108.

Individuals with Disabilities Education Act of 1990 (IDEA), PL 101-476. (October 30, 1990). Title 20, U.S.C. 1400 et seq: *U.S. Statutes at Large, 104* (Part 2), 1103–1151.

Lash, M., & Scarpino, C. (1993). School reintegration for children with traumatic brain injuries: Conflicts between medical and educational systems. *NeuroRehabilitation, 3*(3), 13–25.

Lehr, E. (1990). School management. In E. Lehr (Ed.), *Psychological management of traumatic brain injuries in children and adolescents* (pp. 185–206). Rockville, MD: Aspen Publishers, Inc.

Light, R., Neumann, E., Lewis, R., Morecki-Oberg, C., Asarnow, R., & Satz, P. (1987). An evaluation of a neuropsychologically based re-education project for the head-injured child. *Journal of Head Trauma Rehabilitation, 2,* 11–25.

Nordlund, M. (1994) Transition to postsecondary education. In R. Savage & G. Wolcott (Eds.), *Educational dimensions of acquired brain injury* (pp. 507–518). Austin, TX: PRO-ED.

Pearson, S. (1994, November). *Education issues in school and at home.* Paper presented at the meeting of the National Head Injury Foundation, Chicago.

Rosen, C., & Gerring, J. (1986). *Head trauma: Educational reintegration*. Boston: College-Hill Press/Little, Brown.

Savage, R.C. (1985). *A survey of traumatically brain injured children within school-based special education programs*. Rutland, VT: Head Injury/Stroke Independence Project, Inc.

Savage, R.C. (1991). Identification, classification, and placement issues for students with traumatic brain injuries. *Journal of Head Trauma Rehabilitation*, 6(1), 1–9.

Savage, R.C., & Carter, R.R. (1991). Family and return to school. In J.M. Williams & T. Kay (Eds.), *Head injury: A family matter* (pp. 203–216). Baltimore: Paul H. Brookes Publishing Co.

Savage, R.C., & Wolcott, G. (1988). *An educator's manual: What educators need to know about students with traumatic brain injury*. Southborough, MA: National Head Injury Foundation.

Siantz-Tyler, J. (1990). *Traumatic head injury in school-aged children: A training manual for educational personnel*. Kansas City: University of Kansas Medical Center.

Thomsen, I.V. (1974). The patient with severe head injury and his family. *Scandinavian Journal of Rehabilitation Medicine*, 6(4), 180–183.

Todis, B., & Glang, A.E. (1994, November). *Educating students with traumatic brain injury: Issues and strategies*. Paper presented at the meeeting of the National Head Injury Foundation, Chicago.

Turnbull, A.P., & Turnbull, H.R., III. (1986). *Families, professionals, and exceptionality: A special partnership*. Columbus, OH: Charles E. Merrill.

Tyler, J. (1994, November). *Education issues in school and at home*. Paper presented at the meeting of the National Head Injury Foundation, Chicago.

Walker, B. (1989). Strategies for improving parent–professional cooperation. In G.H.S. Singer & L.K. Irvin (Eds.), *Support for caregiving families: Enabling positive adaptation to disability* (pp. 103–120). Baltimore: Paul H. Brookes Publishing Co.

Willer, B., Allen, K., Durnan, M.C., & Ferry, A. (1990). Problems and coping strategies of mothers, siblings, and young adult males with traumatic brain injury. *Canadian Journal of Rehabilitation*, 2(3), 167–173.

Ylvisaker, M., Hartwick, P., & Stevens, M. (1991). School reentry following head injury: Managing the transition from hospital to school. *Journal of Head Trauma Rehabilitation*, 6(1), 10–22.

9

Substance Abuse and Families of Children with ABI

Roberta DePompei and Julie Weis

We drink every Friday night. When Jeff comes home from the hospital, can he go with us like he used to?

Jeff's friends in first peer counseling session, local high school

I guess I'm not smart enough to be with Jamie and Yvonne. They're always saying I don't act right around our friends. But, if I have a couple of beers, other kids think I'm funny.

Keisha, age 14, who sustained ABI at age 12

Since Jason's accident, I just feel better if I take a couple of the pills the doctor prescribed to help me relax. I don't think it's a problem if I have a glass of wine in the evening too. It's been so hard for all of us since the accident.

Jason's mom, 3 years after his ABI

I can drink beer or wine even though I take seizure medication. That's not the real high-powered stuff!

Yoshiko, age 18, who sustained ABI 3 months ago

After all he's been through, what could it hurt if he has a few beers with his friends?

Father of a 19-year-old survivor of ABI

Although this chapter uses the term *acquired* brain injury in order to remain consistent with the rest of the book, the actual literature and work on which this chapter is based deal primarily with children who have experienced *traumatic* brain injury.

These are real statements from real people dealing with real issues. All of these individuals have several things in common. First, they have experienced an acquired brain injury (ABI) personally or within a family or peer relationship. Second, they have indicated that they are using drugs or alcohol to relieve stress or to belong socially. Third, they have exhibited a lack of information about the relationship between ABI and substance abuse.

A link between substance abuse and ABI has been suggested in the literature for several years. Sparedo and Gill (1989) indicated that alcohol is a precipitant to brain injury. It was also suggested that the use of alcohol and drugs should be a carefully considered factor during postinjury rehabilitation (Kreutzer, Doherty, Harris, & Zasler, 1990; Sparedo, Strauss, & Barth, 1990). DePompei (1991), Karol and Halla-Poe (1987), Kreutzer and Harris (1990), Strauss (1989), and Weiss and Frankel (1989) have all indicated that there are people who may have a dual diagnosis or dual disability, combining both ABI and substance abuse. They have further reported that, because of a lack of information about the relationship between the two problems, many inappropriate diagnoses, placements, and family interventions have been made. They have suggested that family dynamics and intervention may play a significant role in the creation of, or adaptation to, both disabilities.

The dual relationship between children or adolescents and substance abuse is less well documented in the literature than the relationship between ABI and substance abuse. Although the information presented in the above studies focused primarily on adults and their families, it can be assumed—as the majority of ABIs occur in individuals 15–30 years of age—that some of the data were obtained from those in the 15–19 age range. DePompei's study (1991) included data from youth, ages 13–19, that indicated an overlap of substance use and abuse within the population of teenagers with ABI. Mothers Against Drunk Driving (MADD) and Students Against Drunk Driving (SADD) have consistently expressed their many concerns regarding teenagers, use of drugs and alcohol, and motor vehicle crashes. In a study of special education students, the Substance Abuse Resources and Disability Issues (SARDI) program (1994) showed that more than 50% have smoked cigarettes, 54% used alcohol, 25% used marijuana, and 22% used inhalents. Although this study was not directed only at individuals with ABI, the statistics indicate that there is enough substance usage among teenagers with disabilities to validate concerns. The issue of substance abuse should be addressed regarding youth with ABI from the time of injury through rehabilitation and reintegration to home, school, work, and community life.

Kiley et al. (1992) surveyed professionals regarding their knowledge, attitudes, and referral policies for patients with ABI and potential substance abuse. Results indicated that 29% of their clients had a problem with substance abuse; unfortunately, only 30% of the professionals reported that routine screenings for drug and alcohol problems were completed by their facilities. The staffs of facilities were educated about substance abuse and potential dual disabilities in 50% of the facilities, although 59% indicated that client education about substance abuse was available. Although 79% reported that facilities had referral procedures for substance abuse treatment, only 44% reported making such referrals. The results indicated a need to further educate service providers on the relationship between ABI and substance abuse. The facilities surveyed provided services primarily to adults. If this survey were completed in facilities where children and adolescents are treated, the percentages might be even lower and the need to provide information to service providers about ABI and substance abuse even more acute.

In order to effectively address the potential for substance abuse within the youth ABI population, service providers should be prepared to recognize possible problems with substance use and abuse and provide educational information, intervention, or referral when necessary. This chapter focuses on answering the following questions:

1. How might problems with alcohol or drugs develop within the pediatric ABI population?
2. How might children or adolescents and their families respond to ABI and substance abuse concerns?
3. What proactive suggestions can be made for families and children regarding education, intervention, or prevention of substance abuse in children with ABI?

HOW ABI AND SUBSTANCE ABUSE CAN BE PROBLEMATIC

Reintegration to home, school, community life, and work for the child or adolescent with ABI can be further complicated by substance abuse. This abuse can be related to use before or after the injury and includes family members other than the injured child. Service providers should be aware of the potential difficulties with a dual diagnosis of ABI and substance abuse.

Substance Use and Abuse Prior to ABI

It is always possible that the child or adolescent with ABI used drugs or alcohol prior to the injury. In fact, substance abuse has been clearly established as a significant factor in the acquisition of ABI (Jones, 1989;

Sparedo & Gill, 1989). It should be noted that although alcohol use is often reported in conjunction with an injury, there has been little information provided about whether the person was simply a casual user who made a bad judgment about drinking and driving or was, in fact, a substance abuser. It should not routinely be assumed that a child or teenager is a substance abuser; however, information regarding the use of substances prior to the injury should be obtained.

It is difficult to think about children or young teenagers as users and, therefore, questions about possible use often are not asked. Several questions about substance use should be asked routinely of all children, teenagers, and family members involved in an accident resulting in ABI. Questions that may be useful include the following:

1. Before the injury, how much beer or wine did you drink in a week?
2. Before the injury, how many pills or drugs did you use in a week?
3. Before the injury, how much beer or wine did your friends drink?
4. Before the injury, what type of drugs did your friends use?
5. Right now, how much beer, wine, or alcohol do you drink in a week?
6. Right now, do you have a drinking problem?
7. Right now, how many pills are you taking?
8. Right now, how often do you use illegal drugs?
9. Right now, do you have a drug problem?
10. Are there other family members who have an alcohol or drug problem?

These same questions can be adapted for family members or peers to answer about the child with ABI. It may be useful to compare their responses with those obtained from the injured individual. When answers to the questions indicate a possible problem, education, intervention, and referral should be provided.

Potential for Substance Abuse After ABI

There is the potential for children and adolescents to use alcohol or drugs after ABI for a number of reasons.

Use of Prescription Drugs Is Increased   Anti-seizure medications and pain prescriptions are often employed after ABI. The increased availability of prescription drugs themselves can become a problem. Additionally, it is usually recommended that no alcohol be consumed in combination with these drugs. Alcohol consumption has a rapid effect on the central nervous system, disinhibiting higher cortical functions and altering mental processes. When prescription drugs are combined with alcohol, the results can be dangerous, both physically and mentally. However, they can be pleasurable to the individual. Individuals also sometimes assume that beer and wine are harmless to consume, as their alcohol content is lower; this is incorrect information—no alcoholic content is acceptable in combination with prescription drugs for seizures or pain.

Ability to Self-Monitor Appropriate Social Behaviors Is Decreased Disinhibition and poor judgment can be consequences of ABI. Falconer and Tercilla (1985) and Karol and Halla-Poe (1987) indicate that there is a synergistic relationship between the behavioral effects of alcohol and ABI. ABI survivors often have a reduced ability to monitor the social consequences of their behaviors and erroneously conclude that the effects of alcohol or illegal drugs are not a problem for them. They believe they can drink with friends and are capable of monitoring their behaviors when, in fact, they are unable to estimate appropriate amounts for consumption and unable to judge socially appropriate behaviors.

Preinjury Substance Abuse Patterns Can Be Reestablished Where the social reinforcement of children or teenagers has come from peers who drink or use illegal drugs, there is a natural desire to return to friends and social patterns that were routine and acceptable. If friends drink on Friday nights, in order to belong to the group again, the child may want to rejoin them as quickly as possible.

Adjustment to Disability Is Stressful Children may have difficulty dealing with their altered physical, cognitive–communicative, behavioral, or psychological differences after ABI. Adolescence is in itself stressful, with natural changes in friends, parental relationships, and social responsibilities. When a disability is introduced, the permanancy of the injury and its consequences compound the typical developmental stages for youth. The result is stressful and can make adolescents vulnerable to alcohol and drug-related problems. Weiss and Frankel (1989) have suggested that people with ABI could be increasingly drawn to substance abuse in an attempt to escape consequences of the injury, such as depression, anxiety, diminished self-esteem, lack of confidence, and physical limitations.

Children and teenagers who find themselves excluded by old friends may find new friends who will accept silly behaviors more readily because they are all drinking. Seeking friendship and acceptance is normal for all individuals. Unfortunately, where ABI is a factor, it can lead to the development of new social circles where drinking and use of illegal drugs are routine.

Tolerance Levels Are Decreased Individuals who have sustained ABI demonstrate reduced levels of tolerance, regardless of their prior patterns of substance use. Thus, a smaller quantity of chemicals produces a magnified, sometimes uncharacteristic, effect (Kreutzer & Harris, 1990).

Children and their families should be made aware of these factors that may increase the likelihood of substance abuse after a brain injury. Opportunities for frank discussion and alternative social outlets should be outlined prior to their leaving hospitals or rehabilitation facilities.

Family Members' Potential for Substance Abuse

Relatives of children with ABI are at risk for developing a substance abuse problem for primarily two reasons. First, other family members may already have a substance abuse problem. There is a relatively high rate of substance abuse among the general population. Heinemann, Keen, Donahue, and Schnoll (1988) reported the number of people dependent on alcohol to be approximately 13 million. Thus, there is the potential for preinjury family routines to have included drinking, risk taking, or use of illegal drugs. In these circumstances, the combination of ABI and substance abuse can leave the family vulnerable to increased instability and unable to adapt new management skills in order to cope with ABI. In these circumstances, families may also resist information about the use or abuse of substances by their child or adolescent.

Second, some family members may rely on alcohol or drugs to cope with the stress of the injury (Mauss-Clum & Ryan, 1981). Members react differently to stressors on their family system. In some cases, individuals will turn to medications or alcohol in order to feel that they are coping. In situations where long-term care is required, alcohol or drugs can become a means of compensation. Occasionally, these individuals are asked to monitor alcohol or drug consumption of their family member with ABI. They may be unable to do so because of their own substance abuse problems or because of a lack of appropriate information about the importance of such monitoring.

Families should be made aware of the potential for substance abuse in members other than the individual with ABI. They should be encouraged to take an honest look at their own substance use and to monitor use after the injury to determine whether use has increased. Opportunities for frank, nonjudgmental discussions and referrals, when necessary, should be provided.

FAMILY RESPONSES TO ABI AND SUBSTANCE ABUSE

Family systems are as unique and varied as the brain injuries that affect their children. Many have adequate coping skills that will enable them to adjust to the situations before them; others will react to the stress of the ABI in less positive ways. Each of these reactions is a valid response to the dual disability of ABI and substance abuse.

When both ABI and substance abuse are problems, service providers may want to consider the following information. Seaton and David (1990) suggest that the primary focus of family functioning can become either ABI or substance abuse, or both. When families organize their functioning around the disability, characteristic behaviors might include enabling (i.e., providing excuses for the individual's behavior rather than striving to modify it) and co-dependency (i.e., allowing the person with the disability to direct the focus for all family behaviors rather than those related only to the disability). These behaviors may contribute to the family's inability to modify behaviors that would lead to successful interventions.

Families will also respond differently according to their system of involvement and support. Sparedo, Strauss, and Kapsalis (1992) suggest that families with ABI and substance abuse be viewed from a systems model that accounts for family support or nonsupport and involvement or noninvolvement. Adapting this information to children and adolescents with ABI, incorporating the perspective that all family systems have strengths that service providers should consider, and adding suggestions for providing information about substance abuse to the four types of families has evolved into the framework for identifying and dealing with each family type, as presented in Table 1.

PROACTIVE INTERVENTIONS

Service providers should be prepared to work with children with ABI and their families when substance use or abuse is of concern. The following sections give suggestions for providing effective programming.

Educate All Staff Members About Substance Abuse

It is essential that all education or rehabilitation team members understand behaviors related to substance use or abuse, its implications for the individual and the family, and the problems it can cause in treatment. An in-service training session provided by an individual knowledgeable about substance abuse might answer the following questions:

1. What are the problems with alcohol or drug use in children and adolescents?
2. What is alcohol and drug prevention?
3. What is the relationship between substance use or abuse and ABI?

Table 1. Four family types: Strengths, potential problems, and responses to substance abuse information

Family type	Strengths	Potential problems	Approach regarding substance abuse
Involved and supportive	Well-informed, inquiring, follows through, assumes responsibilities	Overprotective, develops dependency in child with ABI, demands excessive staff time	*Service provider approach:* provide written information, encourage joint discussion with child regarding substance abuse potential, provide referral information, and suggest follow-up *Family response:* will accept information, may request information not be shared with child for fear of causing stress, will indicate they will share information with child themselves at right time
Involved and unsupportive	Challenges treatment procedures, wants direct involvement in treatment and decision making	Lacks recognition of limitations other than physical, unrealistic demands and expectations, poor communicators, not open about family	*Service provider approach:* must be concrete in examples and approaches, must be clear and concise *Family response:* demands clear documentation, angry responses, may deny possibility of problem, resists suggestion that there could be potential for abuse in future
Uninvolved and supportive	Relies on recommendations of others, encourages independence, does not interfere with treatment	Allows too much decision making by others, no specific leader, misses appointments, poor follow-through, reluctance to discuss family issues, tends to go along with ideas they do not really believe in	*Service provider approach:* provide written material, suggest joint follow-through for counseling appointments, provide periodic updates on information, provide information to child during therapy, if possible

(continued)

Table 1. (*continued*)

Family type	Strengths	Potential problems	Approach regarding substance abuse
Uninvolved and supportive (*continued*)			*Family response:* passive response, will take information but not respond in any serious manner, will likely take recommendation for future, accepts counseling/education regarding substance abuse but follow-through is questionable
Uninvolved and unsupportive	Ability to disengage from problems, no other notable strengths	Distanced from child with ABI, encourages independence to alleviate burden on themselves, rigid, lack of awareness of the impact of their behavior on child, limited follow-through, resentment of responsibility for child, poor care when sent home, problems between staff and family	*Service provider approach:* provide information that directs anger away from child, provide opportunities for counseling and referral, attempt to identify one service provider who the family may respond to in a positive manner and use that individual to provide essential information, provide substance abuse information to child during treatment sessions, if possible *Family response:* anger directed at child with ABI, lack of follow-through

4. What specific steps can be taken to recognize potential dual disabilities?
5. What interventions might be provided to improve prevention of a dual disability?

This individual should also be given information about the special impairments children may demonstrate as a result of ABI so that this information regarding substance abuse can be tailored to the specific population.

Employ a No-Use Message

If a team is to have an impact, each person on it who comes into contact with the child must send a no-use message to ensure a positive outcome. For example, if a teen asks various team members during therapy whether or not he can "just have one beer" with his friends when he returns home, the answer must be the same: "No, you are taking medication that does not mix with alcohol of any kind." No team member should respond "Maybe, we'll see how your therapy progresses." In addition, no discussion about movies or people who use drugs or alcohol should convey that drug or alcohol use is "macho" or "cool." If one member of the team (including family members) gives a different message, the no-use message can become diluted and the child can be confused about what the correct message is. Whether the desired outcome is prevention of use or intervention for abuse, the no-use message must be a central theme.

Screen for Potential Problems

Numerous screening devices are available from counselors who work with substance abusers and can be adapted for use by a hospital or rehabilitation facility. The questions provided on page 170 can also be used to establish what potential for problems may exist.

Consider the Risk Potential for Substance Use or Abuse

Sparedo et al. (1992) suggest that there are behaviors that indicate both low- and high-risk potential for substance abuse in survivors of ABI. The following risk behaviors have been adapted for the child/adolescent population. Low-risk behaviors may include the following:

- Not currently using
- No history of substance use or abuse
- No family history of substance abuse
- Intact, healthy support system
- Friends who do not report use and who are enabled to maintain contact with the child with ABI

Children at low risk and their families need educational interventions that outline the risks of substance abuse after ABI. In contrast, high-risk behaviors may include the following:

- History of use or abuse prior to injury
- Family history of substance abuse
- Limited family support system
- Friends who report use
- Child who talks about use in past or about reinitiating use when he or she gets home
- History of child as a risk taker
- Isolation from friends during rehabilitation

Children at high risk and their families need intervention approaches that include the use of educational materials, as well as integration of substance use-abuse treatment approaches to the ABI rehabilitation program.

Where a dual diagnosis exists, both disabilities must be addressed. Treatment programs that do not deal with both problems are most likely going to fail the individual and his family.

Provide Education About Substance Use and Abuse

The key to prevention is education. Each team member can determine how she can include alcohol and other drug prevention messages into interactions with the child. In some cases, only one or two team members will provide direct intervention. However, all must reinforce the concept of no use.

In the authors' experience, the use of picture storying is an effective means of providing information in an interesting and nonthreatening format. The chapter Appendix contains a series of pictures, objectives, and suggestions for use that are based on the potential problem areas for children previously suggested, including increased prescription drug use, decreased ability to self-monitor behaviors, reestablished preinjury abuse patterns, stressful adjustment to disability, and decreased tolerance levels. The Appendix can be used in prevention efforts, as well as with individuals who are recognized as users.

Weis, Boros, and Hawkes (1989) have provided a complete manual for working with special adolescent populations regarding the use of alcohol and other drugs. However, if the child is at high risk or found to have a dual disability, additional steps may need to be taken, such as referral or collaboration with a drug and alcohol counselor.

Include Family Members as Part of the Intervention Team

Families can be supportive team members when they have appropriate information and are encouraged to participate actively. In order to know how to participate, families should be given educational information and provided with methods for interacting with service providers.

Family members must be given information about alcohol and other drug use at some point in the rehabilitation process. The importance of highlighting substance prevention is critical regardless of how the ABI was sustained. Abstention from alcohol or other drugs can prevent future medical complications, additional injuries, learning problems, work-related problems, alcoholism, and other mental health problems. The entire family must understand the possible implications for their child and themselves.

It should be remembered that, just as family members may employ different coping styles, they may also utilize a number of different learning styles. It is important to disseminate information in a variety of formats. It may be beneficial to ask each family member what her particular learning style might be. For instance, if one family member learns and remembers better with visuals, the use of pictorial books and videotapes would be useful. If another member likes to read, journal articles and informational pamphlets might be more meaningful. DePompei and Blosser (1991, 1993) and DePompei and Williams (1994) have provided numerous strategies for helping families become active team members.

Refer to Appropriate Resources
When Dual Disability Is Confirmed

When there are indications that alcohol or other drugs are a present problem, referrals to appropriate counselors for team interventions are essential. The best interventions will be concurrent with combined interventions that are designed to meet the needs of the dual disability. Cross-training of drug and alcohol counselors and ABI service providers is essential to provide all professionals with the necessary information to work with people who have dual disabilities. When dual disability exists, methods of referral should be clearly outlined and routinely completed by service providers.

CONCLUSION

It takes a whole village to raise a child.

African Proverb

Just as it takes a whole village to raise a child, preventing the use of alcohol and other drugs takes the efforts of everyone who interacts with a child with ABI. Each member of the rehabilitation or educational team should be aware of the implications of a dual disability and able to act as a preventionist. Effective team members should be able to outline the effects of alcohol and other drugs on a child with ABI, describe the risk factors associated with the use of alcohol or other drugs, suggest intervention approaches for educating the child and family, and activate a referral process for those individuals in need of additional intervention for substance use and abuse. This chapter encourages service providers to consider the possibility of a dual disability in children and to support the development of substance abuse education as a part of staff training and intervention with clients.

REFERENCES

DePompei, R. (1991). *Traumatic brain injury and substance abuse: A comparative analysis of family functioning.* Unpublished doctoral dissertation, University of Akron, Akron, OH.

DePompei, R., & Blosser, J.L. (1991). Families of children with traumatic brain injury as advocates in school reentry. *NeuroRehabilitation, 1*(2), 29–37.

DePompei, R., & Blosser, J.L. (1993). Professional development and training for pediatric rehabilitation settings. In C. Durgin, N. Schmidt, & J. Freyer (Eds.), *Staff development and clinical intervention in brain injury rehabilitation* (pp. 229–256). Rockville, MD: Aspen Publishers, Inc.

DePompei, R., & Williams, J. (1994). Working with families after TBI: A family-centered approach. *Topics in Language Disorders, 15*(1), 68–81.

Falconer, J.A., & Tercilla, E. (1985). *Survival—What next?* Paper presented at third annual meeting of the Washington State Head Injury Foundation, Bellevue.

Heinemann, A., Keen, M., Donohue, R., & Schnoll, S. (1988). Alcohol use by persons with recent spinal cord injury. *Archives of Physical Medicine and Rehabilitation, 69*, 619–624.

Jones, G. (1989). Alcohol abuse and traumatic brain injury. *Alcohol World, Health & Research, 13*(2), 105–109.

Karol, R.L., & Halla-Poe, J. (1987). *Brain injury and alcohol: A workbook for making decisions after injury.* Minneapolis, MN: Thompson & Co.

Kiley, D., Heinemann, A.W., Doll, M., Shade-Zeldow, Y., Roth, E., & Harkony, G. (1992). Rehabilitation professionals' knowledge and attitudes about substance abuse issues. *NeuroRehabilitation, 2*(1), 35–44.

Kreutzer, J.S., Doherty, K., Harris, J.A., & Zasler, N. (1990). Alcohol use among persons with traumatic brain injury. *Journal of Head Trauma Rehabilitation, 5*(3), 9–20.

Kreutzer, J.S., & Harris, J.A. (1990). Editorial: Model systems of treatment for alcohol abuse following traumatic brain injury. *Brain Injury, 4*(1), 1–5.

Mauss-Clum, N., & Ryan, M. (1981). Brain injury and the family. *Journal of Neurosurgical Nursing, 13*, 165–169.

Seaton, J.D., & David, C.O. (1990). Family role in substance abuse and traumatic brain injury. *Journal of Head Trauma Rehabilitation, 5*(3), 41–46.

Sparedo, F.R., & Gill, D. (1989). Effects of prior alcohol use on head injury recovery. *Journal of Head Trauma Rehabilitation, 4*(1), 75–82.

Sparedo, F.R., Strauss, D., & Barth, J.T. (1990). The incidence, impact, and treatment of substance abuse in head trauma rehabilitation. *Journal of Head Trauma Rehabilitation, 5*(3), 1–8.

Sparedo, F.R., Strauss, D., & Kapsalis, K. (1992). Substance abuse, brain injury, and family adjustment. *NeuroRehabilitation, 2*(1), 65–73.

Strauss, D. (1989). Substance abuse treatment often needed in head trauma rehabilitation. *The Psychiatric Times—Medicine & Behavior*, 47–58.

Substance Abuse Resources and Disability Issues (SARDI). (1994, Spring). *Online, special edition*, 5.

Weis, J., Boros, A., & Hawkes, J. (1989). *Prevention curriculum guide for looking at alcohol and other drugs: Special education 7–12.* Kent, OH: Project A.I.D., Kent State University.

Weiss, R.L., & Frankel, R. (1989, January–February). Closed head injury and substance abuse. *Professional Counselor*, 49–51.

Appendix

Potential for Substance Abuse After ABI

The following series of pictures can be employed by team members to begin discussions regarding substance abuse and ABI. Each picture was developed to stimulate thinking and conversation that can provide educational information and opportunities to share a no-use prevention message. Some general considerations for use of the pictures include the following:

1. The cognitive levels of the child should be considered when presenting the stories. One story is longer in length to provide interest for those children with longer attention spans; it can be broken into parts, if necessary. The other stories are shorter in length to accommodate those with poor attention and memory skills.

2. The activities suggested are intended to stimulate other creative means of using the pictures. Any other activities that reinforce the intent of the prevention message should be employed for the individual interests and needs of the child.

3. Each child's learning style will be different. Some will enjoy talking about the pictures; others would rather draw or create written stories of their own. Still others may want to read the stories or act them out with you.

Use of Prescription Drugs Is Increased

Goal: *To increase awareness of the risk factors involved when prescription medications are combined with alcohol or other drugs*

Suggested Activity: Show the child the picture below and tell the following story:

This is Jack (or Jackie, depending on whether the child is a girl or a boy). Jack was riding his bike home from a friend's house last year after drinking a few beers. He was not paying attention when he crossed the street and was hit by a car. Jack was rushed to the hospital after sustaining multiple injuries. While he was in the hospital, Jack's doctor explained that he had sustained an acquired brain injury and would have to take medicine to prevent seizures. Along with all of the other instructions, the doctor told Jack that he should never drink alcohol while he is taking this medication. The doctor emphasized that the combination can be extremely dangerous. Jack told the doctor that he would not drink alcohol while he was taking the anti-seizure medicine. Jack decided that he would do everything that the hospital staff told him to do because he wanted to get better.

After Jack went home, it was time to go back to school. All of Jack's old friends were happy to see him and Jack was glad to be back. Jack's friends asked him thousands of questions about the accident and his injuries. Jack tried to answer all of their questions.

Jack's friends invited him to a party Friday night. Before he left, Jack's mother reminded him about the doctor's instructions and asked Jack to please be careful. Jack assured her that he would be careful. When Jack arrived at the party his friends were there and everyone was drinking beer and wine coolers. Jack's friends offered him some

beer. Jack knew that he was not supposed to drink with the medication he was taking; he also knew that he should not drink because of his brain injury. All of the messages that he received at the hospital and from his parents flashed through his mind about not mixing alcohol with his medication, but he did not want to disappoint his friends and he wanted them to think that he could still do all of the things he used to do with them.

Ask the child what Jack should do next. Discuss Jack's options and list them as the child gives them to you. Storytelling can be a useful tool in engaging the child in a meaningful discussion about the use of alcohol and other drugs and acquired brain injury. Drawing on a large piece of newsprint can also be effective in keeping the child engaged and interested in the discussion. If you are not an artist, stick figures and a little imagination will do the trick. Be sure to ask the child the following questions:

- What would you have done in a similar situation?
- Have you ever been in a similar situation? What did you do?
- Do you know someone who was in a similar situation? What did he or she do?
- Do you know which medications you are taking and what their interaction with alcohol might be?

Have the child role-play the following situations with you, then discuss the experience with him.

1. The child goes to a high school football game and is offered a beer in the woods behind the stadium.
2. The child is offered a wine cooler while he and his friends are driving to a movie.
3. The child's sibling offers him a hit off of a joint (marijuana) when their parents are away for the evening.
4. The child is offered some pills for $5 on the street by a drug dealer.

Ability to Self-Monitor Appropriate Social Behaviors Is Decreased—Option 1

Goal: *To increase awareness of the effects of the combination of alcohol and other drugs and acquired brain injury and the potential for behavior changes when the two are combined*

Suggested Activity: Show the child the picture below and ask him to respond to what he sees. Ask him to tell you what he thinks is happening. Then tell him the following story:

This is Gary and his friend Fred. Gary sustained a brain injury 2 years ago in a car accident. Since his injury, whenever Gary drinks alcohol, his behavior changes and he becomes very wild. He becomes extremely sick and usually tries to start fights with his friends. Before his brain injury, Gary and Fred used to go out and enjoy a beer or two while they watched their favorite movies. Fred is very worried about Gary because his behavior changes now so drastically when he drinks alcohol.

Discuss the story with the child and ask him to finish it for you. Then ask him the following questions:

- What should Gary do?
- Is Gary in danger?
- What kind of medications might Gary be taking?
- Why is his behavior so different?
- Why can't Gary control himself when he drinks alcohol?

Ability to Self-Monitor Appropriate Social Behaviors Is Decreased—Option 2

Goal: *To increase awareness of the effects of the combination of alcohol and other drugs and acquired brain injury and the potential for behavior changes when the two are combined*

Suggested Activity: Show the child the picture below and tell her the following story:

This is Jessica. Jessica sustained an acquired brain injury 3 years ago. Before the accident she would go to parties with her friends, but she would never drink alcohol. Before the accident she would go to parties and dance, laugh, and tell stories with her friends, but now she goes to parties and drinks until she gets drunk. She just sits in the same chair all night until her friends drive her home.

Discuss Jessica's story with the child and ask for her ideas. Create your own story from the picture or use pictures from magazines to create a story.

Preinjury Substance Abuse Patterns Can Be Reestablished

Goal: *To increase awareness of the potential for preinjury substance abuse patterns to be reestablished*

Suggested Activity: Show the child the picture below and tell him the following story:

This is Shelly and Mark. Shelly sustained an acquired brain injury 8 months ago when she fell from a tree in their backyard. Shelly's and Mark's parents are divorced and their mother works at night. It is Shelly's responsibility to watch Mark while their mother is at work. Before she was injured, Shelly used to drink her mother's alcohol when her mother went to work. She got in the habit of having two or three drinks each night; she made Mark promise he would not tell their mother. Shelly stopped drinking after her accident for a few months because her doctor told her she should not drink because of her brain injury. Last week she started drinking again, and Mark is very worried about her.

Ask the child to respond to the story and discuss it. Encourage the child to create his own story about a person who sustained an acquired brain injury and started drinking again after the injury despite the doctor's warnings.

Adjustment to Disability Is Stressful

Goal: *To increase awareness of the risks of using substances to deal with the stress of adjusting to a disability*

Suggested Activity: Show the child the picture below and ask her what she thinks is happening. Develop a story together to go with the picture, emphasizing that there are other ways to deal with stressful situations beyond using substances, including the following activities:

1. Talk to a friend
2. Go for a walk
3. Listen to music
4. Talk to a family member
5. Talk to a counselor
6. Go to a movie
7. Exercise

Ask the child to list the kinds of things she does to relax and avoid stressful situations. Write the list on a big piece of paper and encourage the child to add to the list as she discovers new ways to deal with the stress in her own life.

Tolerance Levels Are Decreased

Goal: *To increase the awareness of the potential for a person's tolerance level for alcohol to decrease after a brain injury*

Suggested Activity: Show the child the picture below and ask him what he thinks is happening to this person. Tell him the following story:

This is Stephanie. Stephanie sustained a brain injury 2 years ago in a tractor accident. Before the accident, Stephanie would go out with her friends on Friday nights to the movies; before the movies they would drink wine coolers and beer. Before the accident, Stephanie could drink three beers before she felt tipsy. After the accident, she feels drunk after her first wine cooler. If she has more than one drink, she passes out.

Be sure to ask the child the following questions:

- What is happening to Stephanie?
- Why is she alone?
- Why does she fall asleep after having one drink?
- What are some of the risks involved with Stephanie's low tolerance for alcohol?

You might find that the child prefers to create his own story about each picture. If this is the case, make sure that you interject the essential information into the scenario.

10

The Needs of
Families with
Children with ABI

Karen L. Kepler

Rehabilitation professionals have long acknowledged that understanding family dynamics and family response to injury is critical to the development of realistic rehabilitation goals, the facilitation of the individual's reintegration into the community, and the family's long-term adjustment. Consequently, comprehensive systems of care for individuals, both adults and children, who have sustained acquired brain injury (ABI) should include an evaluation of family functioning and family needs. Until recently, there was little quantitative data on these needs to guide rehabilitation professionals and community-based agencies in the development of effective programming and resources. However, in the early 1990s, a number of quantitative studies have begun to elucidate the needs of families after a family member has sustained ABI (Kreutzer, Serio, & Berquist, 1994; Marks, Sliwinski, & Gordon, 1993; Waaland & Raines, 1991).

REVIEW OF FAMILY OUTCOME LITERATURE

Historically, empirical investigation has focused primarily on family reactions and outcomes after an adult family member sustained ABI. The research has been flawed by general methodological problems, including small sample sizes, differential criteria for severity of injury, lack of appropriate control groups, and the use of assessment tools with questionable reliability and validity. A brief history of the assessment of family needs and outcomes provides background for the importance of assessing the long-term needs of caregivers of children with brain injuries. One of the first empirical studies to demonstrate the profound effect of acquired brain injury on family outcome evaluated the family members of 30 males who sustained severe acquired brain injury. Results showed that 61% of the family members interviewed required sleep medications or tranquilizers to facilitate coping. The effects of injury affected spouses to a greater degree than parents, and family education and support proved to significantly benefit families (Panting & Merry, 1972).

In a series of studies evaluating long-term family outcomes for survivors of severe brain injuries, Thomsen (1974) concluded that personality changes—characterized by irritability, temper outbursts, restlessness, and emotional lability—represented more significant problems in daily functioning than cognitive or physical impairments. Ten years later, Thomsen (1984) demonstrated that permanent changes in personality and emotional functioning persisted in two thirds of the sample. Similarly, Lezak (1978, 1986) has suggested that neurobehavioral sequelae, including personality changes, produce the greatest disruption in family functioning. Based on extensive clinical work with families of individuals with brain injuries, Lezak reported that relatives demonstrated anger, frustration, and depression at various points in the rehabilitation and recovery process. This sense of burden and emotional distress often remains until the caregiver realizes and reconciles the permanence of the characterological change.

A review of the literature on family outcomes suggests that a majority of families are adversely affected for years following an adult member's brain injury. Family outcome appears to be much more influenced by neurobehavioral sequelae than the physical effects of the injury. Many studies that have made significant contributions to the literature remain methodologically flawed. By the 1990s, investigators had begun to utilize outcome measures with established reliability and validity and multivariate statistical techniques.

FAMILY NEEDS OF ADULTS WITH ACQUIRED BRAIN INJURY

Researchers interested in the evaluation of family needs after brain injury have lacked established assessment tools. Mauss-Clum and Ryan (1981) provided one of the first quantitative studies of family needs following brain injury. In the study, 30 family members—19 wives and 11 mothers of individuals who had sustained a brain injury—completed a questionnaire that ranked family needs according to importance. A "kind, clear explanation" of the child's injury was ranked as the families' first priority. In descending order of importance, the desire to discuss realistic expectations, emotional support, financial counseling, and information about the availability of resources were also rated as meaningful by families.

The Family Needs Questionnaire utilized in both adult and pediatric brain injury research was developed to assess the importance of a variety of family needs and the degree to which these needs have been met (Kreutzer, Waaland, & Camplair, 1988). Individual items survey many areas of need, including the adequacy of education on brain injury sequelae, communication with professionals, the availability of emotional support, and the availability of ancillary support services, such as legal services, financial counseling, and respite care. The questionnaire can be utilized to evaluate change throughout the rehabilitation and community reintegration process. It can also be used to evaluate the efficacy of family education and support programs.

In the largest quantitative study of family needs before 1995, Kreutzer and colleagues administered the Family Needs Questionnaire to 119 family members of individuals who sustained ABI (Kreutzer et al., 1994). In contrast to previous surveys of family needs during the acute stages of injury and rehabilitation, this study sample targeted family members of individuals who were, on average, 16 months postinjury and, therefore, living in their communities. Results indicated that most families demonstrate a continuing need for information and education about brain injuries and ongoing communication with rehabilitation professionals. For example, the needs most frequently rated as important or very important included the following:

- To have complete information on the child's problems in thinking (99%)
- To have their questions answered honestly (99%)
- To be assured that the best possible medical care is being given to the patient (99%)
- To have a professional to turn to for advice when the patient needs help (98%)

In contrast, needs rated most frequently as not important included the following:

- To have help keeping the house (32%)
- To be reassured that it is usual to have strong negative feelings about the patient (19%)
- To have help from other members of the family in taking care of the family (19%)

Approximately 80% of the needs rated as important were also rated as met or partly met; however, needs most frequently rated as not met revealed feelings of isolation, burden, and uncertainty about the future. Similarly, family members of individuals with longer postinjury periods reported a greater amount of unmet needs suggesting that families require more community-based services as time passes.

FAMILY NEEDS OF CHILDREN
WITH ACQUIRED BRAIN INJURY

The Family Needs Questionnaire (Kreutzer et al., 1988) has been modified and utilized in studies of needs of families of children with ABI (Marks et al., 1993; Waaland & Raines, 1991). Although acquired brain injury is the most frequent cause of disability and death in children and adolescents (Waaland, 1990), there are relatively few rehabilitation programs or community-based services specifically designed to meet the specialized needs of these children. Assessment of their caregivers' needs is necessary to delineate the stressors faced by these families as well as the extent to which these needs are met by rehabilitation professionals and service providers (Marks et al., 1993). To provide comprehensive assessment of treatment needs for families with children with neurological disabilities, Waaland and Raines (1991) suggest evaluating three factors: 1) family burden and coping, 2) family functioning and communication patterns, and 3) family resources and support. Families of children with acquired neurological dysfunction, like those with acquired brain injury, have unique needs as they "grieve the loss of a real rather than idealized child" (Waaland & Raines, 1991, p. 24). These families often undergo abrupt and dramatic changes in family roles and functioning. Interestingly, evaluation of the needs of children with neurological disabilities has demonstrated similar findings to the needs reported by family members of adults with brain injuries. Information and understandable explanations from rehabilitation professionals were rated as the most important needs across all socioeconomic levels; instrumental needs, such as household care, child care, and adaptive skills, were rated as least important (Waaland & Raines, 1991). These researchers note that caregivers, who often struggle with feelings of guilt, need permission to attend to the needs of family members other than the injured child, such as spouses, children without injuries, and themselves. To avoid feelings of burnout, they advocate that parents and caregivers protect time with other family members. Additionally, pediatric brain injury researchers and clinicians must understand that caregivers' needs will likely change over time as the child changes and develops as a result of neurological recovery and progression through developmental stages.

In a large study of the needs of caregivers of children with ABI, Marks and her colleagues (1993) endeavored to address the following issues: 1) the long-term needs of families of children with ABI at least 1 year following the injury, 2) the degree to which these needs have been met, and 3) the demographic characteristics associated with families who report having their needs met compared with families who do not report having their needs met. The study sample consisted of 165 caregivers of children with brain injuries who were recruited from the New York State Brain Injury Association. Criteria for caregivers included responsibility for a child with a brain injury under the age of 21 who was injured at least 1 year prior to participation in the study. Demographic variables—including age and gender of the child; and age, gender, educational level, employment status, and income level of the caregiver—were collected. Additionally, caregivers completed several questionnaires assessing the severity of the child's injury, including physical, cognitive, and behavioral sequelae; family coping skills; and family concerns.

Overall, results of the study revealed that of 39 potential needs endorsed by families of a child with ABI, 70% were reported to be important by at least 50% of caregivers. For example, the needs most frequently reported as important included the following:

- To have questions answered honestly (89%)
- To have information on thinking problems (82%)
- To have information on physical problems (80%)
- To have understandable explanations (79%)
- To have professional advice when needed (79%)
- To have enough resources for the child (79%)

In contrast, the needs rated least frequently as important included the following:

- To be encouraged to ask for help (25%)
- To have reassurance about negative feelings (26%)
- To have help keeping house (27%)
- To have help preparing for the worst (29%)
- To have information on drug and alcohol treatment (31%)

Additionally, results demonstrated that importance was correlated with four demographic variables: age of caregiver, level of education of caregiver, sex of caregiver, and age of child with ABI. For example, the age of the caregiver was related to obtaining help from other members of the family and spending time with friends—older caregivers more frequently endorsed these items as important when compared with younger caregivers. Additionally, less educated caregivers reported that being updated daily on what is being done with or for the child and being able to give opinions daily to others involved in the child's care as more important than highly educated caregivers. Notably, female caregivers reported spending time with friends and obtaining understanding from family members regarding their problems and the problems of the child with brain injury as significantly more important than male caregivers. The age of the injured individual was related to the need for information on drug and alcohol problems and treatment—caregivers of older children rated this as more important than caregivers of young children with ABI.

Results of this survey indicated that many needs endorsed as important were unmet. The most frequent needs reported as met included the following:

- To be assured that the best medical care is being given to the child (58%)
- To be told about changes in medical status (57%)
- To have information on medical care of the injury (54%)
- To have questions answered honestly (52%)
- To have explanations from professionals given in understandable terms (46%)

In contrast, a review of needs least frequently met included the following:

- To have help in preparing for the worst (12%)
- To have help getting over doubts and fears about the future (13%)
- To have enough resources for the family (14%)
- To have the child's friends understand the problem (15%)
- To have reassurance that it is all right to have negative feelings about the child (16%)

Additionally, the age of the caregiver was the only demographic variable found to be related to the number of needs met—as only older caregivers endorsed that less of their needs were met, specific demographic variables are not predictive of successful caregiving. Subsequent analyses involving injury characteristics and family coping demonstrated that caregivers of children with significant behavioral and cognitive sequelae had fewer needs met, the longer time since injury was correlated with fewer needs met, and caregivers who are better able to redefine and manage stressful events have more important needs met.

Based on the amount of unmet needs, Marks et al. (1993) conclude that the current service delivery system is ineffective in meeting the needs of families of children with ABI. As no pattern of demographic variables emerged to predict successful caregiving, each family's unique needs must be assessed and treated. Results of this study are consistent with existing literature on family needs of adults with acquired brain injury: Informational needs are reported as important and, in many cases, viewed as met; whereas, critical long-term concerns involving resource allocation, dealing with future uncertainties, and addressing the caregiver's negative feelings about the injured child remain largely unmet. Additionally, the cluster of needs met likely reflects the perceived effectiveness of acute medical care and early rehabilitation treatment. However, it is likely that long-term needs of children and families attempting to reintegrate into their communities and schools have been largely ignored. This study highlights the fact that additional research and program development must be targeted at the postacute needs of families of children with brain injuries.

CONCLUSION: RECOMMENDATIONS AND FUTURE DIRECTIONS

It has been suggested that, to work effectively with families of children with ABI, professionals must assume many roles, including educator, advocate, therapist, and community networker (Waaland, 1990). Rehabilitation professionals are in a unique position to assist children and families in the transition from the hospital or rehabilitation setting to the community and school system. To facilitate reintegration, professionals must provide continuing education regarding the range of cognitive and neurobehavioral sequelae of childhood brain injury. They must effectively communicate the complex interaction of these cognitive and behavioral impairments with the expectations for typical cognitive and personality development to families, educators, school administrators, and community service providers. Additionally, professionals must encourage families to become advocates for their own needs as caregivers and for the needs of the child with a brain injury.

Research initiatives should be directed toward understanding the specific and dynamic needs of parents and siblings of children with ABI. Proactive treatment approaches, such as parenting workshops that address naturalistic or in-home behavior management, should be developed and evaluated. It is recommended that brain injury support groups be expanded to include separate groups for children and adolescents who have sustained a brain injury, their parents, and siblings. These groups could be developed as an ongoing source of support, education, and resource information.

Research to identify the needs of children with brain injuries, their caregivers, and educators during academic reentry is sorely lacking.

Rehabilitation professionals, educators, and families need to work co-operatively to facilitate the child's school reentry after brain injury (Lash, 1994). School administrators, teachers, and educational assessors report that there is a lack of information regarding the specific academic needs of students with ABI, resulting in a lack of appropriate and individualized programming.

Children with brain injuries and their families face many struggles that could potentially be avoided with ongoing communication and cooperation among families, teachers, and service providers. Understanding the changing needs of these children and their families is the first step to providing adequate and innovative programs to optimize recovery, reintegration, and, ultimately, quality of life.

REFERENCES

Kreutzer, J.K., Serio, C.D., & Berquist, S. (1994). Family needs after brain injury: A quantitative analysis. *Journal of Head Trauma Rehabilitation, 9*(3), 104–115.

Kreutzer, J.K., Waaland, P.K., & Camplair, P. (1988). *Family Needs Questionnaire.* Richmond: Medical College of Virginia, Rehabilitation Research and Training Center on Severe Traumatic Brain Injury.

Lash, M. (1994). Families and students get caught between medical and educational systems. *Rehab Update.* Boston, MA: Research and Training Center in Rehabilitation and Childhood Trauma.

Lezak, M.D. (1978). Living with the characterologically altered brain-injured patient. *Journal of Clinical Psychiatry, 39,* 592–598.

Lezak, M.D. (1986). Psychological implications of traumatic brain damage for the patient's family. *Rehabilitation Psychology, 31,* 241–250.

Marks, M., Sliwinski, M., & Gordon, W.A. (1993). An examination of the needs of families with a brain-injured child. *NeuroRehabilitation, 3*(3), 1–12.

Mauss-Clum, N., & Ryan, M. (1981). Brain injury and the family. *Journal of Neurosurgical Nursing, 13,* 165–169.

Panting, A., & Merry, P. (1972). The long-term rehabilitation of severe head injuries with particular reference to the need for social and medical support for the patient's family. *Rehabilitation, 38,* 33–37.

Thomsen, I.V. (1974). The patient with severe head injury and his family. *Scandinavian Journal of Rehabilitation Medicine, 6*(4), 180–183.

Thomsen, I.V. (1984). Late outcome of severe blunt head trauma: A 10–15 year follow-up. *Scandinavian Journal of Rehabilitation Medicine, 3,* 1–4.

Waaland, P.K. (1990). Family response to childhood brain injury. In J.S. Kreutzer & P. Wehman (Eds.), *Community integration following traumatic brain injury* (pp. 225–247). Baltimore: Paul H. Brookes Publishing Co.

Waaland, P.K., & Raines, S.R. (1991). Families coping with childhood neurological disability: Clinical assessment and treatment. *NeuroRehabilitation, 1*(2), 19–27.

Williams, J.M. (1991). Family reaction to head injury. In J.M. Williams & T. Kay (Eds.), *Head injury: A family matter* (pp. 81–100). Baltimore: Paul H. Brookes Publishing Co.

11

The Role of the Family in School-to-Work Transition

Michael D. West, Karen Gibson, and Darlene Unger

The woman's voice on the telephone sounded desperate. Her 17-year-old son had been discharged from postacute care following a serious brain injury sustained in a car crash. His school, after promising to provide in-home instruction so that he could graduate, had reneged. They said his disability was too severe for him to continue school, they could not afford to send a teacher, and besides, they were not required to serve children and youth with acquired brain injury under special education law. She had called a medical college, widely known for its brain injury programs, seeking an adult vocational service agency in her rural area of Virginia where he could go for at least part of the day—a telephone call one might have expected to receive in the 1960s or perhaps even the 1970s. But this call came in 1994, nearly 2 decades after the right to education had been ensured for all children and youth with

The development of this chapter was supported in part by Grant #H235J20014 from the U.S. Department of Education, Rehabilitation Services Administration. The opinions expressed are solely those of the authors and no official endorsement by the Rehabilitation Services Administration should be inferred.

197

disabilities and 4 years after amendments had specified acquired brain injury as a distinct educational impairment.

This story is an extreme example of the difficulties that families can encounter in obtaining appropriate educational services for their children with acquired brain injury (ABI). Although most school districts would not display such ignorance or disregard of the legal rights of these students, families sometimes feel that their visions and concerns are not being adequately addressed in planning meetings or that their comments and suggestions are met with resistance or derision from the education professionals (McNair & Rusch, 1991; Stineman, Morningstar, Bishop, & Turnbull, 1993). As their children approach the age at which they must exit from the school system, parents' anxiety heightens as they foresee discontinuity between educational and adult services, months or even years on waiting lists for employment or residential services, disruption of their own employment, or, if they must work, dependence on friends or other family members or expensive custodial care.

This transition period is a difficult time for the child as well. Because the majority of pediatric ABI cases occur at age 15 and older (Begali, 1987), these students are likely to have already developed expectations for employment, postsecondary education, independence, and social life. In the already turbulent period of adolescence, they may have difficulty coping with their new selves and the modifications to their futures their changes necessitate.

This chapter focuses on school-to-work transitions for students with ABI and is directed toward parents and other caregiving family members who participate in transition planning or in providing supports to the students before or after they exit school. This chapter provides family members with examples of desirable transition outcomes and presents the necessary support services to achieve those outcomes.

A REVIEW OF FEDERAL LAW: KNOWLEDGE REALLY IS POWER

Being an effective advocate for a child with ABI requires an understanding of civil rights and the obligations of local and state service systems. This section briefly reviews five pieces of federal legislation relating to youth and young adults with disabilities in general, and ABI in particular, as well as the legal rights afforded to them and their families.

The Individuals with Disabilities Education Act

The Education for All Handicapped Children Act of 1975, PL 94-142, was amended in 1990 as the Individuals with Disabilities Education Act (IDEA), PL 101-476, and included two changes that affect adolescents with ABI. First, ABI was added as an educational disability—a change that led to more appropriate educational assessment and decisions for this group of students (Carter, 1993) and helped determine the extent of pediatric ABI, which in the past has been clouded by definitional and reporting anomalies (Savage & Wolcott, 1994). Prior to this change, students with ABI were typically classified according to their most prevalent impairment (e.g., emotional or behavior disorder, orthopedic impairment, learning disability, multiple disabilities).

The second major change required educational systems to begin providing transition services to all students with disabilities ages 16 and older, or earlier if appropriate for the student. The individualized transition plan (ITP) is coordinated with the student's individualized education program (IEP) and facilitates movement from school to postschool environments, including postsecondary education and training, employment, continuing adult education, adult services agencies, independent living, and community participation. IDEA also specifies that ITP planning should take into account the student's preferences and interests but does not mandate that student and family choices have primacy in transition planning.

The Developmental Disabilities Assistance and Bill of Rights Act

The Developmental Disabilities Assistance and Bill of Rights Act of 1975, PL 94-103 (commonly referred to as the DD Act), established the Basic State Grant Program to fund projects within states. States set up planning councils that determine how the grants are utilized within the federal guidelines. In 1987, service eligibility was revised from a categorical definition (e.g., mental retardation, cerebral palsy) to a functional definition that included early onset (prior to age 22), chronic impairment, and limitations in performing major life activities. This change has been instrumental in improving access to services for children and adults with an array of physical, mental, emotional, and health impairments, including pediatric ABI. In the most recent version of the act (PL 101-496, 1990), the Basic State Grant Program emphasizes services that support and empower people with developmental disabilities and their families (Wolfe, 1992).

The Medicaid Home- and Community-Based Waiver Program

The Medicaid Home- and Community-Based (HCB) Waiver Program was authorized by the Omnibus Budget Reconciliation Act of 1981,

PL 97-35. This program allows states to use Medicaid funds to provide home- and community-based services to Medicaid recipients, including personal and homemaker services, case management, home health care, habilitation, and respite, residential, and employment services. Most state HCB Waiver Programs are for individuals with mental retardation and developmental disabilities, which include those with pediatric ABI; however, as of 1994, eight states had waivers specifically for individuals with ABI (G. Smith, personal communication, April 30, 1994).

The HCB Waiver Program has reversed the institutional bias of Medicaid-funded disability services, which has profoundly affected residential placement patterns, allowing greater numbers of individuals to return to their families or home communities with necessary support services or avoid out-of-home or out-of-community placements altogether. The program has had far less impact on improving employment opportunities, largely because only those with prior institutionalization are eligible for receiving prevocational or employment services.

The Rehabilitation Act

The Rehabilitation Act of 1973, PL 93-112, is the legislative authority for the federal/state Vocational Rehabilitation (VR) service system. Section 504 of the act was the first legislative attempt to prohibit discrimination toward individuals with disabilities but was limited to organizations that received funds from the federal government. This section requires that postsecondary education and training be made accessible to individuals with disabilities, including modifications to programs of study or degree requirements, alternative testing methods, physical accessibility, and the like.

Also of importance to families of youth with ABI, the act authorizes money for client services, such as assessment, physical restoration, environmental modifications, job placement and training, postsecondary education or training, and adapted equipment, in accordance with an individualized written rehabilitation program (IWRP). In 1986, the act was amended (PL 99-506) to authorize *supported employment* as a service option. This option combines time-limited job placement and job coaching services funded by the VR agency with long-term job maintenance services funded through an alternative source such as the state mental retardation/developmental disabilities or mental health services systems. This option is designed for individuals with the most severe disabilities who would otherwise be excluded from the work force.

Other amendments in 1992 (PL 102-569) have taken the VR system in new and positive directions. Previously, the VR service system required prospective clients to undergo assessments for rehabilitation potential and future employability. In many VR systems, this process prevented individuals with very severe disabilities from having access to services because VR counselors did not have a reasonable expectation that services would result in employment. With the supported employment option, severe disability is no longer analogous with limited employment potential. Title I of the act states unequivocally that all individuals, regardless of the severity of their disabilities, are presumed to be capable of gainful employment in integrated settings with necessary services and supports and, therefore, are presumed to be eligible for VR services.

The 1992 amendments also emphasize consumer choice in planning and delivering VR services. The VR consumer can choose from among service options, providers, and methods. Perhaps most significant, the consumer is allowed to directly secure her own services, including using family members, friends, or co-workers as support providers as long as their functions are consistent with the IWRP. This change allows consumers to go outside of the established service delivery system if they feel it is in their best interests or increases their comfort levels. For example, an individual who needs personal assistance on the job may elect to hire a family member who already provides assistance at home (and perhaps is paid with VR funds), rather than utilize professional assistants or co-workers to provide these functions.

The Americans with Disabilities Act

The Americans with Disabilities Act (ADA) of 1990, PL 101-336, is a broad-based civil rights law designed to promote full inclusion in employment and community participation for people with disabilities (Wehman, 1993). Title I of the ADA relates to employment in businesses of 15 employees or more—prohibiting discrimination against an individual with a disability in hiring or promotion if the person is otherwise qualified for the job. Title I also requires that businesses provide reasonable accommodations for qualified workers with disabilities, such as restructuring job duties or modifying equipment or work spaces. Businesses can opt not to provide accommodations if an undue burden would result, but there is insufficient case law as of 1996 to provide guidelines about what constitutes a "reasonable" request for accommodation or what types of burdens are "undue." Titles II and III of the ADA require accessibility in bus and rail transportation and in public accommodations (e.g., hotels, restaurants, offices), respectively.

Prior to transition planning, students, parents, and other family members can prepare in the following ways:

1. Parents can obtain copies of the above pieces of legislation, or concise summaries, and review them prior to the ITP meetings. Knowledge of federal laws and their requirements on educational and adult services systems sends a clear message to other ITP team members that the family is concerned about their child's future, aware of their need for services, and determined to succeed even if it means making waves in the system.
2. Parents can learn their area's specific legislative guidelines, as states and localities are unique in how they implement the legislation previously described. For example, each state's service and eligibility requirements under the HCB Waiver Program will be different, and each school system will have different types of agreements with the regional VR office. For this reason, families should contact appropriate state offices about the services that are available to them and their child in transition and how best to gain access to them.
3. Families should understand that, unlike education, adult services are not entitlement programs. For example, if VR or HCB Waiver case service funds run out, then no new cases can be taken. In addition, there may be income or age restrictions on services funded by the state planning council or the VR agency. However, many service systems such as VR have an order-of-selection process that specifies which groups have priority for services when funds begin to run low. Each program's order of selection should be investigated to see if the student with ABI fits into one of the priority groups.

BEYOND INVOLVEMENT: LEADERSHIP

Research has generally found that family participation in ITP meetings is a good indicator of successful completion of the plan and that educational personnel want parents to be involved in transition planning (McNair & Rusch, 1991; Sale, Metzler, Everson, & Moon, 1991). However, this same body of research has also found that school personnel do not necessarily value the suggestions or concerns of family members or feel that they can contribute substantially to the process (Gallivan-Fenlon, 1994; Stineman et al., 1993). In fact, more vocal and concerned family members are often perceived to be troublesome, obtrusive, or even delusional about their child's potential. A common example is planning for postschool employment, with parents pushing for competitive employment and educators suggesting sheltered employment at best.

Federal law requires that the student and parents (or other family members) be allowed to participate as members of ITP teams, if appropriate. However, if the goals and concerns of the family and student are to be fully addressed, then participation is not enough. They must assume the leadership role in planning, including determining appropriate postschool goals, environments, and support services. This may produce some skepticism or resistance from the school ITP team members and will likely be difficult for parents who are used to allowing the education professionals to control the IEP or ITP process. The following are some tips for families and students with ABI in assuming transitional leadership:

1. Parents should prepare school personnel for the shift in leadership roles by being active in educational planning and learning activities throughout their child's educational career. As the student approaches age 16 (or the first ITP meeting, if the injury occurred after age 16), parents should inform either the teacher or the school's transition coordinator of their intention to take responsibility for guiding the ITP meeting.

2. If met with resistance, parents should remind the school personnel that it is the student and family, not the other ITP team members, who will have to live with the consequences of ITP decisions for many years to come; therefore, it is in everyone's best interests to let the concerns and preferences of the family take priority in decision making.

3. Parents should do their homework prior to their first ITP meeting. They should make notes of their concerns about life after school for themselves as well as their child with ABI and how they believe the school can address those concerns. They should also investigate adult services and other forms of assistance that are available and eligibility criteria. They should ask the school's transition coordinator for advice about which adult services representatives to invite, such as vocational rehabilitation or residential service providers, based on their perceptions of postschool needs.

4. They should prepare an agenda for the meeting that follows a clear, logical path from problem identification and goal setting to developing activities and responsibilities. Most school systems should already have an ITP form that follows this process and can be obtained and reviewed prior to the meeting.

5. If members of the ITP team bring prepared education or transition goals to the meeting, the parents should dispose of them as discretely or pointedly as they wish. This is a clear violation of the team process that is spelled out in the IDEA regulations.

6. Finally, students and family members should assume that the other members have the interests of the student and family at heart and be prepared to listen to their concerns and ideas.

Case Studies in Community and Workplace Supports: Jacob

Jacob is a 22-year-old young man who resides with his retired parents in a suburban area of a major metropolitan city. He sustained ABI at age 18 when he was a passenger in a single-car accident that occurred on a rural, ice-covered road. During the accident, he was ejected from the car and pinned under it in a stream. The driver of the car was unable to locate Jacob and went for help. It is unknown how long Jacob was pinned.

Jacob was unresponsive for 5 months but was released from the hospital within 7 months of his injury. He returned to school as a part-time student within 10 months and returned full time at 11 months postinjury. At that time, Jacob's limitations included loss of speech, contracture of the right side, spasticity of the limbs, limited range of motion, and severe short-term memory loss. He utilized a wheelchair and required help with adaptive behaviors. Jacob is ambulatory without physical aids but has difficulties with stairs and uneven surfaces. He has severe long- and short-term memory problems and is reported to be functioning at low intelligence levels in all areas. Although Jacob has limited verbal communication, he can proficiently use a portable augmentative communication device that gives a printed message tape. He chooses, however, to express himself through verbal responses and gestures. He understands what is going on around him and directions given to him. He is unaware of his limitations and has no concept of time.

According to Jacob's mother, who retired to care for her son, Jacob's school did not know what to do with him when he returned. The school had a special education curriculum but did not have a specialized track for students with ABI. Jacob was assigned a full-time aide to assist him with academics, adaptive skills, and mobility. His IEP included augmentative communication, speech therapy, physical therapy, occupational therapy, adapted physical education, and resource classes.

Jacob's transition program is guided by a team that includes Jacob, his mother, an instruction specialist, a personal aide, a case manager, a speech-language therapist, a physical therapist, an occupational therapist, a VR counselor, a rehabilitation engineer, and a job coach from a local supported employment provider. The team meets biweekly to review Jacob's progress on his tasks, stamina, preferences, needs, and any other issues that arise. The job coach informs the group about assessment information and any updates on job development. The team incorporates any tasks that may have marketable and transferable skills that could benefit Jacob's experience or assist with formulating a résumé. The team works together to modify Jacob's tasks or make accommodations so that he can better perform them. Jacob is very vocal and gives his input regularly. During one meeting as the team was discussing a product that Jacob was assembling for assessment purposes, someone sug-

gested that Jacob continue making the product that could then be sold. There was much debate over this, with questions relating to the costs and what to do with the proceeds. Jacob became very rambunctious and typed out on his communication device, "I would like to see me get the money."

Jacob is in his last year of school. He is targeted for supported competitive employment and is in the job development phase. Through the cooperation of the school, the state VR office, and the local supported employment provider it is estimated that Jacob will begin a competitive job before the end of the school year. Jacob's aide will assist him on the jobsite with work and nonwork issues. He will be trained by the employing company, with assistance from the job coach and all community or workplace support resources that are available. At the end of the school year when his aide is no longer available, alternative resources will be utilized and long-term, follow-along services will be incorporated.

REAL WORK FOR REAL PAY: ACCEPT NO SUBSTITUTES

Students in need of long-term employment support face a dual system of vocational services in which segregated, facility-based employment services and integrated, community-based services compete for resources and participants (Mank, 1994; McGaughey, Kiernan, McNally, Gilmore, & Keith, 1994). This dual system survives despite public policy initiatives, such as the Rehabilitation Act and the ADA, that encourage integrated employment for all individuals with disabilities and growing acceptance of people with disabilities in the work force (Rees, Spreen, & Harnadek, 1991).

Since the 1960s, sheltered workshops, work activity centers, and other segregated employment options have been scrutinized and criticized. As critics of segregated facilities have pointed out over the years (Garner, Lacy, & Creasy, 1972; Gersuny & Lefton, 1970; Mallas, 1976; Schuster, 1990), these facilities have taken on two incompatible goals: 1) providing services to individuals with disabilities to optimize their employment potential, and 2) operating a business enterprise. This conflict results in low wages, lack of movement to less restrictive settings, disregard of client preferences and goals, and low expectations of client employability on the part of workshop staff, local businesses, and the community at large.

In 1996, after over a decade of research, the evidence is overwhelming that adults with disabilities who require relatively permanent employment services fare better in supported employment than in sheltered work. Supported employment participants have been shown to increase their earnings by 200%–500% over sheltered work

(Helms, Moore, & McSewyn, 1991; Kregel, Wehman, & Banks, 1989; Thompson, Powers, & Houchard, 1992) and also to increase their job satisfaction (Test, Hinson, Solow, & Keul, 1993), community participation (Helms, Moore, Powell, & Gould, 1990), and quality of life (Sinnott-Oswald, Gliner, & Spencer, 1991).

With the advent of supported employment, a real job is a viable option for any student regardless of the severity of his impairments. For this reason, parents of youth with ABI should never be satisfied with sheltered employment or other segregated prevocational activities as a transitional goal. The following tips can reassure them that the ITP team settles for nothing less than a real job for real pay:

1. If employment skills, behavior problems, or having access to adult services are foreseeable problems, the family can ensure that community work experiences are a prominent component of the ITP. On-the-job training programs can help students develop a résumé of work skills and references prior to exiting the school system and perhaps achieve full employment.
2. If loss of medical or income supports is an issue, school-based job development can focus on either full-time employment with health insurance or part-time employment that will not jeopardize government benefits. A case manager from the Social Security Administration can be invited to be a member of the team to help determine exactly how much the student can earn before this becomes problematic.
3. Many states provide VR services to youth with disabilities in transition, and many have VR counselors or case managers who specialize in assisting people with ABI. One of these VR representatives should be invited to be a member of the ITP team and open a case for the student, even if services are not anticipated before or at the time of school exit. The student may want to change jobs or may experience job loss at some point in the future, and having a knowledgeable counselor or an open VR case file can speed up the process somewhat and perhaps allow the person with ABI to remain in the competitive work force.
4. Job exploration and placement services should be career oriented. Preliminary work experiences or assessments should be conducted in real work settings and varied enough to help students make choices about the types of jobs or work settings they prefer that match their strengths. Figure 1 provides a sample assessment sheet for a work experience program operated by a center for youth and adults with ABI, showing the different types of work environments utilized and the factors assessed within each setting. Job

	Library	Central Supply	Print Shop	Finance	Grounds	Gym
Physical abilities		■			■	■
Sensory abilities			■		■	
Communication abilities		■				■
Cognitive abilities	■	■	■			
Academic abilities	■					
Equipment/tool use	■		■	■		■
Productivity	■				■	
Response to hazards			■		■	■
Response to environmental conditions					■	
Work traits and behaviors	■			■		
Response to supervision		■			■	
Accessibility needs		■		■		■

Figure 1. Sample assessment factors and work environments utilized for assessment in a work experience program for individuals with ABI.

tryout programs can be specifically designed to increase work tolerance so that a student who is easily fatigued can work up to maximum employment levels. The closer the student approaches school exit, the more refined his career goals and work experiences should be. The ultimate goal should be for students to graduate into jobs that put them on their chosen career paths.

5. Family members and friends are, and always have been, a major source of employment contacts for students with and without disabilities. Families should begin networking their own employers and those of their friends to identify school-based training sites and future job openings that might interest their children as they approach school exit.

6. Like many members of the general population who are beginning their careers, young adults with ABI often do not keep their first job but achieve success in second, third, or later positions (Wehman, West, Kregel, Sherron, & Kreutzer, 1995). Thus, parents should not allow their children's employment potential to be judged by results from one or two jobs—repeated placements may be necessary for individuals to learn or relearn work skills and behaviors and decide what types of jobs or work environments they like.

Case Studies in Community and Workplace Supports: David

David is 19 years old and has acquired brain injury. He resides at home with his parents and a 13-year-old sister. David presents himself as being meticulously groomed and extremely talkative and sociable. Just prior to David's 10th birthday, he was hit by an automobile while walking. He was in coma for 3–4 days, with further coma induced to reduce his pain and discomfort. He sustained damage to the right frontal part of the brain with generalized swelling. David reportedly did not have a history of serious injury, illness, or seizures prior to his injury and reached developmental milestones well within typical or advanced limits prior to his injury. As a result of his injury, David has no peripheral vision and a hearing loss in his right ear that is not correctable with a hearing aid. Often, his voice tone and volume are loud, possibly due to his hearing loss. Although he speaks clearly and in sentences, he appears to have some difficulty with expressive language, especially in formulating his thought process and word retrieval. David also has significant difficulties in both short- and long-term memory and a limited attention span.

Prior to his current educational placement, David had been integrated with the assistance of a full-time aide. David was able to maintain progress for many years following his injury because there were minimal demands for higher-level, independent reasoning. However, as educational demands increased, David encountered extreme difficulty in advanced reasoning skills. He currently attends a self-contained class for students labeled as having mild to moderate mental retardation. The class focuses on teaching students functional academics and appropriate work behaviors and also provides students with nonpaying, community-based work experiences. David has participated in a community-based work experience at McDonald's and worked in a cafeteria performing stocking.

A representative from the school system met with David and his parents to discuss referring David to a local supported employment program for job placement and training while David was in still in school. After hearing about the program, David and his parents decided that they were interested in him receiving these services. David's VR counselor made the referral to the supported employment provider, and a home visit was scheduled so that a representative from the supported employment program and the state Department of Rehabilitative Services could meet with David and his parents.

During the home visit, the job coach described the services that the program offered and asked David and his parents questions regarding David's prior work experiences, his general likes and dislikes, what types of things might be important to David in working in the job of his choice (e.g., location, type and size of business, work hours, transportation), his vocational goals and experience, and who might be available to assist David in any areas where support might be needed. For example, David said that he was interested in working full time and would like to work during school at a business close to where he went to school. His parents had suggested that it might be good for David to begin working part time and build up his stamina and then he could ask for more hours if the job permitted.

After the home visit, the job coach initiated a community-based situational assessment with David. At one assessment site, a buffet-style restaurant, David worked side by side with another employee who prompted David on what to do. He was responsible for filling pans and bowls with food items and then placing them in the appropriate spot on the buffet table. David needed frequent prompting in order to remember where to return the leftover food items after he was through filling the pan or bowl. He had no difficulty reading the chart that showed where the item was to be placed on the buffet table and was able to count the number of spaces to place the pan or bowl accordingly. The co-worker did not seem to mind that after David returned from the buffet table he needed to be prompted to the next task. The job coach noted that a checklist would be extremely useful for David in making him more independent on the job.

Because David was very social and wanted contact with the public, his school teacher, parents, and job coach agreed that David would need a job where there would be a lot of interaction with people and support from co-workers to stay on task. From the information that the job coach obtained from the assessments and David's records, it was evident that David would also require a job that was repetitive in nature and would be performed in a predictable environment. David would also benefit from the use of memory strategy training techniques, such as notebooks or calendars and schedules.

After the job coach visited the restaurant, the teacher called and said that David had asked the employer for a job at the restaurant. The teacher felt that the employer was very receptive to working with a supported employment program and might be willing to hire David. The job coach is currently in the process of following up on the lead that was provided by both the consumer and the teacher and hopes that a potential job for David can be identified at the restaurant.

ALLOWING OPPORTUNITIES TO CHOOSE

A key feature of both IDEA and the Rehabilitation Act is the encouragement of consumer self-determination in planning and delivering services. Self-determination occurs when people experience choices in their lives and control over decision-making processes and outcomes (Deci & Ryan, 1985; Lovett, 1991). Most people develop self-determination as children and adolescents as they are given greater responsibilities and freedoms by their parents and teachers. However, research on children and adults with disabilities tends to show that they have fewer opportunities to participate in decision making than their peers who do not have disabilities (Guess, Benson, & Siegel-Causey, 1985; Houghton, Bronicki, & Guess, 1987). As Bannerman, Sheldon, Sherman, and Harchik (1990) write, limitations on choice may be the result of a number of factors, including convenience of the family or school staff, regulatory and accountability pressures, and fear that the choices and decisions made by people with disabilities will hinder or conflict with habilitative efforts.

Since the 1990s, choice making and self-determined behavior have been recognized as valuable for people with disabilities and have become a focus of educational and habilitative programs. A growing number of parents, professionals, and individuals with disabilities themselves are convinced that all people can and should be taught to express preferences, make choices, and exert greater control over the decisions that affect their lives; they have also demonstrated methods for enabling these behaviors for people with even very severe and multiple disabilities (Reid & Parsons, 1990, 1991; Wacker, Wiggins, Fowler, & Berg, 1988).

The weight of empirical evidence indicates that individuals with disabilities participate more appropriately in learning and social activities that they can choose or control (Dyer, Dunlap, & Winterling, 1990; Ip, Szymanski, Johnston-Rodriguez, & Karls, 1994; Koegel, Dyer, & Bell, 1987; Parsons, Reid, & Baumgartner, 1990). Student self-determination can improve successful transition also. Families can foster self-determination in transition in the following ways:

1. Students with ABI can be provided instruction in identifying goals, options, and preferences across the array of life experiences. There are some commercial and educational training programs available for this purpose.
2. Students with ABI should be encouraged to participate in educational planning, including the IEP and ITP meetings, and should be rewarded for their participation.
3. Parents, teachers, and other caregivers can incorporate choices and decision making across all facets of the educational program and in other activities in the school and at home. This could include decisions about classes to take, schedules, friendships and dating, clothing, after-school activities, meals, and a multitude of other major and minor decision areas. Like all adolescents and young

adults, youth with ABI will make some decisions with which parents or teachers disagree; but, being a good decision maker requires practice in making decisions and experiencing both the positive and negative consequences.

4. Parents and teachers can provide instruction in self-advocacy skills, self-expression, decision-making skills, and assertiveness, which will help students put choices into action.

5. Students should be given all of the information necessary to make an informed choice. Making good decisions requires information about the available options so that students can weigh positive and negative aspects. Informed choices can be facilitated through direct exposure to vocational, social, and independent living options.

Case Studies in Community and Workplace Supports: Joe

Joe, age 21, sustained two closed brain injuries within a 1-month period at the end of his senior year of high school. His first injury (a moderate injury) occurred when he jumped from a moving car. His second injury (a mild injury) occurred as the result of a hit-and-run traffic accident when Joe was riding a moped. Prior to these accidents, Joe had an extensive history of medical conditions, including numerous childhood illnesses, behavior and emotional problems, attention-deficit/hyperactivity disorder, adjustment disorder, impulse control disorder, dysthymic disorder, and mild cerebral dysfunction that may have resulted from a blow to the head from a student in junior high school. He has a chronic history of substance and alcohol abuse for which he has received treatment through numerous inpatient and outpatient programs.

Joe completed his high school class credits and graduated. At the time of his second injury, he was working part-time in a restaurant and was attending courses at a community college. He felt he was unable to return to college following the second injury and has not pursued postsecondary education since that time. He was referred to an out-of-state community rehabilitation program 6 months after his injuries. However, the family was planning to relocate due to a job transfer, so Joe moved alone. He received rehabilitation services from that program for approximately 5 months and was discharged with no individualized supports in place. He was referred to the state VR agency, which recommended him for supported employment.

During the time without supports, Joe continued his heavy use of alcohol and became increasingly involved in serious legal issues. He was arrested numerous times for, among other charges, driving under the influence of alcohol. He was unable to manage his finances and was in jeopardy of losing his apartment. He often went days without eating as a result of a lack of skills and an inability to remember.

Upon referral, the supported employment program immediately made contact with Joe and began the assessment process. Within a matter of weeks, Joe was employed in a restaurant as a prep cook. Job training was provided primarily through the employer using a mentor. The job coach provided assistance to the employer to enhance the training to accommodate Joe's learning needs. This included developing checklists, implementing compensatory strategies, and arranging other supports in an organized and consistent manner to eliminate the element of chance or reliance on memory. Unfortunately, the work environment was not conducive or supportive in averting Joe's poor impulse control and he often had interpersonal conflicts with his co-workers. As a result of this increasing frustration, Joe quit his job after a few months.

He began working at another restaurant as a dishwasher. He was not eager to have assistance from his job coach at this job and relied more on his father, who had recently moved to the area. Joe continued to abuse alcohol excessively during this time and was arrested on more than one occasion. The job coach provided assistance to the employer and off-site assistance to Joe as he would allow. The environment at this restaurant and his co-workers promoted Joe's continued alcohol consumption as they would often socialize after working hours and drink heavily. Joe also continued to have interpersonal conflicts with co-workers and again quit his job.

Throughout this time, Joe was appearing in court for his numerous offenses. He would be given suspended sentences, license suspension, or community work hours. Joe was also beginning to have other symptoms, such as seizures and an inability to sleep. Joe became increasingly frightened of his court appearances, as it was only a matter of time before he would be incarcerated. He recognized that his behavior was out of control and began to ask for help. Joe met with his job coach and a neuropsychologist and agreed to develop a treatment program. He began seeing a substance abuse psychotherapist and attended a weekly substance abuse group meeting. He also agreed to attend Alcoholics Anonymous (AA) meetings for an extended period of time.

Joe and his job coach identified work environments that would be supportive of his treatment and conducive for positive working relationships. Such supports would include high company standards, close employer–employee relations, and procedures for handling stressful job duties, among other characteristics that would aid Joe in getting his life in order. Joe and his job coach located such a job and Joe was hired. During the interview, it was made clear that Joe had pending court dates that could result in jail time. Joe was employed approximately 3 weeks and had moved to a new apartment within walking distance to his new job when he was sentenced *to jail. By that time, Joe had become a valued employee and his employer was willing to allow him to continue working through the work-release program.*

It is suspected that Joe will continue to work for this employer and that his recovery program will continue. His job coach is very involved in the coordination of resources to assist Joe in maintaining his employment. Long-term, follow-along services will include community and workplace supports as intensive service is no longer needed.

POSTSECONDARY EDUCATION AND TRAINING

Students with disabilities are enrolling in postsecondary education and training in increasing numbers, but they still lag far behind those without disabilities (Fairweather & Shaver, 1991). As with students without disabilities, completion of postsecondary education and training improves employment prospects and potential earnings for students with disabilities. Many students with ABI have the academic potential to pursue postsecondary education and training but may have physical, sensory, or behavioral issues that need to be addressed by both the ITP team and the postsecondary institution (Savage, 1987). For those students, parents should advocate for postsecondary education as a transition goal.

Despite the mandates of Section 504 of the Rehabilitation Act of 1973, students with disabilities encounter significant barriers in postsecondary educational endeavors, such as poor access within and between buildings, limited numbers of parking spaces for people with disabilities and poor enforcement of parking regulations, limited numbers of paid or volunteer staff to assist with school-related functions, and poor compliance in program accommodations (West et al., 1993). These barriers have the following implications for students with ABI who wish to continue their education:

1. The transition planning team cannot assume that services and accommodations at the postsecondary level will be available when they are needed. Any number of factors, including funding and staff shortages, inflexible instructors, historical architecture, and overburdened disability services, can intervene and result in students with ABI being denied their legal rights to services and accommodations. Students who will be entering postsecondary education or training and their families must be empowered with knowledge of their rights under Section 504 and the ADA, as well as with self-advocacy skills training.

2. The transition planning team should thoroughly investigate potential postsecondary institutions for services and accommoda-

tions, including the size and location of the school, services and accommodations for the student's particular limitations, availability of therapeutic services, costs, and financial assistance available (Nordlund, 1994). The ITP should include specific educational institutions to which the student will apply for admission, based on each school's track record of accommodating students with similar impairments and needs, as well as the student's educational goals.

3. The student and his family should be encouraged to arrange visits to each school under consideration to meet with disability services coordinators and, if physical accessibility is a concern, tour the campus and buildings in which the student will have classes. If scheduled far enough in advance, the disability services coordinator can arrange for the student and parents to talk with others who have similar accommodation needs; a coordinator who is unwilling or unable to arrange such a meeting may signal that the school's disability services are deficient or the coordinator is overburdened. If accessible student housing will be needed, this can be investigated with the school's residential office, along with the availability of personal assistance. These site visits will provide more valid information for the student and his family than any college catalog.

4. The coordinator of services for students with disabilities at that school should be invited to become a member of the ITP team so that proactive planning can occur, even if services will not be sought immediately upon admission. If the student's mental health or physical abilities worsen and problems with attendance or classwork arise, prior knowledge of the student and his impairments will help the coordinator make arrangements with the student's instructors before the student's grades are affected.

FOCUS ON SUPPORTS

A major movement in disability services, particularly transition and VR, is the use of existing community and workplace supports, also referred to as natural supports, in lieu of or in addition to formal supports provided by educational, rehabilitation, or other adult services professionals. Natural supports can include employer resources such as employee assistance programs, training programs, co-workers, and supervisors; natural supports may also include friends, family members, personal care attendants, generic community services (e.g., public transportation, subsidized housing), and other existing resources that may be used to provide assistance in employment and community living. Natural supports have been advanced as a cost-effective means of achieving maximum social integration at work and in other integrated environments (Nisbet, 1992).

Social supports in the workplace appear to play a significant role in long-term job retention for employees with ABI. Using the Vocational Integration Index (Parent, Kregel, & Wehman, 1992), West (1995) compared jobs for individuals with severe brain injuries who retained a job for 6 months or more versus those who did not achieve the 6-month milestone. Successful job retainers had been placed into positions that offered higher levels of physical proximity with co-workers without disabilities, more opportunities for socialization (e.g., breaks, off-duty recreational events), formal employee assistance programs, fringe benefits (particularly health benefits and paid leave), and opportunities for regular raise reviews and advancement. The latter two factors, although economic in nature, can also be considered as supportive aspects of a job in that they provide assistance to the employee that would otherwise need to be sought either through a governmental source (e.g., Social Security, Medicaid) or through job changes.

Since 1992, the Rehabilitation Research and Training Center on Supported Employment in Richmond, Virginia, has operated a research and demonstration project for developing community and workplace supports for students making transitions, including those with ABI. The natural supports model that has emerged from this project is presented in Figure 2. Using this model, the role of the educational and adult services agencies is transformed from direct skills training and job maintenance activities to identifying and facilitating an array of formal and informal support systems, including family members, friends, neighbors, employers, co-workers, the school, VR and other adult services agencies (Parent, Unger, Gibson, & Clements, 1994).

The three case studies included in this chapter are students who have been served by the Natural Supports Demonstration Project, and examples of how community and workplace supports can be utilized for students with ABI who are making transitions. These cases illustrate the themes of effective and continuing transition planning, facilitating student choice, and ongoing support through and beyond transition.

CONCLUSION

Family members of a child with ABI have survived an arduous, stressful, and confusing time. As their injured son or daughter approaches

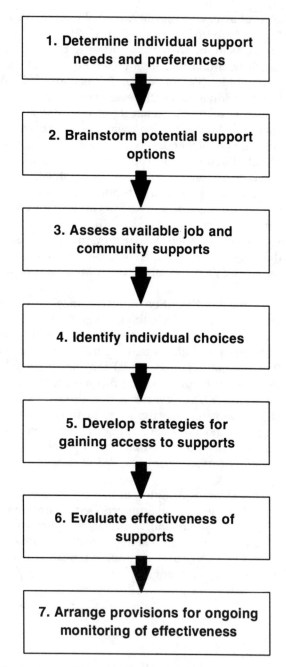

Figure 2. The Community and Workplace Supports Model. (Adapted from Parent et al., 1994.)

adulthood, many questions arise over the futures of both the child and the family. Without oversimplifying the process of transition, it is—in essence—the same process that all families go through at this time in a young person's life. The brain injury and the resulting problems and impairments may make the process more difficult, but not fundamentally different. Families can ease the transition of children with ABI in the same ways they intended to do so before the injury—by giving them the resources and the freedom to choose and supporting their choices in whatever ways they can.

REFERENCES

Americans with Disabilities Act of 1990 (ADA), PL 101-336. (July 26, 1990). Title 42, U.S.C. 12101 et seq: *U.S. Statutes at Large, 104*, 327–378.

Bannerman, D.J., Sheldon, J.B., Sherman, J.A., & Harchik, A.E. (1990). Balancing the right to habilitation with the right to personal liberties: The rights of people with developmental disabilities to eat too many doughnuts and take a nap. *Journal of Applied Behavior Analysis, 23*, 79–89.

Begali, V. (1987). *Head injury in children and adolescents: A resource and review for school and allied professionals.* Brandon, VT: Clinical Psychology Publishing Co.

Carter, S. (1993). *Traumatic brain injury: The role of the school in assessment.* Eugene: University of Oregon, Western Regional Resource Center.

Deci, E.L., & Ryan, R.M. (1985). *Intrinsic motivation and self-determination in human behavior.* New York: Plenum.

Developmental Disabilities Assistance and Bill of Rights Act of 1975, PL 94-103. (October 4, 1975). Title 42, U.S.C. 6000 et seq: *U.S. Statutes at Large, 89*, 486–507.

Developmental Disabilities Assistance and Bill of Rights Act Amendments of 1987, PL 100-146. (October 29, 1987). Title 42, U.S.C. 6000 et seq: *U.S. Statutes at Large, 101*, 840–859.

Developmental Disabilities Assistance and Bill of Rights Act of 1990, PL 101-496. (October 30, 1990). Title 42, U.S.C. 6000 et seq: *U.S. Statutes at Large, 104*, 1191.

Dyer, K., Dunlap, G., & Winterling, V. (1990). Effects of choice making on the serious problem behaviors of students with severe handicaps. *Journal of Applied Behavior Analysis, 23*, 515–524.

Education for All Handicapped Children Act of 1975, PL 94-142. (August 23, 1977). Title 20, U.S.C. 1400 et seq: *U.S. Statutes at Large, 89*, 773–796.

Fairweather, J.S., & Shaver, D.M. (1991). Making the transition to postsecondary education and training. *Exceptional Children, 57*, 264–270.

Gallivan-Fenlon, A. (1994). "Their senior year": Family and service provider perspectives on the transition from school to adult life for young adults with disabilities. *Journal of The Association for Persons with Severe Handicaps, 19*, 11–23.

Garner, R.E., Lacy, G.H., & Creasy, R.F. (1972). Workshops—why, what, whither? *Mental Retardation, 10*(3), 25–27.

Gersuny, C., & Lefton, M. (1970). Service and servitude in the sheltered workshop. *Social Work, 15*, 74–81.

Guess, D., Benson, H.A., & Siegel-Causey, E. (1985). Concepts and issues related to choice making and autonomy among persons with severe disabilities. *Journal of The Association for Persons with Severe Handicaps, 10,* 79–86.

Helms, B.J., Moore, S.C., & McSewyn, C.A. (1991). Supported employment in Connecticut: An examination of integration and wage outcomes. *Career Development of Exceptional Individuals, 14,* 159–166.

Helms, B.J., Moore, S.C., Powell, T.H., & Gould, B.F. (1990). A preliminary study of a statewide effort to develop supported employment services for people with severe and prolonged mental illness. *Psychosocial Rehabilitation Journal, 13*(3), 45–57.

Houghton, J., Bronicki, G.J., & Guess, D. (1987). Opportunities to express preferences and make choices among students with severe disabilities in classroom settings. *Journal of The Association for Persons with Severe Handicaps, 12,* 18–27.

Individuals with Disabilities Education Act (IDEA) of 1990, PL 101-476. (October 30, 1990). Title 20, U.S.C. 1400 et seq: *U.S. Statutes at Large, 104* (Part 2), 1103–1151.

Ip, S.M.V., Szymanski, E.M., Johnston-Rodriguez, S., & Karls, S.F. (1994). Effects of staff implementation of a choice program on challenging behaviors in persons with developmental disabilities. *Rehabilitation Counseling Bulletin, 37,* 347–357.

Koegel, R.L., Dyer, K., & Bell, L.K. (1987). The influence of child-preferred activities on autistic children's social behavior. *Journal of Applied Behavior Analysis, 20,* 243–252.

Kregel, J., Wehman, P., & Banks, P.D. (1989). The effects of consumer characteristics and type of employment model on individual outcomes in supported employment. *Journal of Applied Behavior Analysis, 22,* 407–415.

Lovett, H. (1991). Empowerment and choices. In L.H. Meyer, C.A. Peck, & L. Brown (Eds.), *Critical issues in the lives of people with severe disabilities* (pp. 625–626). Baltimore: Paul H. Brookes Publishing Co.

Mallas, A.A. (1976). Current workshop strengths and weaknesses. *Education and Training of the Mentally Retarded, 11,* 334–348.

Mank, D. (1994). The underachievement of supported employment: A call for reinvestment. *Journal of Disability Policy Studies, 5*(2), 1–24.

McGaughey, M.J., Kiernan, W.E., McNally, L.C., Gilmore, D.S., & Keith, G.R. (1994, April). *Beyond the workshop: National perspectives on integrated employment.* Boston: Children's Hospital, Institute for Community Inclusion.

McNair, J., & Rusch, F.R. (1991). Parent involvement in transition programs. *Mental Retardation, 29,* 93–101.

Nisbet, J. (Ed.). (1992). *Natural supports in school, at work, and in the community for people with severe disabilities.* Baltimore: Paul H. Brookes Publishing Co.

Nordlund, M.R. (1994). Transition to postsecondary education. In R.C. Savage & G.F. Wolcott (Eds.), *Educational dimensions of acquired brain injury* (pp. 507–518). Austin, TX: PRO-ED.

Omnibus Budget Reconciliation Act of 1981, PL 97-35. (August 13, 1981). Title 31, U.S.C. 1331 et seq: *U.S. Statutes at Large, 95,* 357–933.

Parent, W.S., Kregel, J., & Wehman, P. (1992). *Vocational Integration Index: Measuring the social integration of supported employment workers.* Boston: Andover Medical Publishers.

Parent, W.S., Unger, D., Gibson, K., & Clements, C. (1994). The role of the job coach: Orchestrating community and workplace supports. *Rehabilitation Administration, 20*(3), 2–11.

Parsons, M.B., Reid, D.H., & Baumgartner, M. (1990). Effects of choice versus assigned jobs on the work performance of persons with severe handicaps. *Journal of Applied Behavior Analysis, 23,* 253–260.

Rees, L.M., Spreen, O., & Harnadek, M. (1991). Do attitudes towards persons with handicaps really shift over time? Comparison between 1975 and 1988. *Mental Retardation, 29,* 81–86.

Rehabilitation Act of 1973, PL 93-112. (September 26, 1973). Title 29, U.S.C. 701 et seq: *U.S. Statutes at Large, 87,* 355–394.

Rehabilitation Act Amendments of 1986, PL 99-506. (October 21, 1986). Title 29, U.S.C. 701 et seq: *U.S. Statutes at Large, 100,* 1807–1846.

Rehabilitation Act Amendments of 1992, PL 102-569. (October 29, 1992). Title 29, U.S.C. 701 et seq: *U.S. Statutes at Large, 100,* 4344–4488.

Reid, D.H., & Parsons, M.B. (1990). Assessing food preferences among persons with profound mental retardation: Providing opportunities to make choices. *Journal of Applied Behavior Analysis, 23,* 183–195.

Reid, D.H., & Parsons, M.B. (1991). Making choice a routine part of mealtimes for persons with profound mental retardation. *Behavioral Residential Treatment, 6,* 249–261.

Sale, P., Metzler, H.M.D., Everson, J., & Moon, M.S. (1991). Quality indicators of successful vocational transition programs. *Journal of Vocational Rehabilitation, 1*(4), 47–63.

Savage, R.C. (1987). Educational issues for the head-injured adolescent and young adult. *Journal of Head Trauma Rehabilitation, 2*(1), 1–10.

Savage, R.C., & Wolcott, G.F. (1994). Overview of acquired brain injury. In R.C. Savage & G.F. Wolcott (Eds.), *Educational dimensions of acquired brain injury* (pp. 3–12). Austin, TX: PRO-ED.

Schuster, J.W. (1990). Sheltered workshops: Financial and philosophical liabilities. *Mental Retardation, 28,* 233–239.

Sinnott-Oswald, M., Gliner, J.A., & Spencer, K.C. (1991). Supported and sheltered employment: Quality of life among workers with disabilities. *Education and Training in Mental Retardation, 26,* 388–397.

Stineman, R.M., Morningstar, M.E., Bishop, B., & Turnbull, H.R. (1993). Role of families in transition planning for young adults with disabilities: Toward a method of person-centered planning. *Journal of Vocational Rehabilitation, 3*(2), 52–61.

Test, D.W., Hinson, K.B., Solow, J., & Keul, P. (1993). Job satisfaction of persons in supported employment. *Education and Training in Mental Retardation, 28,* 38–46.

Thompson, L., Powers, G., & Houchard, B. (1992). The wage effects of supported employment. *Journal of The Association for Persons with Severe Handicaps, 17,* 87–94.

Wacker, D.P., Wiggins, B., Fowler, M., & Berg, W. (1988). Training students with profound or multiple handicaps to make requests via microswitches. *Journal of Applied Behavior Analysis, 21,* 331–343.

Wehman, P. (Ed.). (1993). *The ADA mandate for social change.* Baltimore: Paul H. Brookes Publishing Co.

Wehman, P., West, M., Kregel, J., Sherron, P., & Kreutzer, J. (1995). Return to work for persons with severe traumatic brain injury: A data-based approach to program development. *Journal of Head Trauma Rehabilitation, 10*(1), 27–39.

West, M. (1995). Aspects of the workplace and return to work for supported employees with brain injuries. *Brain Injury, 9,* 301–313.

West, M., Kregel, J., Getzel, E.E., Zhu, M., Ipsen, S., & Martin, E.D. (1993). Beyond Section 504: Satisfaction and empowerment of students with disabilities in higher education. *Exceptional Children, 59*, 456–467.

Wolfe, P. (1992). Challenges for service providers. In P.J. McLaughlin & P. Wehman (Eds.), *Developmental disabilities: A handbook for best practices* (pp. 124–141). Boston: Andover Medical Publishers.

12

The Role of Self-Help and Social Support in Assisting Families

Janet M. Williams

Social support for families of children with acquired brain injury (ABI) comes from a variety of sources—professional and nonprofessional, familiar and unfamiliar. Mobilizing these resources can provide the means and tools by which families can create appropriate environments for their children.

This chapter defines social support, demonstrates the need for social support for families of children with ABI, presents a family situation, and offers four social support strategies, including family-to-family programs, self-help groups, action planning groups, and family outreach and advocacy. In addition, suggestions for professional involvement in each model are offered and implications for professionals and families aiming to incorporate social support as an integral part of the lives of children with ABI and their families are given.

This chapter is based upon three basic assumptions about families. First, families are viewed from a strengths perspective, which operates on the premise that families are competent or have the capacity to become competent (Dunst, Trivette, Gordon, & Pletcher, 1989). Second, the use of the word *family* includes the child with a brain injury. Third, social support is presented as a way to work in collaboration with professional support, not as a way to supplant professional support. In this model, families and professionals work together to seek out social support.

DEFINITION OF SOCIAL SUPPORT

All families need support to carry out their roles (Williams, 1996). When a child experiences a brain injury, the family may require social support in addition to financial and professional support. Social support includes help from families' immediate network of friends and relatives as well as from professionals. To better understand how this support can be offered, it is important to start with an understanding of the concept.

Caplan and Killilea (1976) consider social support to be attachments among individuals or between individuals and groups, that serve to promote competence in dealing with short-term crises and life transitions as well as long-term stress. Dunst et al. (1989) define social support as a multidimensional construct that includes physical and instrumental assistance, attitude transmission, and resource and information sharing, as well as emotional and psychological assistance. Both of these definitions of social support are incorporated into communities that are described by DeJong, Batavia, and Williams (1990) as whole networks of friendships, schools, religious institutions, self-help groups, and various businesses and civic organizations. McKnight (1987) further defines *community* as the structure by which social attachments and interactions, as defined by Caplan and Killelea (1976), are carried out. In short, *social support* is the support provided in communities through attachments or interactions with other people that helps families increase their competency to meet challenges (Williams, 1991b). Professionals play a vital role in social support, not as experts who fix families, but as supporters who allow families to obtain the mastery required to seek out resources and meet challenges.

THE NEED FOR SOCIAL SUPPORT

There are at least four reasons that families require social support after a child experiences a brain injury (Williams, 1991a). First, the American family is undergoing unprecedented changes (Vincent & Salisbury, 1988). The traditional nuclear family that lives among close extended kinship bonds is not as common or widespread as it was in the past. Smaller families, family members living farther apart from one another, institutions that often take on the traditional role of families, and the high cost of professional intervention (DeJong et al., 1990) all force families to look to the community for support.

Second, families need social support to bridge the gaps among service delivery systems after a member experiences a brain injury. For example, when a child returns home from the hospital or rehabilitation facility, the family will require social support and assistance while they attempt to gain access to and educate new service delivery systems. Some service systems families may require after brain injury rehabilitation treatment, such as schools or vocational rehabilitation agencies, often do not know enough about brain injury to effectively support the child without assistance (Savage, 1985). Additionally, there may be a multitude of staff involved in the planning of individualized education programs (IEPs) as a child moves from grade to grade. During each transition, it may be important for the family to have supportive people available while the new personnel become acquainted with the child and family, as continuity of history can be invaluable.

Third, all families experience life cycle changes; when combined with the stresses of brain injury, additional social support is essential. Williams (1991b) identified the following as the eight primary challenges for families after a child's brain injury:

1. Changes in the child as a result of the brain injury
2. Lack of information
3. Lack of services
4. Role changes
5. Social isolation
6. Financial stress
7. Uncertainty of the future
8. Prolonged caregiving

Professional support is not always available nor is it always the most effective intervention when one of these challenges is present in a family's life. Therefore, for most children, family and community support remain essential on a long-term basis (Beals, Mathews, Elkins, & Jacobs, 1990).

Fourth, each team of professionals participates in a child's life for only a short period of time when compared to other significant relationships in a child's life. The team members provide expertise in brain injury, intervention, and education but do not always know about the child's life, history, or home environment (Beals et al., 1990). Conversely, family and friends are with a child before, during, and after a brain injury and often live in the same community as the child. Existing significant relationships are the logical link that children—with and without disabilities—have for support.

STRATEGIES FOR SOCIAL SUPPORT

In examining strategies for social support, it is important to understand the link families have to their social environment and begin to understand ways in which the social environment may provide support to them. Through family-to-family programs, self-help groups, action planning groups, and family outreach and advocacy, families can use community resources in ways that allow them to receive social support.

The Carter family's story illustrates a common family scenario after a member experiences a brain injury. By using each of the four social supports listed above, the Carters were better able to adjust to and cope with their situation. The following section illustrates the real-life applicability of these supports.

The Carter Family At age 8, Sam was a lively second grader who loved to play pranks. One day after school he decided to hide behind a parked car and jump out to scare two of his friends. He did not see the oncoming car rounding the corner and was hit just as he began his daring prank. His sister witnessed the whole incident. Sam was flown by air ambulance to the nearest trauma center an hour from the family's home where he remained in coma for 2 months. His parents arrived soon after the flight and stayed at the hospital 6 days before returning home to regroup and take shifts at the hospital. The doctors used words like "vegetable" and "brain-dead" on a regular basis to prepare the family for the worst. For the next 3 months, there was a family member at the hospital night and day. Sam's 10-year-old sister, Julie, and his 4-year-old brother, Adam, asked many questions and were understandably confused about why they couldn't see their brother and why their parents were so upset. After 3 months, Sam was medically stable and the hospital recommended a rehabilitation program another 3 hours from the family home. Sam could mouth words and was beginning to sit up on his own and receive therapy. He was in rehabilitation for 9 months and went home in November, 3 days before the first anniversary of the incident. He could walk and talk but had slowed motor movements and could remember little of a day's events. The transition home to a hectic household that had continued without him for a year and to a school semester already underway was a great challenge for Sam, his parents, and his sister and brother.

Family-to-Family Programs

Family-to-family programs use a person's actual experience, which can be unique and yet still similar to the experience of others with the same challenges (Borkman, 1976). The approach is pragmatic rather than scientific or theoretical, oriented to the here and now, and holistic rather than totally segmented. In a family-to-family program, a family who has already gone through the cycle of recovery from ABI offers support and information to other families experiencing brain injury for the first time. O'Brien (1987) was able to benefit from this exchange of experiential knowledge and expresses its benefits as the following:

> Meeting other people who had already experienced what I was going through was enormously helpful to me. Meeting Jean Bush, for instance, was a major breakthrough. Jean and her husband, Gerry, also have a son who has experienced brain injury. The information I began to receive became a lifeline. I knew I wasn't alone. (p. 424)

The program aims to provide emotional support and information from one family member to another; it does not provide counseling or supplant professional assistance (Iscoe & Bordelon, 1985). Families find offering one-to-one support to be a way in which they can help other families and also help themselves. Family-to-family programs have been shown to be one of the most helpful supports that can be offered (Winch & Christoph, 1988). Only another family can say, "I have been there and I know what you are feeling" (Borkman, 1976). It is also mutually rewarding for families to be able to give to others. Not only do parents become involved in family-to-family programs, but matches are made among siblings, spouses, children of people with ABI, and people who have experienced brain injury themselves.

The family-to-family program formalizes the matching process so that families can meet other families as soon after an injury as possible—a service for which families are often grateful. In many situations, a formalized training program can be set up for families who want to provide family-to-family help, which allows families to learn the most supportive techniques. Training also helps to show families that they are emotionally ready to provide such support. Ongoing sessions provide on-the-job updates and brainstorming after the program has started.

Cultivation of referral sources and a systematized referral process are crucial to a successful family-to-family program. Referrals usually come from a head nurse or social worker in an intensive care unit directly linked to the program. With permission of the family whose child is in the hospital, a call is made and a trained family member is often available within 48 hours. Matches are made based upon a variety of criteria including severity of the injury, age of the child injured, and where the child lives. Often, the family member offering support simply gives the family an information packet and telephone number. The new family is encouraged to call as questions arise. This process allows families to provide help that is not intrusive.

The family-to-family program can also greatly benefit families at various points long after the initial injury. For example, as a family decides what rehabilitation hospital to use, it is helpful for them to talk to other families who have utilized the various programs available. Or if the education team has recommended a new learning technique, it is helpful for a family to contact another family who has already used the technique. And as a child returns home, families are often encouraged by talking to someone who has already negotiated that milestone. Families can always offer a different insight to help others with decision making, based upon what they have done or would have liked to have done.

Family-to-Family Programs and the Carter Family The Carter family was able to benefit from a family-to-family program. In those first uncertain days, their feelings of isolation and lack of information were decreased by Marge, the mother of a young girl with ABI. Marge sat with the Carters in the intensive care unit's waiting room to validate their feelings and give information that let them know they were not alone in their fear and uncertainty. As the Carters began to search for rehabilitation programs, other families suggested numerous programs for Sam, which provided them with the options and choices to make the most informed decision. While in rehabilitation, the Carters found others who lived a long way from the program and learned new coping strategies. As the move home approached, Carla, Sam's mother, was able to prepare the family based upon the experience of other families she met through the local Brain Injury Association. Each of these matches really helped the Carters negotiate through the systems, giving them some degree of assurance and control.

Professional Involvement in Family-to-Family Programs There are several ways that professionals can be involved in family-to-family programs. First, professionals can be constantly on the lookout for families who would benefit from a family-to-family program, as well as continually considering possible matches. Second, professionals can serve in an advisory capacity to family-to-family programs; involvement in training, grant writing, and referral are a few possible roles. Finally, professionals can encourage other professionals to make referrals to family-to-family programs to help increase the credibility of the service. Relating specific success stories and educating about the role of families in the program can help dispel fears about nonprofessional support.

The Kansas City Person-to-Person Program The Person-to-Person program of the Brain Injury Association of Kansas and greater Kansas City is one example of a successful family-to-family program (D. Delyonas, personal communication, August, 1994). With the support of the Brain Injury Association, a core group of people with ABI, families, and professionals joined to form a resource coalition available to families in hospitals in greater Kansas City. Initially, the group focused on the content of and training for the program. The training included information on brain injury, how to provide emotional support, and community resources. A packet is now given to each family that includes information on brain injury, some loose change for the telephone, and toiletries such as a toothbrush and toothpaste. Families make one initial visit and one follow-up visit. The Brain Injury Association Helpline then serves as a resource link to families.

The group's greatest initial challenge was gaining access to the hospital units. It was important that the hospital staff understand that the program is credible and worthwhile. Yet after a series of in-service meetings to answer all questions that hospital staff raised, the program started in only two area hospitals. However, support soon followed and the program is now available in six hospitals.

Self-Help Groups

Group settings can provide highly supportive environments in which families can share feelings and explore alternative ways of coping with difficult situations (Winch & Christoph, 1988). Stewart (1989), in describing social support, suggests five attributes of social support that are helpful to understand when thinking about self-help groups: attribution, coping, equity, loneliness, and social comparison. *Attribution* is a family's search for meaning and mastery in threatening events. There are few events more threatening to a family than their child experiencing brain injury. The family soon needs to find meaning in the event (e.g., Why us?) and mastery of the situation (e.g., Why can't you tell us?). *Coping* is the family's ability to draw the resources from their environment that will allow them to manage specific external and internal demands. The constant need to cope forces families to continually draw upon the same resources of family and friends for prolonged periods of time. *Equity* suggests that there is a desire to maintain equity of exchanges in relationships. Over time, families begin to question their own ability to make decisions and offer help to their family member because so many experts are available to provide help. In addition, they find few opportunities in which they can give back to professionals all that has been given to them. *Loneliness* is a subjective, unpleasant experience resulting from a perceived deficiency in social relationships or relational provisions. As families travel through many systems that are unfamiliar to their personal network of family and friends, the journey can become lonely. *Social comparison* is the tendency for people to evaluate themselves and their situation through comparisons with similar others. Seeing how others handle similar situations can help families negotiate circumstances.

All five attributes have great importance when considering the role and function of self-help groups. Families, including people with ABI, find that they can develop mastery and find meaning in their situations, develop coping strategies, have mutual and reciprocal relationships, find new social relationships to replace loneliness, and meet other people in similar situations with whom they can say, "Things are getting better." Maureen Campbell-Korves, a woman with a family member with ABI, relates her experience in a self-help group:

> By August of 1983, when the first brain injury support group meeting for the New York City region was held, I was desperate. I wanted—and needed—this meeting so badly. I found people going through pain on all levels and I found hope. I have met wonderful people willing to share what they went through and how they were coping with their ordeals. (Williams & Kay, 1991, p. 6)

There are various philosophies on the best approach to developing and maintaining self-help groups (Jacobs & Goodman, 1989; Williams, 1987). Generally, the group should be held away from a hospital setting at a time most convenient for the members, and the group should be led by an individual who has had similar life experiences to the group. Many families will not attend meetings in a hospital or rehabilitation facility because it reminds them of previous struggles and situations. The best time to hold the meeting, the site of the meeting, and the format of the meeting should be determined by surveying all members and potential members.

Leadership comes from the group itself. If the group requests a professional facilitator, the issue of maintaining group cohesion and control is important. Some groups function best when the professional fades out over time, delegating leadership and control to the members of the group with similar life experiences. Other groups choose to keep a professional facilitator present; group members may decide that coordinating a group along with all of their own family responsibilities is too much to handle at a given time.

Self-Help Groups and the Carter Family Mrs. Carter attended one self-help group meeting while Sam was in rehabilitation and several more after Sam returned home. She enjoyed the groups but found it difficult to get time away from her family. She began to think about why this happened to her family (e.g., the meaning in her situation) and found the resources she needed to help her cope with the overwhelming tasks involved in caring for Sam. Sam's father, Joe, did not attend the groups, but he did learn a lot from his wife as she shared the information presented in the group. The family's greatest frustration was in not finding a group for their other two children, especially Julie who witnessed the accident.

Professional Involvement in Self-Help Groups Generally there are five possible roles of the professional:

1. Facilitating the group
2. Providing referrals
3. Serving as guest speaker
4. Serving as group advisor
5. Creating a new group

As mentioned previously, professionals are often crucial in helping to get a group started. It is important to clarify the professional's role in the group. A common pitfall for professionals is continuing to play the traditional role of leader at this time, which may promote ongoing dependence on the professional while stifling the members' own senses of responsibility and ownership that spark the energy and dynamics of self-help groups.

Action Planning Groups

After experiencing brain injury, a child's social network increases in density over time, with a corresponding decrease in size (Kozloff, 1987). Friends, neighbors, and extended family members tend to slowly drift away and lose contact with the injured child, leaving the majority of caregiving and socialization tasks to a few people with more intense involvement (i.e., parents and siblings). Caregiving is most likely to have positive influences when it comes from people with whom the child has positive emotional ties, most notably, personal social network members (Clark, 1983). By their nature, hospitals and rehabilitation programs will not be able to provide the close personal relationships families need for several reasons. First, families seldom have time to establish long-term and lasting relationships with professionals or other families in these settings. Families often know that their stay will be short, and they may not want to invest in personal relationships that they perceive are temporary. Second, if families must travel great distances to see their child, it is difficult to focus on maintaining social ties while devoting energy to the child's rehabilitation program. And last, the very nature of rehabilitation focuses on the individual with ABI, rather than on the family—dealing with the short-term goals of individual habilitation, not the long-term circumstances families face over the life cycle. A family outreach program supports the family's long-term need to maintain personal ties while understanding the need to focus on the here and now.

Regardless of the severity of a child's brain injury or the personality and coping abilities of the family, usually the most important determinant of a family's normalization is the availability of supportive resources in the community (Seligman & Darling, 1989). O'Brien (1989) has defined this community as where a child who depends on services lives, learns, works, and plays; other crucial dimensions are the activities that fill a child's day, with whom the child becomes acquainted, and where the child belongs. Probably most important, after the experience of brain injury, is the way people, including that child, perceive that child's identity. If a child lives in an institution following therapy every day without any other aspects of life, brain injury will begin to define that child. If the child lives in the community and participates in activities with all other community members, brain injury will become only one aspect of the child's life; the child and family will begin to understand that the child is still a contributing community member.

To enhance a child's capacity to be a contributing member of a community, Dunst et al. (1989) define five strategies to enhance social support:

1. It is necessary to identify existing natural ties as well as untapped resources. These ties may include people the child has worked with in the past, school friends, or family members. New resources can be identified by first clarifying the child's current interests.
2. The identification of resources should be needs based, family identified, and consumer driven. If a family says that they need laundry detergent to help them deal with an increase in laundry, they should be provided with laundry detergent—not counseling to discuss why they are having a hard time doing the laundry.
3. A major emphasis should be placed upon building on existing family capabilities as a way of strengthening family functioning. Too often people tend to see only those families that cannot manage well and overlook the families that are learning to cope themselves.
4. The exchange of resources should occur among individuals who come together around shared interests and common causes.
5. Professionals who work with families should not mobilize resources on behalf of the families but rather should create opportunities for them to become better able to do so for themselves.

Action Planning Groups and the Carter Family As Sam's family began to realize that the rehabilitation process was going to take months rather than days, they tried to create strategies to keep all of their extended family and friends up-to-date on his progress. The family wrote monthly updates on his progress in the form of a newsletter. The newsletter included a description of his typical day and notes on how much he appreciated the mail he received. As time passed, the family sent the updates every 3 months and included messages from Sam. They found that their interaction with friends became easier over time because people began to understand the consequences of Sam's brain injury. Rather than offering generic support, friends offered creative options for support. When he was ready to return home, the family sent an update and wish list of items and supports they needed. They were happily surprised to find that all of the people who said they wanted to help came through at the time of discharge from rehabilitation. This is one of many creative strategies a family–professional collaboration can accomplish by anticipating the known stressors families face over time. It can begin while a child is in the hospital and continue as the child returns to the community.

Now that the Carter family is back in the community, a program to enhance and build relationships is crucial. Developing a group of friends that consists of people concerned about Sam has helped him to participate in the community and see himself not as a brain-injured child, but as a child who has experienced brain injury. It also has provided a basis of support for the family to rely on during the transitions ahead. A few friends from school who were close with Sam before the crash were brought together to understand how they could help Sam; a few teachers from school and a few members of the family's church were also included. Sam had just joined a scouting troop before the incident and the troop leader also gladly became involved. The group met casually at the family's house and concentrated on figuring out how Sam could be involved in the same kinds of activities and relationships other children his age participate in. Sam is involved in all of the meetings and on occasion his brother and sister sit in. The group meets monthly and has some creative strategies and solutions to the challenges Sam faces.

Professional Involvement in Action Planning Groups A program that truly seeks to build on community ties creates a provocative and challenging role for professionals. Professionals do not serve in the traditional role of paid counselor or therapist; rather, they bring their unique skills to the circle as a friend or volunteer just as any other circle member. For example, a person who works as a counselor by profession may choose to be a friend to a child with ABI and offer skills that support the child. At the same time, he or she can step out of the role of professional and truly have a friendship with the child. Professionals can also work to support families to problem-solve by talking with them about their options and choices. Instead of doing for the family, the professional supports the family to do for themselves. Knowing that families may experience social isolation and loss of support from extended family and friends, professionals can begin early to help the family maintain these important ties. Additionally, professionals can offer support in enlisting additional help.

Family Outreach and Advocacy

The development of family advocacy groups is an important factor in the overall development of family support for people with ABI and their families. The growth of the Brain Injury Association and its state associations is indicative of the ability of family advocacy to create solutions for families beyond their own personal situations. Marty Beaver, a mother of a child with ABI, relates her experience:

> It was during that time I learned of the National Head Injury Foundation (NHIF [now known as the Brain Injury Association]), a newly formed organization for survivors of brain injury and their families. I sent in my membership and shared my trials of lack of resources and understanding. I attended a conference on brain injury and, after meeting Marilyn Spivack, came back to Georgia with the commitment to begin an NHIF chapter. I was soon put in touch with two other family members who shared my frustrations. Together we started the Georgia Head Injury Foundation. When not working full time, caring for two children, or visiting my husband, I was talking to people, groups, and sending out information about head injury and its consequences. (Williams & Kay, 1991, pp. 21–22)

There are many issues that prompt families to become involved in advocacy organizations. For the most part families seek to make changes in a system that did not provide what they needed at a crucial time. Some families choose drinking and driving as an important issue; others choose seatbelt laws or the development of community-based services as their personal crusades. The desires to make changes in the system and give back what was given to them provide the motivation to make important contributions to other families and professionals.

Family Outreach and Advocacy and the Carter Family For the Carters, both outreach and advocacy are important to the family. Mr. and Mrs. Carter have tried to be involved in providing some of the supports that were provided to them. Mr. Carter attended a self-help group meeting where someone from the local Brain Injury Association spoke about the programs of the organization. Mrs. Carter is now available to other families through the family-to-family program. In addition, Mr. Carter has become involved in some legislative testimony for increased funding for community programs he knows his son will need in the future.

Professional Involvement in Family Outreach and Advocacy As in self-help groups, professionals can serve several roles in family outreach and advocacy. However, here professionals work side by side with families. For example, with legislative testimony, the professional may coach the parent on procedure and demeanor but it is ultimately the experience of the family member that is critical in demonstrating the experience of brain injury. In other instances, such as organizing a conference or holding a fund-raiser, there is no need to distinguish one role from the other—parents and professionals act as equal partners. The specialized talents individuals can bring to advocacy groups help make the combined effort effective.

CONCLUSION

All families seek a sense of balance in their lives, often by working toward control, predictability, and opportunity. When a member of the family experiences brain injury, any sense of control and predictability is usually destroyed, at least for the immediate future. For families to gain the mastery and predictability they need, they require a strong social support network. Traditionally, families have been forced to rely on professional support during rehabilitation and on social support once professional support has ended. Social support should be mobilized with professional support immediately after brain injury through the use of family-to-family programs, self-help groups, action planning groups, and family outreach and advocacy. As families acquire the skills to mobilize resources, they will begin to create their own social support. It is this family-enlisted social support that will enable them to succeed.

REFERENCES

Beals, M.P., Mathews, R.M., Elkins, S.R., & Jacobs, H.E. (1990). Locating community resources. *Journal of Head Trauma Rehabilitation, 5*(1), 31–39.

Borkman, T. (1976, September). Experiential knowledge: A new concept for the analysis of self-help groups. *Social Service Review,* 445–456.

Caplan, G., & Killilea, M. (1976). *Support systems and mutual help.* New York: Grune and Stratton.

Clark, M. (1983). Reactions to aid in communal and exchange relationships. In J.D. Fisher, A. Nadler, & B.M. DePaulo (Eds.), *New directions in helping: Recipient reactions to aid* (Vol. 1, pp. 281–304). New York: Academic Press.

DeJong, G., Batavia, A.I., & Williams, J.M. (1990). Who is responsible for the lifelong well-being of a person with a head injury? *Journal of Head Trauma Rehabilitation, 5*(1), 9–12.

Dunst, C.J., Trivette, C.M., Gordon, N.J., & Pletcher, L.L. (1989). Building and mobilizing informal family support networks. In G.H.S. Singer & L.K. Irvin

(Eds.), *Support for caregiving families: Enabling positive adaptation to disability* (pp. 121–141). Baltimore: Paul H. Brookes Publishing Co.

Iscoe, L., & Bordelon, K. (1985). Pilot parents: Peer support for parents of handicapped children. *Children's Health Care, 14*(2), 103–109.

Jacobs, M.K., & Goodman, G. (1989). Psychology and self-help groups. *American Psychologist, 44*(3), 536–545.

Kozloff, R. (1987). Networks of social support and the outcome of severe head injury. *Journal of Head Trauma Rehabilitation, 2*(3), 14–23.

McKnight, J. (1987). Regenerating community. *Social Policy, 6,* 18–26.

O'Brien, B. (1987). A letter to professionals who work with head-injured people. In M. Ylvisaker & E.M. Gobble (Eds.), *Community reentry for head-injured adults* (pp. 421–430). Boston: College-Hill Press.

O'Brien, J. (1989). *What's worth working for? Leadership for better quality human services.* Lithonia, GA: Responsive Systems Associates.

Savage, R.C. (1985). *A survey of traumatically brain-injured children within school-based special education programs.* Rutland, VT: Head Injury / Stroke Independence Project.

Seligman, M., & Darling, R.B. (1989). *Ordinary families, special children: A systems approach to childhood disability.* New York: Guilford Press.

Stewart, M. (1989). Social support: Diverse theoretical perspectives. *Social Science and Medicine, 28*(12), 1275–1282.

Vincent, L., & Salisbury, C.L. (1988). Changing economic and social influences on family involvement, *TE CSE, 8*(1), 48–59.

Williams, J.M. (1987). *Head injury support groups.* Southborough, MA: National Head Injury Foundation.

Williams, J.M. (1991a). Family reaction to head injury. In J.M. Williams & T. Kay (Eds.), *Head injury: A family matter* (pp. 81–100). Baltimore: Paul H. Brookes Publishing Co.

Williams, J.M. (1991b). Family support. In J.M. Williams & T. Kay (Eds.), *Head injury: A family matter* (pp. 299–312). Baltimore: Paul H. Brookes Publishing Co.

Williams, J.M. (1996). The relative nature of brain injury. In G.H.S. Singer, L.E. Powers, & A.L. Olson (Eds.), *Redefining family support: Innovations in public–private partnerships.* Baltimore: Paul H. Brookes Publishing Co.

Williams, J.M., & Kay, T. (Eds.). (1991). *Head injury: A family matter.* Baltimore: Paul H. Brookes Publishing Co.

Williams, J.M., & Savage, R.C. (1991). Family, culture, and child development. In J.M. Williams & T. Kay (Eds.), *Head injury: A family matter* (pp. 219–238). Baltimore: Paul H. Brookes Publishing Co.

Winch, A.E., & Christoph, J.M. (1988). Parent-to-parent links: Building networks for parents of hospitalized children. *Children's Health Care, 17*(2), 93–97.

13

Stress Management Training to Help Parents Adapt to a Child's ABI

George H.S. Singer
and Laurie E. Powers

This chapter, which describes a group intervention to help parents of children with acquired brain injury (ABI) cope with stress, is based on a set of studies conducted with parents of children with severe disabilities and parents of children with acquired brain injury (Singer et al., 1994; Singer, Irvin, & Hawkins, 1988; Singer, Irvin, Hawkins, & Cooley, 1989). The chapter presents a contemporary theory of stress and coping, briefly touching upon the stressors that family members encounter when a child experiences a brain injury. It describes the content of a stress management training class for parents and reviews recent evidence for the efficacy of this approach to helping parents.

STRESS COPING

Everyone is familiar with stress. A Harris Poll found that 89% of all adult Americans report experiencing high stress (Harris, 1987). Of

The research reported in this chapter was funded in part by Grant #HO86P90023 from the U.S. Department of Education, Office of Special Education and Rehabilitative Services. The views expressed herein do not necessarily reflect those of the funders.

them, 59% said that they experienced great stress at least once or twice a week, and 30% reported living with high stress every day. The concept of stress in the popular vernacular as well as in the voluminous literature is often vague, encompassing many different meanings. One way to understand what people typically mean by "stress" is to ask them how stress manifests itself. Harris reported that 26% of the respondents said stress led to a seizure of nervousness, anxiety, and tension. Another 24% said they got headaches as a result of stress, while 19% experienced anger and irritation in response to stress. An additional 11% explained that stress was accompanied by a sense of depression. Other symptoms of stress that Harris reported were muscle aches, stomachaches, an overall feeling of upset, an increased heartbeat, insomnia and loss of sleep, a rise in blood pressure, a feeling of frustration, crying, sweating, yelling and screaming, compulsive eating, and loss of appetite (Harris, 1987).

Although there is not one universal definition of stress, most people seem to have a shared concept of events and circumstances that pose difficulties and often result in a set of interrelated unpleasant physical, cognitive, and emotional reactions that are interpreted as stress. Still, stress remains a diffuse and broad concept that is associated with a variety of different reactions. Instead of causing a specific set of symptoms, it is associated with many different symptoms that tend to be physical and emotional states that people do not typically prefer compared to feelings of rest, enjoyment, relaxation, pleasant excitement, and the other hedonic states.

Stoyva and Carlson (1993) have presented one theory that explains stress and its array of symptoms, arguing that human physiological functioning is characterized by a rhythmic alteration between states of activation and states of rest. When faced with a challenge from the environment, people characteristically react with elevated arousal. The neuroendocrine system is central to these activated states. Considerable evidence indicates that stress is marked by elevated blood levels of adrenaline and other hormones that function to place the body on full alert. Although extreme alertness has an important function, the body maintains this state at considerable cost. Sustained arousal is associated with rapid heart rate, sleep loss, disruption of short-term memory, and depression of immune functioning. In regard to arousal, a little of a good thing goes a long way and too much of a good thing exacts a high price. In fact, a number of serious physical and emotional conditions are associated with long-term stress.

Stoyva and Carlson (1993) also argue that states of restful alertness function as modes of recovery from stress. They review several traditional practices from both Western and Eastern cultures that promote states of restful alertness. For example, in laboratory studies biofeedback has been effective in relieving stress-related symptoms such as tension headaches. People learn to relax head and shoulder muscles and sustain a relaxed state. Similarly, meditation practices from several cultures produce a state of wakeful, but calm, alertness in which respiration and the heart rate slow and the brain's electrical functioning changes from rapid disorganized patterns to slower, more regular wave-like patterns. Hormonal secretions become more regular and levels of blood cortisols decline. Uncontrolled and unpredictable aversive events are more stressful than controllable events for both laboratory animals and humans. Practices such as biofeedback or meditation provide people with tools that allow them to have more control over their own responses to difficult circumstances. This combination of restfulness and control seems to serve as a counterweight to stressful, uncontrollable events.

STRESS AND A CHILD'S BRAIN INJURY

It is evident that a brain injury is stressful for the entire family. Parental accounts of children's brain injuries are replete with the most difficult kinds of experiences. The following three types of stressors stand out from these accounts:

1. Trauma and its immediate aftermath
2. Grief and the need for cognitive adjustment to a changed child
3. Ongoing disruption of typical living routines

A child's brain injury typically begins with an accident. Severe brain injury almost always entails the possibility of death from the trauma or its complications and the immediate aftermath of the injurious event usually takes place in hospital emergency rooms and intensive care units. These experiences evoke in parents and many siblings the most extreme kinds of hyperalertness, anxiety, and emotional disruption.

Recovery from coma and the return of functioning is an unpredictable and largely uncontrollable set of processes. As a child emerges from coma and enters a prolonged period of rehabilitation, parents and other family members must come to terms with a changed child—often a slow and difficult process that can tax coping resources in the extreme. A child can regain lost skills and abilities for many months and even years after the trauma so that the extent of the change is ill-defined for a long time. Eventually, however, family members must completely reconcile the dramatic changes in the child's personality, behavior, and expectations regarding the child's future; grief is a common and natural part of this accommodation. In addition, family members must grapple with the sense of loss of the former child while accepting a changed person in their midst—a highly stressful cognitive and emotional process. This kind of stress is different from the practical challenges that beset the family in that it is centered on the cognitive and emotional problems of meaning and acceptance.

The third form of stress that families encounter consists of the many ongoing practical hassles that brain injury entails. These may include paying enormous medical bills, arranging transportation to therapy sessions, working out an appropriate school plan, assisting the injured child with adaptive skills, and dealing with the child's behavior problems.

In the process of caring for a child's brain injury, many typical relationships, family customs, and routines often get set aside. Accustomed practices for relaxing and socializing with others can erode as parents focus on the injured child's needs. These leisure-time activities are the ones that provide states of rest that, according to Stoyva and Carlson (1993), are so necessary for physical and mental recovery from stress. By the time parents seek help from a counselor or support group, some of them are worn out and experiencing the consequences of prolonged stress, including anxiety, depression, disrupted sleep, and physical symptoms such as headaches, repeated colds or infections, and other stress-related symptoms.

PSYCHOEDUCATIONAL SUPPORT GROUPS

The social and emotional support services offered to families with a member with ABI ought to include ways to help families deal with stress. One type of support group emphasizes skill training and education. The psychoeducational support group's purpose is to teach coping skills in an environment where parents can also learn from one another and share common concerns and feelings. Theorists who have studied self-help groups agree that one of the important functions of groups is to allow participants to develop new norms of behavior (Katz, 1993). A norm is a social standard for how to behave. Groups also provide parents with ways to think about new situations that are often outside the bounds of their experience or that of anyone they know.

In the authors' experience, many parents of children with ABI seem to believe that they should expect themselves to be unstinting in their caregiving and to give little concern for their own well-being while faced with the crisis brought on by a child's brain injury. An initial pattern of extreme commitment—to the point of exhaustion—is sometimes established during the acute phase of hospitalization when parents understandably wish to be at their child's bedside around the clock. Parents may forget to eat meals, rarely go out for walks, and are often too distressed to keep in touch with friends or other sources of social support. In two-parent families, the demands of hospitalization sometimes put a severe strain on the marriage because of the high stress and need to be apart for extended periods of time.

As the child's recovery progresses, often the initial pattern of extreme commitment continues. There is little time or social support for self-care, and changing this pattern is not simple. The demands of the child's care are so compelling and the unwritten norm that parents should first and foremost attend to their injured child is so strong that efforts to persuade parents to take time for themselves and their other family members are sometimes futile.

The dynamics of self-help groups are particularly helpful in addressing the kinds of problems that require standards of behavior to change in order to make the caregiving arrangement sustainable on a long-term basis. A helpful feature of these support groups is the inclusion of parents at all different stages of trauma and recovery. For example, parents who have already undergone the reintegration of their child into their home and neighborhood school are sometimes able to convey a sense of perspective about ABI to more inexperienced families (see Chapter 12). Parents are far more likely to serve as effective models for each other than professionals because of their commonality of experience and their immersion in the day-to-day lived reality of caregiving.

In a psychoeducational support group, the power of shared experiences can be harnessed to teach parents new self-care skills. The psychoeducational orientation means that group meetings are designed as learning experiences. Meetings are advertised as stress management classes and the group leaders present lectures and demonstrations and assign homework. This orientation contrasts with support groups where the emphasis is mostly on the expression of emotion and the sharing of emotional support. In the psychoeducational groups, parents do talk openly about their difficulties and are often highly expressive, but the context places emphasis on effective ways to cope with adversity and take care of oneself in the middle of extremely challenging circumstances. Most important, the group can help parents to accept a new norm for caregiving behavior: They will take care of their injured child and their family most effectively if they also take care of themselves. This norm is communicated as a meta-message while the group focuses on learning and practicing specific stress management skills.

The stress management classes meet eight times, usually once a week, and aim to teach the following skills:

- Self-monitoring
- Progressive muscle relaxation (PMR)
- Brief forms of relaxation in natural settings
- Cognitive coping and modulating emotions
- Utilization of social support

Each class lasts for 2 hours. Classes have been held in rehabilitation hospitals, community centers, and psychology clinics. A professional psychologist, clinical social worker, or counselor leads the groups, but they can be co-led by an experienced parent who has taken the course previously.

Each class begins with a brief lecture about a new coping skill. The leader then demonstrates the skill and leads the group through an example of its application. The second half of the meeting is devoted to a review of the previous week's homework. Because the homework always involves keeping a brief daily diary, this portion of the meeting gives parents a chance to talk about difficult experiences, share practical solutions, and support one another emotionally. Because the emphasis is on coping skills, whenever a parent describes a difficult experience, the leader asks for information about how the parent coped with the situation. She also asks other parents if they have encountered similar problems and, if so, what they found helpful. In this way, the emphasis stays on adaptation. This emphasis on coping prevents the group meetings from becoming demoralizing.

The following discussion reviews each of the main coping strategies that make up the stress management curriculum.

Self-Monitoring

The stress management course begins by teaching parents self-monitoring skills. Parents learn to keep a brief diary of daily stressors and successful coping efforts. They keep this log during the 8 weeks of the course and are invited to share their notations during each meeting. Prior to using self-monitoring skills, many parents are not able to identify the specific circumstances or times of the day that are stressful. Monitoring allows them to identify recurrent stressors. When parents identify situations that are repeatedly stressful, the instructor and the group offer suggestions for coping with them. As the course progresses, the instructor recommends ways of applying stress management skills to deal with these situations. The instructor is careful not to make exaggerated claims about the power of individual coping efforts. Often she will say, "The circumstances that you are describing would be difficult for anyone. I don't have any way to make them go away or remove the pain you feel. However, sometimes by making small changes you can at least take the edge off and make these situations more bearable and easier to endure." This attitude protects the parents from feeling that their challenges are being minimized.

Parents have reported many different kinds of stressful situations. Mothers commonly report that two times of day are particularly difficult: the hour before children go to school in the morning and the hour before dinner. In both of these instances, the primary caregiver is under time pressure to perform multiple tasks—her attention is divided among competing activities, making these prime settings for problem behaviors. When parents identify a particular daily routine as stressful, the group leader encourages a wide-ranging approach to problem solving. For example, she might recommend one family purchase a microwave oven to reduce the time in meal preparation; for another, she might recommend a behavior management intervention.

Another example of a recurrent stressful situation often reported in the diaries involves going out in public places with a child who has ABI. Parents report a variety of unpleasant social interactions with strangers, including staring, unwanted questions, rude comments, or intrusive advice. The group members often have several practical coping strategies to recommend. In addition, the leader—usually later in the course—will recommend using cognitive coaching and brief relaxation to cope with these situations.

One feature of the self-monitoring procedure is very important: In addition to noting and reporting stressful events, parents are asked to share anything they did to cope. They rate the efficacy of their coping responses on a scale. The group leader, and eventually the other group members, make a point of praising and encouraging effective coping responses. Again, this emphasis helps to create a productive and optimistic tone in the class.

Another factor that contributes to a positive tone is the selection of group participants. It is helpful to include a few members in the group who have already made some progress in adjusting to their child's brain injury. The presence of these more experienced parents provides a model for the other group members and lends veracity to the group leader's implicit claim that a difficult, even tragic, life circumstance can become less painful and, at least partially, be interpreted in a positive light. Clinical experience suggests that some parents come to terms with their child's disability and find valuable lessons learned and abilities developed.

Progressive Muscle Relaxation

As previously discussed, the prolonged activation of the neuroendocrine system that is associated with stress can lead to negative physical and emotional outcomes. Periods of rest allow for recovery and reduce stress-related disease. Several ways of relaxing have been studied for their benefits. Methods as diverse as transcendental meditation, progressive muscle relaxation, controlled diaphragmatic breathing, autogenic training, biofeedback, stretching, and mindfulness meditation have been effective in controlled studies of stress-related problems such as insomnia, low back pain, anxiety, and depressive symptoms (Woolfolk & Lehrer, 1984).

One of the best researched of these methods is progressive muscle relaxation (PMR). Developed by Jacobson (1938) in the first half of the 20th century, PMR has been used as a regular component of behavior therapies for phobias, posttraumatic stress disorder, social anxiety, and stress-related illness. PMR consists of alternatively tensing and relaxing major muscle groups. For example, in the stress management classes, parents are taught to tense the muscles of their hands, arms, and shoulders by making fists and bringing them to their shoulders while tightening the muscles of their arms. They are asked to feel the tension and then slowly open their hands and let their arms and hands settle to a resting position. They concentrate on the physical sensation of relaxation as it replaces the feeling of muscle tension. Parents are instructed to alternate between tension and relaxation in all of their major muscle groups (i.e., head, neck and shoulders, arms, torso, lower body, legs and feet). After 20 minutes of PMR, they are instructed to use guided imagery to visualize a place where they feel safe and restored. Guided visualizing adds a cognitive element to the relaxation practice that allows some people to calm their thoughts and feelings.

After this first instructional class, the leader guides the group through a session of PMR at each meeting. In order to facilitate its learning and encourage its use, parents are provided with tape-recorded PMR instructions and loaned tape recorders if they do not have them at home. Also, if necessary, the taped instructions are translated into the family's first language. The tape serves as a guide through a 20-minute relaxation session. Parents are asked to commit to practicing by listening to the tapes for as many sessions as they can work into their schedule. In order to keep a record of how the sessions felt and any difficulties they encountered, parents are provided with a data form that asks them to rate their state of relaxation before and after listening to the tape and practicing PMR.

The classes emphasize that progressive muscle relaxation is a skill, much like learning to swim or shoot baskets. It requires repeated practice until it begins to induce a pleasant, restful state. Often busy parents need to discuss and carefully plan times to practice. The authors suggest a time when distractions are at a minimum—often this means early in the morning or late at night. Taking the telephone off the hook and turning off the radio or television is also a good idea, although some people prefer to play music as they practice.

Progressive muscle relaxation can be, at least initially, counterproductive for a small number of people. It can lower internal defenses and lead to heightened feelings of anxiety or other suppressed emotions. If PMR makes someone uncomfortable, he should call the group leader and arrange to meet with her in order to assess the nature and possible causes of the discomfort. Some people are able to work through relaxation-induced anxiety by persevering with the procedure. Others find it too uncomfortable and, for them, alternative ways to relax are recommended.

Using Short Forms of PMR in Daily Settings In order to make relaxation a portable coping response that can be used in daily life, parents are gradually introduced to the short forms of relaxation. However, these methods are usually not very useful until class members have developed some proficiency in the longer form of PMR. They must have some memory of how it feels to release tension before they are likely to develop proficiency at relaxing in the middle of challenging events. In order to teach relaxation as an active coping skill, parents are provided with colored stickers and advised to place them in locations where they are likely to feel stress, such as above the kitchen stove, on the telephone, on a computer screen at work, or on the car steering wheel. The colored marker is meant to serve as a reminder to scan for tension, breath deeply, tense and release a muscle group such as the hand or the shoulder muscles, and coach oneself to relax. Again, class members are provided with self-monitoring forms to keep track of when they use this short form of relaxation and how well it works for them.

Encouraging Familiar Forms of Relaxation In addition to encouraging them to develop new relaxation skills, parents are also asked to do an inventory of their current activities and are invited to talk about those activities that give them a sense of rest and recovery. These commonly include talking with friends, taking baths, running, reading, going for walks, and enjoying hobbies. Often, parents have had enjoyable activities as part of their schedule in the past but have lost these pastimes to the time demands of caregiving. To reestablish these healthy habits, participants are asked to make a commitment to engage in a relaxing activity in addition to practicing PMR. They report on these other recreations each week as a way of supporting behavior change.

The discussion of informal forms of stress relief occasions a brief discussion about alcohol and other drug use. Group leaders should point out that sometimes people under ongoing stress will develop forms of stress management that are, in the long run, unhealthy. They should suggest that, if people are using substances to relax, they take care to examine how much and how often they are consuming alcohol and other drugs. In order to maintain the emphasis on skills training rather than therapy, parents are told that they may talk to the group leaders privately if they would like to talk about their substance use. The group leader should be trained in conducting screening interviews for alcohol and other drug addiction and should be prepared to refer participants for treatment.

Grieving: Cognitive Coping and Modulating Emotions

Qualitative research (see Chapter 2) as well as clinical experience indicate that many parents experience grief at the change that ABI causes in their injured child. Children with severe brain injuries usually undergo dramatic personality changes, particularly with respect to social and emotional behaviors. The process of family accommodation to ABI involves a gradual acceptance of the child's changed cognitive, physical, and social-emotional status. Because children can regain skills, learn new ones, and develop ways of accommodating to their disabilities, the child's postinjury condition poses considerable uncertainty. Family members may not be able to easily characterize their injured relatives because their statuses change so rapidly. This kind of uncertainty or ambiguity can impede cognitive adaptation to the changed child.

Cognitive Coping *Cognitive adaptation* refers to the intellectual and emotional process of coming to terms with a child's disability. Successful adaptation is marked by a realistic sense of acceptance. Although difficult emotions such as fear, shame, and sorrow may arise, they do not dominate the emotions of one who has cognitively adapted. Often adaptation involves giving a meaning to the child's injury that is consonant with a belief system that the parent held prior to the trauma. For some parents, the belief system is religious; for others, it may be a more homespun, secular philosophy.

In order to encourage the process of cognitive adaptation, group leaders work to stimulate discussions of the meanings that parents give to living with a child with ABI. Many people are not used to thinking about their own cognitive processes; therefore, the class should begin with examples of how thought mediates experience. Give numerous examples such as the following vignette about two friends, which illustrates that one's thinking about a situation can shape emotion and affect perception.

> You encounter a friend at the grocery store. She walks right past you without saying hello. You start to worry that she is angry at you and you begin searching through your memory to see what you might have done to offend her. Finally, you call her on the telephone and she laughs and explains that she had lost her contact lenses that morning and didn't see you clearly enough to recognize you.

After hearing several examples, the class members are asked to keep a diary during the week of stressful situations and the ways they think about them. These diary excerpts often provide vivid glimpses into parents' thinking processes. As the class progresses, parents are asked to add to their diaries cognitive coping statements that they employ in stressful situations. The diaries are the focus for discussions during some of the classes and afford an opportunity for parents to learn from one another about effective ways to cope with daily stressors.

Two class sessions are devoted to identifying negative self-statements associated with daily stress and countering them with positive coping statements. In order to give the reader an understanding of this cognitive component of cognitive behavioral intervention, data are presented from a study conducted by Singer, Cooley, and Hawkins (1989). Table 1 presents excerpts from the diaries of 36 parents of children with severe disabilities who participated in the 8-week stress management classes. In order to develop a profile of the kinds of negative cognition and counterstrategies that parents learned to deploy, a content analysis of the parents' stress management diaries was conducted for the information in Tables 2, 3, and 4. Table 2 presents the coding categories derived for the stressor entries. Table 3 presents the coding categories for negative thoughts in response to stressful events, while Table 4 presents codes for positive coping statements. In all, 99 entries were coded. These entries primarily illustrate parental responses to daily hassles. They do not directly address cognitive coping in regard to the larger issue of grief.

Based on her work with bereaved parents and widows, Powers (1993) contributed a set of structured discussions and homework exercises aimed at encouraging parents to consciously grapple with the larger questions of loss and meaning that a child's ABI raises for many parents. It uses a modified version of the ABC format illustrated in Table 1, which concerns stressors of relatively small, daily events—commonly referred to as *hassles*. For the discussion of coping with

Table 1. The ABC log

A Stressful situation	B Negative thoughts	C Positive coping self-statements
Child gets sick in the car.	If I wasn't in such a hurry to leave, this wouldn't have happened.	Just change him. He will be better soon.
Erica stayed out late and was drinking.	Where have I gone wrong? Maybe one parent is not enough.	She is trying her wings. This may have little to do with me.
Sarah was carrying a bowl with milk to the table. She poured it on the floor.	Why me? Why do I let small things bother me so much?	I need to calm myself. It wasn't that big of a deal.
I am doing housework.	I'll never get all the work done.	Take a break. Start again more calmly.
People are watching while my child has an attack of coughing.	It's never going to quit.	Relax until she's done coughing. Carry on. Don't worry about them.
My boss is being sarcastic and putting me down.	What's wrong with me?	He must be antsy today. It's his problem. I know the truth of the matter.
Mike is sick with a bad cough.	He could be seriously sick. I'm anxious.	Every time he gets sick, it isn't necessarily critical. Think over the symptoms. They don't seem that bad. Calm down.
I did not receive the support check when it was due.	I'll always have this problem. I feel tense and hopeless.	I'll work out a plan that I think will succeed for getting the check.
Bill screamed in the car with my sister and nieces.	He's doing it on purpose. He wants to embarrass me.	I decided to let my sister drive. I sat in the back with Bill, which made him happy. We had a great day.

Source: Singer, Cooley, and Hawkins (1989).

Table 2. Stressful situations

Category	Definition	Number of entries
Child problem behaviors	Aberrant behavior exhibited by a child with disabilities, including whining, fighting, hyperactivity, and self-injurious behavior	21
Child caregiving demands	Assistance provided to a child with a disability for an activity of daily living, including eating, dressing, toileting, grooming, and cleaning	3
Child medical problems	Minor or major illness or medical appointments, including dental visits for children with or without disabilities	7
Child-centered meetings	Meetings concerning the child with disabilities with school personnel, service coordinators, and other nonmedical professionals	4
Finances	Problems with money, bills, or taxes	2
Environment	Concerns about the weather, pollution, or neighborhood crime	1
Intimacy	Problems with spouse or other cohabitating adult	2
Medical issues	Illness, dental or doctor appointments not related to the child with disabilities	8
Household problems	Concerns about cleaning or maintenance of the household, including cooking, cleaning, repairs, and the breakdown of automobiles	14
Work	Problems arising at the place of employment	11
Child problems	Difficulties associated with raising a child without disabilities	14
N/A	Items that cannot be coded by other categories	12
Total		99

Source: Singer, Cooley, and Hawkins (1989).

Table 3. Negative thoughts

Category	Definition	Number of entries
Negative view of self	Self-criticisms, derogatory or self-deprecating comments	41
Negative view of one's experience or others	Complaints or negative comments about a situation or other people	42
Negative view of the future	Negative comments about the future or long-term continuation of a difficult situation	11
Uncodable		5
Total		99

grief, the idea that there are larger-level stressors and more expansive categories of both negative and positive cognition relating to these larger issues is introduced. Parents are then asked to share what meanings they give to their child's injury and disabilities. Although some parents have not previously thought about these questions, typically, several parents will have developed well-thought-out points of view. Here again, the group format provides an opportunity for sharing private material that would be otherwise unavailable to parents.

Modulating Emotions Cognitive coping is only partly a matter of self-statements. There is also a large emotional component to the cognitive adaptation process. Again, based on her clinical work with bereaved parents, Powers (1993) has emphasized the importance of modulating strong emotion in the grieving process. Parents of children with ABI may experience periods of overwhelming emotion in which feelings of sorrow or anger dominate their consciousness. In addition, there is no particular statute of limitations on these feelings: Some parents may experience them intensely during the period immediately following the child's injury whereas others may experience these feelings many years later. Based on their clinical experience, the authors believe that it is important for parents to allow themselves to fully feel these emotions as well as develop ways to compartmentalize them so that they do not disrupt daily living for prolonged periods of time. In the classes, the value of allowing oneself to feel is discussed, as well as viewing the emotions as something that can—at least to a limited extent—be managed. The recommended method for managing the strong emotions associated with grieving is modulation of feelings. It is suggested that parents allow themselves a special time and place each day to feel their grief-associated emotions. For example, one be-

Table 4. Coping statements

Category	Definition	Number of entries
Taking action	Statements about performing actions on the environment in order to alter the unpleasant situation, problem solving	16
Reframing	Redefining a difficult situation or interpretation of the situation in a more rational and acceptable way in order to make it more manageable	65
Relaxing	Deciding to take action upon oneself to relax tense muscles or alter other physiological reactions, including progressive muscle relaxation, resting, or taking a break from a difficult situation	10
Passive appraisal	Ignoring a problem, setting it aside, deciding to "let it pass" or to "ride it out"	0
Uncodable		8
Total		99

reaved mother talked about how she allowed herself to cry while taking a shower in the morning and then set aside the feelings when she went to work. If class members report that they are having great difficulty in coping with daily life because of overwhelming emotions that are not lessened by stress management methods, they are often spoken to privately and referred to individual or couples' counseling as more intensive therapeutic intervention is needed.

CONCLUSION: EVALUATION DATA

A series of studies of stress management training have been conducted as an intervention for parents of children with severe disabilities including the aftereffects of ABI (Singer et al., 1988). In a 1994 study, the efficacy of two kinds of support groups for parents of children with ABI were compared (Singer et al., 1994). One group of parents participated in the 8-week stress management class described above. A second group participated in a support group that emphasized information about ABI and emotional coping. Parents were randomly assigned, and both groups met for equal lengths of time. Outcomes were measured on the Beck Depression Inventory (Beck, Steer, & Garbin, 1988) and the State-Trail Anxiety Inventory (Spielberger, Gorsuch, & Lushene, 1970). There were seven parents in the stress management group and eight in the information- and emotion-focused group.

The parents in the stress management group showed significant reductions in self-reported depression and anxiety, whereas the parents in the other group actually experienced an increase in symptoms. The authors caution that this study should be viewed as a preliminary investigation because the small number of subjects and the fact that married couples participated in the groups pose threats to the statistical validity of the study. However, this series of studies on the efficacy of stress management training with parents of children with multiple disabilities can be reasonably assumed to hold real promise for assisting parents of children with ABI as they encounter the many challenges associated with a disabling brain injury. In summary, support groups that focus on coping skills aimed at helping parents take care of themselves can be an effective part of family support services.

REFERENCES

Beck, A.T., Steer, R.A., & Garbin, M.G. (1988). Psychometric properties of the Beck Depression Inventory: Twenty-five years of evaluation. *Clinical Psychology Review, 8,* 77–100.

Harris, L. (1987). *Inside America.* New York: Vintage.

Jacobson, E. (1938). *Progressive muscle relaxation* (2nd ed.). Chicago: University of Chicago Press.

Katz, A.H. (1993). *Self-help in America: A social movement perspective.* New York: Twayne Publishers.

Powers, L.E. (1993). Grief and disability. In G.H.S. Singer & L.E. Powers (Eds.), *Families, disability, and empowerment: Active coping skills and strategies for family interventions* (pp. 119–150). Baltimore: Paul H. Brookes Publishing Co.

Singer, G.H.S., Cooley, W.C., & Hawkins, N.K. (1989). *Parents of children with disabilities: Cognitive distress and coping.* Unpublished manuscript, Oregon Research Institute.

Singer, G.H.S., Glang, A., Nixon, C., Cooley, E., Kerns, K., Williams, D., & Powers, L. (1994). A comparison of two psychosocial interventions for parents of children with acquired brain injury: An exploratory study. *Journal of Head Trauma Rehabilitation, 9*(4), 38–49.

Singer, G.H.S., Irvin, L.K., & Hawkins, N.K. (1988). Stress management training for parents of children with severe handicaps. *Mental Retardation, 26*(5), 269–277.

Singer, G.H.S., Irvin, L.K., Hawkins, N.K., & Cooley E. (1989). Evaluation of community-based support services for families of persons with developmental disabilities. *Journal of The Association for Persons with Severe Handicaps, 14*(4), 312–323.

Spielberger, D.C., Gorsuch, R.C., & Lushene, R.E. (1970). *Manual for the State-Trail Anxiety Inventory.* California: Consulting Psychologists Press.

Stoyva, J., & Carlson, J.G. (1993). A coping/rest model of relaxation and stress management. In L. Goldberger & S. Breznitz (Eds.), *Handbook of stress: Theoretical and clinical aspects* (pp. 724–755). New York: Free Press-Macmillan.

Woolfolk, R.L., & Lehrer, P.M. (1984). *Principles and practice of stress management.* New York: Guilford Press.

Index

Page numbers followed by "f" indicate figures; those followed by "t" indicate tables.